in
SUNSHINE
and in
SHADOW

in
SUNSHINE
and in
SHADOW

A Mother's Story of Autism & Addiction

Dixie Miller Stewart

Dixie Miller Stewart
3-19-12

TATE PUBLISHING
AND ENTERPRISES, LLC

Published by Tate Publishing & Enterprises, LLC
127 E. Trade Center Terrace | Mustang, Oklahoma 73064 USA
1.888.361.9473 | www.tatepublishing.com

Tate Publishing is committed to excellence in the publishing industry. The company reflects the philosophy established by the founders, based on Psalm 68:11,
"The Lord gave the word and great was the company of those who published it."

Book design copyright © 2012 by Tate Publishing, LLC. All rights reserved.
Cover design by Erin DeMoss
Interior design by Chelsea Womble

Published in the United States of America
ISBN: 978-1-61862-293-8
1. Biography & Autobiography / Personal Memoirs
2. Family & Relationships / Autism Spectrum Disorders
12.02.20

DEDICATION

To my sons:

Robert Bowers, for his courage in allowing his story to be told.

Patrick Bowers, whose loyalty to his brother and to me gave me the courage to tell the story.

To mothers and fathers everywhere who weep for their children.

And to those sons and daughters in prison for whom no mother weeps.

Drawings by Robert Bowers. These are some of
the long, lonely roads he traveled through life.

CHAPTER 1

Winter mornings are my favorite times in Southern California. The mist from the ocean plays a game of hide-and-seek with the sunshine, knowing it cannot win, but basking, as do I, in the exquisite joy of the chase. Today, we both surrender: the mist to the warmth of the sun and I, uncharacteristically, to the yellow caution light.

The red traffic signal lasts two minutes. This morning I am grateful for the delay and the chance to look out at the land-scape instead of traffic. The view is splendid: mountains boasting golden halos and valleys preening beneath veils of silver fog. I am smugly aware that the rest of the nation is digging out of snow-storms and scraping ice off windshields.

As my attention is drawn to a young man walking ahead alongside the roadway, sudden powerful emotions flood over me; tears blur my view of him and I grip the steering wheel. Memories begin to flash in rhythmic order across my mind. The rhythm seems to correspond to the "tick tock" sound of my turn signal. It is as if I am watching a series of family slides on a rap-idly changing projector. Each slide reveals a life scene; each scene contains pain and sorrow. I switch off my radio, but I cannot silence my heart; I have accidentally turned on my windshield wipers, but they don't wipe away my tears.

My journey backward in time has been triggered by the lone figure whose back is to me as he walks forlornly onto the on-ramp of Interstate 5. His long blond hair is matted and parted in jagged lines, uncombed at seven-thirty on this still chilly morning. His stride and posture are painfully familiar, seeming permanently molded by a lifetime of inner torment; yet they seem also to reflect a private dignity.

There is about him something that suggests vulnerability, contained despair, and loneliness. I recognize him first by the flood of my feelings before I recognize the dingy white jacket he wears. He is my son; his name is Robert. As Rob came into focus, the mountains and valleys became only a backdrop for the drama of his life.

This is his story. No, it is our story.

It is not a tale of heroics, success, or courage as society defines those; neither is it one about the transcendence of the human spirit over evil to some higher plane. It is instead a story about the mere survival of the broken spirit of a very shy, strangely disabled, usually gentle, and almost always tormented young man.

You know him. You see him in every park, in every city across the United States. He is the disheveled young man who retrieves the aluminum cans you have discarded, or the one you barely notice sweeping the parking lot of a restaurant in exchange for a meal.

He is the stranger on a street corner whose eyes you avoid, or the one whose profile you see as he rides woodenly in the back seat of a police car. But make no mistake about him; he has a home. He lives in the heart of his mother and there, if only there, he is a hero. And because my son has killed a man, it is only there that he is free.

Rob's story is written to give voice to him and the men and women like him who don't fit any molds, neither those society sets for them, nor those of "criminal." They are the lost people who, in desperate moments, made awful decisions for which they will pay the rest of their lives. And his story is to express for him what has become his fervent hope: "Mom, if just one person is helped from reading my story, it will all be worth it."

So I begin with acknowledging the courage of the man who is willing to have his most intensely personal flaws exposed to the condemnation of a population he hopes to help, but to which he has never felt he belonged. My personal hope is that the reader will gain insight into others who struggle with burdens they cannot lay down.

Rob is autistic. He has always been autistic so he doesn't comprehend a time when he might ever perceive things differently. But he hasn't always been an addict and so he sees alcohol as the cause of all his problems and wrong decisions.

Autism is a strange disorder. Many speculate, but no one knows its cause. Perhaps no two autistic individuals are alike, but the disorder is primarily characterized by the *inability* to effectively relate to other people in a mutually beneficial or socially acceptable manner. The consequences of such a disability can be pervasive and tragic when they result, as they have with my son, in a life spent outside any sense of intimacy with or belongingness to others. The life of an autistic person often represents only an accumulation of painful, failed efforts to be a somebody to someone else.

Along with Rob's autism are other disabilities and disorders that effectively clouded his early childhood diagnoses and further isolated him from his fellowman. He is like a crippled submarine deep beneath the surface of the water: contained, but lacking an emotional lifeline to those he feels any attachment to: his brother, his father, and me.

Until this morning, I had not seen Rob in several weeks. He was supposed to be in an alcohol and drug treatment program. My tears today are also in part because I see now that my last desperate hope has been dashed again.

I must make a decision before the light changes: I can continue straight ahead, and pull over and invite him into my car. He will welcome that; it is typical of what I have done all his life. Or I can commit another act uncharacteristic of me: I can turn and continue on my route and leave Rob behind, alone to experience whatever consequences derive from his decision to walk away from another treatment facility. I am still recalling quick, clear memories from his childhood, his young adulthood…the tragedies of them. It is an unusual, surreal experience.

My light turns green and I make my turn, astonished that a lifetime has "happened" in that one hundred and twenty seconds. My decision haunts me for many days. I have knowingly abandoned my son.

The memory of that decision returns with fierceness when I learn not very long afterward that he had killed a man. It is as difficult now to wrap my mind around that truth as it was when I first learned of it.

Ultimately, I believe it is my son's disabilities that led him to take the life of another. Autism itself may not increase the risk of doing harm to others, but rejection and ridicule do.

The news of what he had done came in a phone call on a pleasant Sunday afternoon. That call redefined my life and plunged my son's into unimaginable despair.

"Is this the mother of Robert Bowers?" The caller's voice has an air of gentle authority, as have most of the voices asking that same question over the past forty years. I hold my breath and try to still my heart so I can hear only with my "professional mind." Doing so allows me a small bit of control over words that are about to undo my life, again.

This voice belongs to a detective with the San Luis Obispo California Police Department. As I listen to his beginning remarks, I try to recall the name he gave. I can't, but amidst the gripping tension, I cling to the kindness already apparent in his tone.

"Robert," he is saying, "has been..." Here, he seems to hesitate; my heart pounds furiously, as I wait to hear him finish telling me that Robbie has been severely injured or killed. I have rehearsed this call many times, but I sense now how very poorly prepared I still am.

"...arrested for stabbing a man."

Stabbing a man! Deliberately harming *someone else*?

In two previous such phone calls, Robbie has been the stabbing victim. Have I misheard this time? I have lived many years with a constant dread that Rob will some day take his own life out of despair or cause his own death through reckless decisions, but I never believed he would deliberately hurt someone else, least of all by such a violent act as stabbing. Except for the deliberate savagery done against himself in car wrecks, Robbie is the least violent person I know.

He has so many times been the target of violence; I marvel that he is still patient, even gentle, under the kinds of conditions I find most frustrating. His bruised and battered face, black eyes, and the smell of alcohol and sweat have all told me when he has been in a fight. But even then, it is never fights he knowingly starts for he knows too well how poorly he fights. I have read police reports describing Rob as an intoxicated someone I don't know, but his violence is mostly directed against himself, not other people. He has been a funny and whimsical or secretive and ashamed drunk around me. Listening now to the voice on the phone, I cannot believe Rob could ever knowingly harm another.

Yet, Rob believed it. In fact, in hindsight, I realize he has long been trying to communicate how great has been his fear that he might actually do harm to someone some day. He fears it because doing so is the content of many unbidden, unwanted, hideous-to-him fantasies he has experienced for years. Not until he was thirty-two years old did he tell me he had been experiencing them since he was eight, and that he thought it meant he had demons inside him. Has none of us to whom he finally, shamefacedly, sobbingly confessed his fears grasped that he was begging to be more than just understood? Wasn't he also begging to be stopped?

Although I dread his answer, I make myself ask the detective how seriously the man was injured.

"He has died."

Died.

A man is dead. Robbie has killed another person.

I don't exhale in the practiced manner I've acquired from such calls; my breath is sucked out of me. Tragedy does that; it steals the spirit from the lives it assaults. Still holding the phone to my ear, I stumble to the nearest chair, almost missing it and falling.

Robbie has killed someone. I can't even force my mind to comprehend this. The man's words all seem to bounce around inside me colliding with fears and wild emotions as though frantically searching for an escape from this seeming fiction back to truth. The enormity of this most hideous act will take weeks and weeks to completely reach the center of my heart, that part of me where finally it seemed even hope now wept.

The detective is kind; he is saying such nice things about Rob that I can almost believe in listening to him that everything is going to be all right. After all, I have almost believed that since Rob's birth. My heart grabs the words he is using to describe Rob: polite, cooperative with the police, has voluntarily confessed to stabbing the man.

A sob slips out as I hear that Rob had been badly beaten by the man several hours earlier. I learn how after he had stabbed him, my son had slowly bent and picked up his guitar and backpack and begun walking across the street in front of dozens of cars filled with stunned witnesses. One witness noted that he had "looked directly at me as though nothing had happened."

In his calm, gentle manner, the detective is continuing to tell me things I know I need to hear, but I don't think I can bear anymore. It has fallen to him to report the facts that speak of our now shattered lives. How odd—I feel sorry for him too.

Still sitting beside my dining table, still listening to the circumstances surrounding the killing, my eyes and mind go to my backyard where the late afternoon sunshine dances through tree leaves and bright flowers bloom; how incongruous they now seem. Yet this way I can listen to him without being stabbed by his words. My attention rests for a moment on the ivy climbing over my fence. It was the reason I bought this place. I look at the cascading splash of rocks and small boulders that trail down the side of the hill, boulders that Rob patiently delivered to me. He had lugged each one up my back stairs and up the steep hill, placing them just so. There had been a ton of them in all. He had been so proud of himself for creating that effect, especially knowing that I loved the look.

I am crying. Such innocent times will never come again.

My attention turns back to the caller: "Even though Rob wasn't going anywhere in a hurry, some 'do-gooder' jumped him from behind, knocked him down, and began kicking him in the face with the toe of his boot. He'd already been beaten pretty badly; his eyes are swollen closed." I gasp at hearing this, and again protectively shift my mind, this time to the small kindness of the detective now using the name, "Rob," instead of "Robert."

I see Rob lying on the sidewalk being kicked in the face and I involuntarily flinch. I wonder if he lay there in submission to punishment he thought he deserved, or if he had curled up in a fetal position and endured yet another assault. I think of his naked, vulnerable soul, the lifelong rejections as if he were a pariah, and I hear nothing else the detective is saying. We end our conversation somehow. I am in blackness.

Darkness falls while I still sit here, aware that it seems to be brighter in the moonless backyard than within the circle of grief that shrouds me. Like bolts of lightning out of a distant, dark sky, other things the detective said pierce my consciousness. I want to push them away but they are relentless. I recall things said about the man Rob killed and feel shame that I care more about my son than about his mother's son.

Sitting here, I know I should move, feed Rob's cat, make my dinner. I think, too, that I should call someone: Patrick, Rob's brother, and his dad, at least. I desperately want someone to help carry my burden of pain, but I also want to protect Patrick from this violation. I can't protect him; he has to know. But I don't call anyone just yet because when I do, it will be real. It will mean I am not simply having a nightmare; I am living one.

———◆◆———

Pulling into the parking lot of the motel in San Luis Obispo, I wonder how I have gotten to this town and how I have now found the motel. I am three hundred miles from San Diego, but I don't remember the drive. I remember the tumbling of thoughts and memories and the crying and nose blowing.

Nor do I remember finding the attorneys' offices, yet I have just come away from a meeting with them and the investigator feeling some encouragement from their seeming confidence and certainly by their compassion. Tomorrow, I will finally be allowed to see Rob; I have to get through tonight. I have grieved that I have not been able to comfort or talk to him at all since learning of his arrest two weeks ago.

Tonight, I will read the loaned copies of the police interrogation and other relevant arrest documents. I have been told about Rob through all of this. I will now finally get to read his words, but I am both desperate and terrified to do so.

My hands are shaking and my heart is pounding as I try to make myself comfortable on the bed. I have a bottle of water and a roast beef sandwich on rye from a nearby deli. I cannot recall when I last ate. I open the folder and scramble through until I find the running dialogue of the police interviewing Rob as well as his replies. I begin reading somewhere in the middle, too anxious to organize the sheets. A glob of mustard falls on the paper. I wipe it off and smear some on my cheek when I wipe away the tears that come as I read my son's words.

Interrogator: "Did you want to hurt him or kill him?"

"…Just stab him…I didn't like the way it felt when it went into his body. It felt ugly and it was gross. It's just a sick feeling when it went into his body, a sickening feeling, I didn't like it and I never want to do it again."

"I was gonna die anyways." *I was gonna die anyways, I was gonna die anyways…* The pages drop from my hands and scatter all over the floor as I fall sobbing back on the pillow of the motel room bed. I pull the other pillows over my face to stifle sobs and try very hard to empty into them the life-sized reservoir of tears that have for days been pouring down my face. They are not like ordinary tears; these come from somewhere in the deepest regions of my soul, down there where grief and motherhood are synonymous.

For three sleepless days and nights now, sobs have come out of me in sounds that I can't even recognize as coming from myself, as though some giant monster of grief trapped inside me is roaring for freedom. But I know it will never be set free because I am Robbie's mother.

Mothers go to war with their sons; they go to emergency rooms with them, or to bankruptcy courts. They're standing alongside when they get fired from a job half a world away or when the girls that weren't good enough for them anyway have dumped them. Wherever his decisions propel the son, it doesn't matter that she is neither seen nor invited, so too, goes his mother, though only in spirit. It has nothing at all to do with enmeshment or codependency; it has everything to do with the unbreakable bonds of motherhood. This mother was going to prison because that's where Robbie was going.

The strewn papers are gathered haphazardly from the floor and I settle this time in a chair to read on in the arrest documents, the self-condemning near monologue of my drunken son being allowed to, as he finally realized, verbally hang himself there in the deliberately very cold interrogation room.

"Fight? Yeah, I lost. I'm a poor fighter. He beat my ass like they always do."

Interrogator: "Did you think about going back and just punching him in the face?"

"I can't do that. I don't have the ability to fight like normal people. I wasn't sure I stabbed him more than once but I didn't want him to… I wanted to make sure he couldn't attack me."

"I didn't like it. I don't like it, but it's too late; it's already been done. I did a bad crime and I'm thinking you'll hear my honesty and my sincerity and maybe I'll get five years or so…I should talk to a lawyer. I'm gonna hang myself."

Rob still did not know that his victim had died from the stabbing. He was asked here how many times he thought he'd stabbed his victim: "…Two or three times. It was an ugly feeling, oh so gross!"

"I'm tired of being treated like a punk. I was gonna just scare him…but ended up stabbing him."

"I'll be in prison for the rest of my life; I guess that's what I wanted. I was drinking Southern Comfort. I'm a little bit more intoxicated than I'm used to being, so bad things happened, and a person ended up in the hospital. It's my fault. Here's my neck, so hang me."

Interrogator: "What did you think would happen?"

"I didn't think about it."

"I think honesty should prevail and whatever I deserve for this crime I should get."

"My mom and brother live in San Diego…so sad that I'm going to have to tell them."

"I drank a lot, but I'm not trying to use that as an excuse, so shoot me. It was premeditated. I'm not…I'm not going to lie to you."

"I just, I just ended my life." *I just ended my life.*

These things are too hard to read. He has indeed just ended his life! Again, the folder and sheets scatter to the floor, tossed further by the blower from the nearby heater.

Neither the nice detective on the phone, the nice attorneys, nor the nice investigator had told me that Rob was being allowed to dig his grave without the benefit of an attorney. He had not known during all his confessing that the man he had stabbed was dead. After all, Robbie had survived being stabbed all over his body and left for dead on two separate occasions. He had once joked to me that he was living proof that stabbing couldn't kill.

I stare at the papers scattered again across the floor and the thought flashes through my mind that if I just leave them there, it will be as though they really don't contain horrible truths, only trashy fiction. Inside that ever-so-brief moment of thought is a feeling almost like normalcy, as if it really is fiction or maybe only a nightmare. Robbie hasn't killed anybody and he isn't going to prison. I want to hold on to the thought, but it vanishes as quickly as it appeared and I am swept back into the dark realm of personal insanity where mothers' minds do crazy things, too, when their sons have gone crazy and killed a man. The sorrow returns, rushing over my heart with the force of Niagara Falls. I remember visiting Niagara Falls as a family when Robbie was ten or so and how when we weren't looking, he'd tried to climb out to the falls.

I shut my eyes, recalling not only the fear I'd felt for his safety, but also a more haunting and ever-present one that his life was going to continue in the same pattern: impulsive actions followed by bad consequences. I feel again the same guilt, as if I should have been a better mother, that I should have paid more attention to something… but what? What?

Do all other mothers know things about parenting that I somehow missed out on? And so, once again, I relive that awful sense of failure, as if Rob's killing the man was due in part to my own personal failing. My mother's heart wants too much to protect my child from suffering, yet I'm flooded with the struggle over whether or not I am the cause of it. I cannot bear the added pain but it keeps coming, in silence this time. I learn that sometimes agony makes no sound at all.

I slump back and stare at the ceiling, wishing this drama was all fiction, wishing that the phone call hadn't happened, thinking, again, how strange it still seemed that being his mother was so often punctuated with *that* question: "Is this the mother of Robert Bowers?" Whatever follows will always break my heart. However I answer, I will always struggle with fear, guilt and confusion about how I ought to respond. Is Rob safe? Should I be angry with him? Should I defend him? And, perhaps worst of all, will I be able to cope with what I'm about to hear? I am so afraid that I won't be.

Once, though, many years ago, the voice asking that question on the other end of the phone line was female. She identified herself simply as "I live two blocks away." She was calling, she said, to tell me that she had just seen my son, four-year-old Robbie, playing in the middle of the busiest avenue in Jacksonville, North Carolina.

I didn't like the woman's voice or attitude. She seemed accusatory and self-righteous. I thought she was probably one of those mothers whose kids never lie down in mud puddles in their best clothes or pour a cup of bleach on a neighbor's carpet or impulsively throw bric-a-brac at Mormon elders who come to the door.

Playing in the middle of a busy street was definitely not something Robbie would have avoided, so I would have easily believed her had I not been holding his just-bathed, deliciously sweet-smelling, towel-wrapped little body in my arms. It was so rare that he would let me hold him that I savored the moment and recall its sweetness even now.

But that was then, when Robbie still believed in his autistic way that he was a real car instead of just a little boy. It was before he came to believe that he was a *damaged* car and before he had ever stolen old cars to wreck so as to "kill the bad Robert in me."

That sweet moment of bathing and holding him tightly happened before he ever learned he might seek solace from a human. Instead, he learned that humans deceive and ridicule; so he learned, too, to drown his pain from those and many more awful events in alcohol and learned that he could actually, and only, "be like the other kids" when he used drugs.

As I write his story here, I find I am picking up one piece of his life at a time much as one might gently touch an old photograph of a loved one before selecting the next one from the pile tucked helter-skelter in a velvet-lined box. Like sorting photos for a family album, not all pieces of Rob's life immediately fit together. Rather, they flow on waves of memory where emotion selects the order.

CHAPTER 2

"Mom, I'm worried about my cellie. He's a lifer like me. He says he's innocent and I believe him…I gave him your address so he can write you. I told him you would help him. His family abandoned him years ago. I'm so very glad my family stands by me." Rob from prison, 2006.

"Mom, I've been really down. My cellie who wrote you died of a heart attack. Terrible, seems like he'd just given up. Then, right after he died, his case did go to appeal and he was found innocent, just like he said. I cut out all the newspaper stories about it and sent them to his parents. I wanted them to know that all this time he'd been innocent and they hadn't believed their own son. So sad. Rob from prison 2007.

Twice imprisoned for auto thefts, Robbie returned each time to live with me in San Diego. At least, I thought of him as living with me. He seemed to think of himself as being homeless, perhaps because he wandered the United States either driving an old car he'd managed to purchase or been given, or hitch-hiking and working odd jobs here and there. He might be gone a night or two or sometimes for one or two months at a time. Perhaps thinking of himself as homeless meant he didn't have to think of himself as still being dependent on his mother.

In truth, he had been wandering away since before he could walk. Strangely, I used to feel rejected by him when he left. I would conjure and explore deep motives I thought he might have for wanting to leave a nice home where he was loved. Once, to reassure me, he told me he wandered in search of himself. I was impressed by the self-insight but as with most such hints of his underlying pain, he had no more to say about that.

Finally, I accepted that wandering the country is just what Robbie does. Still, he lived with me for more months at a time than not, too often holing up in his room, not often enough playing funny tricks on me, and always making sweet music with his guitar. But sometimes he lived in prison, when his need to destroy the "bad Robert" clashed with the laws against stealing muscle cars of the sixties, the kind he once thought he was.

Here in my motel room, I read again the interrogations. And I spend long minutes reflecting on how little it will matter to anyone involved in Rob's proceedings what losing that fight meant to him.

Losing it loosed an avalanche of life-long pain that went beyond the capacity of Rob's power to reason. It was deep, deep wounds, not meanness, that wielded the knife. The alcohol merely set free the inhibitions that had prevented him from hurting anyone before now, inhibitions that had also kept him an isolated man carrying the heavy burdens of the secret shames known only to the very lonely.

I know that what I am reading in this motel room, three hundred miles from home, are words that are finally deciding the fate of a wandering soul who has lived his life daring unseen forces to either stop him or set him free. I weep again for my son, for the man he has killed, for myself, and for lonely little boys everywhere who everyday fight battles much too big for them just because, in the words Robbie had once used to define himself, they're "not like all the other kids."

Rob's jail monologue continued. I had seldom known him to be so verbose with strangers; I guessed it was the alcohol. He had to have been hurting from the beatings and freezing from the cold. It is left only to a mother to care deeply that the son who has just killed a man himself needs comforting and medical help.

In some tiny place inside I want to at once chuckle and sob at the "tough guy" demeanor my son has assumed here. I do not doubt he learned it as a means to survive in the streets and in prison, and while over his forty years I have seen this side of him, such glimpses have been rare.

"I know when I did that, that I was going away for a long, long time. And when people mess with me in prison, I'm going to do exactly the same thing, 'cause I don't care!"

I know Rob. This is posturing. He cares maybe more than he's ever cared in his life because now he knows from experience what lies ahead for him. He's scared; he's fighting not to cry. He knows that his immediate future is going to be hell; he knows his life of roaming, exploring the nature he so loves has forever ended. And I think that just on the outer edges of his weary, weary mind he knows some small relief that he has finally been stopped, his fury contained, if not understood.

"I've been picked on all of my life. You know what? When kids get picked on, you'd better watch out! Sometimes, s**t like this can happen. I don't want it to, but…that man beat me up, or his brother did. Apparently I got the wrong man."

"I've always been picked on; that's why I did that s**t. That's all I got to say. Put me in jail the rest of my life, cause I was gonna die anyways."

It is precisely midnight; I finish the second reading and leave the room to walk the several blocks to the downtown intersection of Nipomo and Broad Streets, where "it happened." I still cannot bring myself to say, "Where Rob killed a man." I need to see it, to try to replay the events; I need to go there. I want to know how it can possibly have happened that in this incredibly beautiful little city that my incredibly loved son had killed a human being. I can more easily imagine his death than his causing a death.

It is much colder here than it is in San Diego and windy. I am shivering as I approach the bus bench where Rob had sat with the men with whom he had first talked about politics and then quarreled. It is as I pictured it in my mind while reading about the "crime scene:" A charming, park-like corner, too pleasant, too busy with life to be the scene of death. My mind still tries hard to bend truth so that I will believe it really hasn't happened at all, but the tears running down my cheeks tell me it has.

I sit on the bench imagining Rob sitting there only days before. I reach out and touch the cold hardness of it, imagining how the man had also sat there talking after the fight and after his son had been arrested and mine had stumbled off somewhere continuing to drink. I try to imagine how my son had finally thought to purchase a knife as much to *be* even with it as to *get* even, obsessing on his most recent humiliation. I wonder what had been the man's last words and if he had any strange notion that his life was about to end.

Across the street from the bench is the brightly lit corner liquor store where Rob had purchased his second bottle of Southern Comfort. Perhaps he drank more in order to gain courage, but I think he drank more, at least a little bit, because the last shreds of self-respect had been knocked out of him, the consequence of his having insulted a woman in a wheelchair. She had been siding with Rob's adversary. Not many months earlier, Rob had spent almost a year in a wheelchair.

How many swallows had burned down his throat before the liquor stopped comforting and began fueling a rage in him so forceful that it would take a man's life? How many fights must a drunken man provoke before he understands that provocation is not a substitute for manliness? How many fights must a man lose before he becomes crazed by his imagined impotence, his *nothingness*?

If in times past Rob's battered face told me he had been in a fight, his knuckles told me he had not struck many blows, which was an unrelenting source of shame for him. Clumsiness and poor coordination are common in individuals who have some minimal brain dysfunction or autism, but to Rob his lack was just one more insurmountable barrier between himself and his peers.

I knew his not being able to fight well represented a life-long struggle with his image of himself as masculine. If he couldn't fight, he wasn't a man. No amount of logic could dissuade him of that. And if he didn't have a woman's love, he wasn't a man, either, to his way of thinking.

He has lived through many wild and dangerous things that would make another man cower, but he is deeply ashamed of his awkwardly flailing fists that rarely make sound contact with the jaw of any adversary. He tends to regard most adversaries as much more worthy than he. And he believes he is not manly enough to ever have the love of any woman other than his mother; although not even that, he is sure, is born of anything worthy in him but rather simply because "love is what mothers do."

Rob's having somehow concluded that fighting was the primary test of masculinity was all the more odd because fighting was not something anyone in our family did, short of the earlier playground fights his seven-year-old brother, Patrick, had fought on Rob's behalf. Patrick deemed those fights necessary because already Rob, though three years older, was the brunt of hostile taunting and rejection by kids his age. It frequently went well beyond what Rob told the police as being simply "picked on;" it was bullying in every sense of the word. Patrick's budding manliness demanded that he defend his brother, and no doubt the family name.

Finally, Rob's ten-year-old sense of manliness demanded that he fight his own fights and he asked Patrick to stop defending him. So Patrick stopped, bewildered for a season that his help was no longer wanted when it seemed so apparent to him that the help was needed.

But that was a telling and memorable moment in Rob's life, that moment, that day of choosing to defend himself even though he knew he would be ganged up on many more times and that he would lose every time. He never grasped, as Patrick and I did, that the courage he showed in accepting such a fate was far above that shown by the other kids who called him names, threw rocks at him, and ran him down with their bikes.

Rob didn't merely stab the man because of that day's pain. He stabbed him with the force of an awesome accumulation of humiliations becoming gargantuan and awful and, yes, sickening, over forty years spent mostly sucking it all in. He stabbed what that man represented: someone bigger and badder; someone who didn't play fair; someone who sexually violated his body and innocence; someone who had repeatedly robbed him of all his belongings and twice left him for dead from stab wounds; and someone who countless times mocked and humiliated him in public. He finally stabbed *those* men back.

He doesn't excuse himself and I'm not excusing him. Decisions have consequences, but decisions also have reasons that only make sense when the broken pieces of a defeated man's life are fit back together.

A friend of mine, a successful and self-confident man, at peace with God and himself, recently told me that a "humiliated man is the most dangerous thing in the world." Do others know that? Do prison guards know it? Do wardens and police and teachers and wives, angry friends and covetous neighbors? Do we know that words really can kill? Words kill the soul and spirit and vitality of a life that surely must once have had hope and dignity.

———◆◆◆———

It is my first time to be in the San Luis Obispo Jail visiting area, but the surroundings are painfully familiar and dismal with human longings. My son is brought to me on the opposite side of a window in a tiny private room. He is brought with his hands cuffed behind his back. He is wearing the same ugly, misshapen orange jump suit of everyone else in the jail. He patiently waits while his cuffs are unlocked and he is allowed to enter his side of the glass-walled cubicle, to pick up the phone through which we will communicate. I have already lifted mine. I have already read on the wall the notice that tells me the calls are being recorded.

His face is still cut and bruised; his eyes are open but still swollen. I want to cry, but I smile. Perhaps he wants to cry, but he smiles broadly. We gaze silently into each other's eyes for a time, drawing comfort in finding that love remains sturdy and eternal. Rob thanks me for coming and tells me he was scared I might not. We assess each other's mood, determining what verbal path to take as we each continue to pretend that a man does not lie dead somewhere because of the deeds of one of us.

I cannot touch or hug him. I must rely on words and facial expressions to offer comfort. Although I have come to console him, it is he who consoles me. He thanks me again and again for coming. He tells me I am beautiful and that he had been afraid that I would look older. Only a few weeks have passed since we were together, but it must seem like years to him. As he talks, I recall how he always worries when he has not seen me for a while that I will show great signs of aging which will mean that I am that much closer to death and abandonment of him. He has told me many times in the past that he does not know how he will cope with my death because he is sure he will be utterly alone then, more alone than the aloneness he has lived all his life. He often said he had a mother with strong mom power when it was needed. But mom power is rendered impotent in a jail visiting room when your son has confessed to killing a man.

He tells me he is doing well and that his cuts don't hurt. He wants to know if I will remain loyal to him, but he asks that in roundabout ways. He thanks me profusely for "always standing by me." The hour is up and I leave, to return for another one tomorrow. He is allowed a one-hour visitation per week, which amounts to one hour on Saturday, the last day, and one hour on Sunday, the first day of the week.

Again tonight, I walk the back streets of San Luis Obispo until well after midnight. I walk down alleys and along a little bending river, into dark crevices and under bridges. I am searching for homeless people who might know Rob, for some who would have witnessed the events some days earlier. I meet dozens of homeless, most of them drinking or seeking money to drink, some smoking. I make small purchases from them of crafts they have made from bits of foil or twigs and string, in order to buy drugs or alcohol, I guessed. I smile gladly at their pride and at their efforts to have something to exchange for money instead of asking outright for a handout. Rob has told me that it is so important to him to work or sell his belongings in order to eat.

I ask again and again, each time disappointed that none knows his name. Apparently, homeless folks don't read the local paper, either. I am not afraid of them or of the night; I know and love one of them, although he is locked away now.

As I walk, I also look for the telltale signs that Robbie has been here: I look for perfectly crafted question marks on street signs or light poles. Rob draws question marks everywhere he goes. This quirk comes to my mind now and I smile with love for this harmless habit that holds some secret meaning for him. I think about the question marks he has drawn on signposts all over the United States: "So that the kids who picked on me would drive by, see, wonder, and *know*, but not have their lives hurt or anything."

Our Sunday visit is much the same as Saturday's, but heavy in the absence of a promise of another one tomorrow. We say goodbyes that wrench out the pieces of my broken heart as I watch him being handcuffed and led away. I drive back to San Diego realizing that we have said very little about the killing. I wanted to follow his lead on that; I don't know how to ask him things because I am afraid that the recorded conversations will be used against him. I am preoccupied with my wishes that he was back home, playing his guitar. Who will hang my Christmas lights come December?

Every month for over eighteen months I spend a weekend in San Luis Obispo, waiting my turn in the lobby of the jail for the one hour each day with Rob. One of the questions Rob asks every visit is how San Luis Obispo looks on that day; he has no windows. Hell for him is a frenzy of men whose intentions he has never understood, and the idea of never again getting to wander and explore earth and nature. Almost as painful is the lack of a view of the majestic mountains, emerald green meadows, and tree-lined streets that surround him *out there*, a place that he has learned to call the free world.

I ache when he asks that because it is a reminder of the terrible price he will continue to pay for the taking of a man's life. The price isn't merely his freedom; it is being denied one of the two things in his life that gave it meaning: nature's beauty and making music. His guitar is missing, and would not be allowed anyway, so he listens each day to the clamor and misery of incarcerated men and he passes the nights remembering.

Each time, I make careful note of points of interest, of how the sunshine colors the meadows differently depending on the time of day, or how the shadows transform the very shape of the mountains and how sweet and soft is the air. He wants to hear those things, but it feels cruel to be describing them from the perspective of my freedom. And I feel oddly detached from the landscape I paint for his mind because it is always a scene filled with tragedy.

Cruel, too, is dining alone on those Friday and Saturday nights. San Luis Obispo is a college town. I see parents and young adults at adjoining tables in the charming restaurants I visit. They are laughing and happy, engrossed in conversations rich with hope, promise, and a future. They have spent the day together shopping or walking in the parks or enjoying a movie. I have spent the day in jail. I want what these parents have; I want that experience with Rob. I will never have it and so on Fridays and Saturdays, once a month, I blink back tears of self pity.

In between my visits, after work, and on the other three weekends, I fight lethargy and hopelessness. Friends made suggestions about things I might try in order to help put together a defense, but somewhere over the past several months I have stopped believing there could be one. I can only call his attorney from time to time for reassurance.

I have stopped something else, too: I have stopped believing that God will intervene even though he has always done so in the past. Yet now, when I need to more than ever, I don't trust him with my burdens. My thoughts about him are as crazy as my moments of hoping that none of this is true: *Rob has killed a man, he has confessed to it, he has an arrest history and that is that; there's nothing God can do about it now.* But there is something more. It is the guilt and regret I have carried for a long, long time that I did not trust God with Rob in his childhood.

I didn't know God very well then. He was my 9-1-1 crisis call in the many times of desperation about both my sons, but I didn't really think he involved himself in the lives of people like me: people whose parenting is somehow so bad that their kid goes to prison. It is the shame of knowing that I have let both God and Robbie down that keeps me from turning to him now. Even worse, it is the fear that I might discover that I'm right, that he really doesn't care.

Finally, roused by the need to provide Rob's history, I search on the Internet for things that might be legitimately used to help his case. I look for other cases of individuals charged with killing someone for whom autism, learning disabilities, attention deficits, addictions, or other social and educational challenges are part of their defense.

I tell myself I am not trying to keep him from the consequences of all he has done. But deep in my heart, I know that if

I could, I would serve his sentence for him. If I could, I would throw my arms around him and keep him from all that lies ahead.

While I wish desperately that he had never killed and therefore did not have to go to prison, I cannot help him avoid righteous consequences. I just don't like the options, given his problems. I definitely do not want him in the main stream of prisoners. He will be highly vulnerable to injury, assault, and the same kinds of treatment from peers he has mostly received throughout his life, only it will be ramped up to fiendish levels in a prison surrounded by others who feel they have nothing left to lose.

I believe that a jury will have sympathy and see that he needs to be in a treatment program rather than mainstream. In sensing the compassionate reactions of others to my son's situation, I begin to believe that a jury's decision will recognize Rob's suffering and restore some dignity.

In recent months, I have come back to hope. It crept back in while out on a walk in which I was searching for the right words to pray for Rob and for myself. Romans 8:1 came to mind as it often had. This time, I listened. By the time I returned home, I felt the first bit of peace I'd experienced in months and months: "Therefore, there is now no condemnation for those who are in Christ Jesus." God wasn't condemning Rob or me!

The trial is postponed several times while his attorneys seek additional psychological examinations and any history that might be useful for his defense. We wait for archived, often discarded, or lost medical and other treatment records to arrive at the attorney's offices. Rob's childhood treatment records from psychiatrists, psychologists, and residential and other special schools are only trickling in. Records from more recent addiction treatment centers and other mental health reports arrive as slowly. No one seems to care that a man's life is depending on those records!

Yet, amid writing and preparing and grieving, peace is continuing to visit my heart. It arrived first during that late night walk. Because I cannot keep from crying when I pray for Rob, I take my walks around 10:00 p.m. Nevertheless, I wear sunglasses so no one will see my tears, yet they stream down underneath the glasses.

My pattern is the same: I walk the two miles to the center boundary of a nearby golf course crying, grieving, and praying about all my many fears for Rob's welfare, pouring my heart out to God. Then I walk the two miles back, crying and thanking him for his help and his comfort, giving him my burdens to hold… at least until morning when grief reaches out and draws them to me again. But, little by little, over many months, I quit taking them. I'm learning that God does intervene in the hearts of grieving mothers, and in the lives of sons who cause them grief. He reminds me that sorrow is the price of loving. I would not have it any other way. And, though not just yet, soon I will learn that sorrow is also an invitation to the indescribable sweetness of walking with God.

CHAPTER 3

"You are my sunshine, my only sunshine, you make me happy, when skies are gray, you'll never know, dear, how much I love you, please don't take my sunshine away." Rob singing to me during a visit in jail awaiting trial, 2003.

Tomorrow morning is the deadline for Rob's decision: He will either accept the offer made by the district attorney or he will choose to go to trial. The DA's offer is that Rob waives trial, pleads to a lesser charge, and receives a minimum prison sentence of seventeen years. The DA tells him if he goes to trial and loses, his minimum sentence will be fifty-two years. He is now forty-two years of age.

He has largely grappled with this conflict between two evils alone. How can I advise him to do what I only hope is best when he is the one who will live out the consequences? I want him to go to trial. I believe there are many extenuating circumstances. I have by now been preparing for a trial for months.

He phones from jail to tell me his decision to accept the DA's offer. His voice is flat, less with despair than finality. He has been in limbo for almost two years waiting while the rest of us in the free world try to manipulate his choices, one of which will decide the most important challenge he's ever faced. In the end, he chooses not to gamble that a jury will sympathize with him and give him a better sentence than the seventeen years to life he is offered. Although I am very disappointed, I dare not dissuade him from that decision because I don't know, either, if a jury will feel compassion for my son or see him only as someone who has killed another. I wince at the truth in that, but I try to offer hope before we are automatically disconnected due to the time limit set on his phone calls.

How can I offer him hope? His decision just trampled mine, even though it was his to make in the first place. I sit here almost paralyzed because my mind is trying to do two contradictory things at once: accept the fact that Rob is really going to prison and reject that fact. I hang up and find that I've been looking at Rob's kindergarten picture here beside my bed the entire time we talked. Seeing his innocence, remembering how even then his life's burdens had been much too heavy for him, my mind searches for some moment in his childhood that I can point to and say, "That's where it all began." I stand and walk down the hall into his room. All his belongings are still as he left them. I begin to pack his personal things away in boxes. I do that so my mind will get the message that he is not coming back home for a very long time.

Even seventeen years is an incomprehensible lifetime to be in prison, assuming he is released then. I already know what prison does to a man in just four years. I wish desperately that all of society understood that prisons are dehumanizing and that they erode a person's spirit and soul. I recall things I've read with outrage and frustration, letters to editors and other commentaries on the so-called amenities of prisoners. These writers have a misguided notion that treating felons as human beings is somehow coddling them.

I think about the problems Rob has had with society and I ache, imagining what he might become in prison in his efforts to fit in. I don't want him in that environment, and I don't want my imagination assaulting me this way. I want to be numb, but I'm not. I don't want to feel any more pain, but I do. Rob is entering a world where he cannot weep for himself so I must weep for him.

And I do. And the memories stream again in the flow of love for him that is always the color of sorrow.

—————◆◆◆—————

The beginning: from birth Rob seemed so very unlike my friends' babies. I think about his neurological and developmental problems and his isolative loneliness in childhood, and I wonder how much to attribute to "nature" and how much to "nurture." That was the essential debate when I was in college. Autism as a spectrum in which there are varying degrees of impairment was not known by many practicing professionals at the time of Rob's birth. I knew almost nothing about it. But I came to know that somehow my baby was different and I lived with a secret fear for his future.

The feel of his little eight-pound, eight-ounce body laid on my abdomen just after delivery was intensely, joyfully intimate. I was certain on that long ago. Tuesday afternoon that I would be able to know this was my own infant from that of any other. He felt like he belonged! The delivery had been difficult with some unexpected complications and even the physicians grew tired, but in the single moment before I got to see him I knew I had just participated in a miracle! I smiled, travails of labor forgotten, but I wished his daddy was there. A lieutenant in the Marine Corps, he had been on orders in Okinawa since I was six months pregnant. He would not be home until our firstborn was eleven months old.

Robbie slept very little and cried very much. His sleep times were rarely more than maybe three hours, with several hours of crying in between, although he cried less when I held him. So, I held him while I did everything else I needed to do. From the outset, he had a very weak sucking response, but I didn't yet know the implications of that on his ego development. I knew only that my nursing him seemed somehow not to nurture. Nurtured instead was a galloping self-doubt about my mothering.

The seeds of the fear that I was not a good enough mother were planted in those first days and weeks. No one had prepared me for a baby that cried all the time or one that slept only half the amount of time indicated in books. I'd read a lot about tending to a newborn and two things seemed clear: they brought joy and they needed a lot of sleep. Although I was in awe of the miracle of my child, and could not imagine life without him, there was little of the joy that I'd read about. Because there was more doubt than joy, I felt guilt. Guilt steals joy.

It didn't occur to me that if his daddy had been there, we could have shared in the care and commiserated together over the worry and fatigue of a baby who seemed to always be in pain. Instead, I wondered how in the world a new mother could also be a wife or have any other life!

I had thought loneliness was epitomized in my husband's leaving me behind to go to Okinawa. I'd cried buckets of tears from missing him and felt like a part of me had gone with him. Thirteen months there plus a month absence prior to his departure was a lifetime. He'd driven me back to my mother's home to stay and flown back to California.

My return to Oklahoma was to a town from which I'd moved eight years earlier when I was fourteen. I considered it my "hometown," but had no close friends there anymore. Like me, most of them had gone away to college or married and moved to other places. My mother and I chuckled over how my circumstances might appear to the local folks who hadn't seen me in eight years. I drove a new, bright red, sporty car, was six months pregnant and growing, I had fluid retention that caused swelling in my fingers (and elsewhere), which prevented me from wearing my wedding rings, and there was no husband in sight.

Mother left for a three-week vacation when Rob was three weeks old. I'd been worried that his crying day and night was bothering her, so it was almost a relief to have her gone.

Loneliness was redefined for me on a Friday when Rob was a month old and had screamed all day. I'd nursed, burped, rocked, walked and changed him over and over. That was all I knew to do and none of it was working. I was alone and felt completely helpless in my inability to soothe and comfort him. After all, weren't those the essentials of being a mother of an infant? *What was wrong with me?*

He was finally quieted and fell asleep around 10:00 p.m. Without showering or even brushing my teeth, I crawled into my bed, next to his bassinette, and lay there in despair. In the stillness, I heard from far across town the roaring crowd cheering our high school team on to victory. The contrast of that with the lonely and frightened hopelessness I'd experienced all day brought stinging tears to my eyes that streamed down my temples as I lay there. I was afraid to sob audibly for fear that the sound would wake Rob.

I hadn't spoken to anyone in days. It seemed to me that night that everyone else had something in life I had lost: fun, laughter and confidence. My old team won, but I felt defeated. I'd fallen to the bottom of a dark pit and feared I would have a whole year ahead before I'd see sunshine again.

My instincts that something was wrong with Rob were reflected in concern by his new pediatrician, but the same comment was often repeated: "He'll probably grow out of it. Give him time."

Rob's legs were significantly turned inward, which without treatment would interfere in his being able to walk. To correct it, he required full leg casts for nine months. He would not have control over bladder and bowels for many, many years. His fine and gross motor and hand-eye coordination were impaired. By only a few months of age I began to wonder if he had a short-circuited nervous system, whatever that is.

To thrive, babies need the touches and cuddling and nestling and murmurings of their mother or loving caretaker. Moms need that too. And moms, to thrive, need the joy of their child making eye contact, showing pleasure at the sight of her face, cooing in response to her voice, reaching for her and reaching the necessary developmental stages. Most babies do those things. Robbie did not. He cried. And I cried, inwardly and silently, with an aching hunger and a terrible fear. What was wrong with my baby? *Was it me?*

I obsessively followed the instructions in *Your Baby*, my most recent baby book. *Babies for Dummies* was probably never going to be a popular title, but right then, it was the kind of book I needed. I had already thrown away two "how to" baby books.

The first one I'd tossed had been during my fifteenth hour of labor. I had done everything I was supposed to for natural childbirth. In fact, to assure a healthy, happy baby, I had given up my vices: candy, sugar, bologna, sodas, salt, alcoholic beverages, and smoking. I retained only my right to have a chocolate ice cream sundae after each doctor visit and weighing-in.

The picture of a *smiling* mother supposedly experiencing a contraction at the precise moment the camera flashed had admittedly prompted me to hurl the book out the open door of my labor room. As if on cue, my smiling (male) obstetrician came through the door less than a second later: "Now are you ready for something for pain?"

His dad returned and we relocated to a Marine Corps Air Base in Yuma, Arizona. This was before the days of cell phones, email, Skype, and imbedded reporting. Therefore, when my husband left to go overseas it had seemed in some ways as though he'd simply disappeared. In the eleven months following Rob's birth before his return, he'd missed out on very important bonding experiences of sharing the care and nurturing our son.

I had mailed him Rob's umbilical cord, with some humor but also with the thought that the bit of flesh, would symbolize for the new daddy the realness of his son.

Just as important, I had missed out on the experience of sharing our son's care with a father who was an equal parent. By the time my husband returned, I was so accustomed to meeting Rob's needs, I just continued to do that; it felt normal for us both. I think I must have felt like Rob was *my* responsibility. That feeling, too, had origins in actual experiences. As I said, my mother was uncomfortable with Robbie because of his crying day and night. To spare her, Rob and I drove to Biloxi, Mississippi, to stay with my husband's parents.

These grandparents were loving and accepting of Rob and me, but only up to a point. As my mother and friends had been, so did they become: very awkward with a baby who cried a lot and didn't respond with their best efforts to amuse him. No grandparent ever changed his diaper or gave him his bottle. If I left him in a playpen to go to a neighbor's, I was called home to wipe his nose or change him. For that difficult year, I was essentially alone in the care and tending of our son. I sometimes cried at night after Robbie had fallen asleep because there was the ever-present nagging concern that something was not right and I didn't know how to make it so. He'd met no markers or milestones such as reaching, cooing at me, or patty-caking.

If life with Rob had not brought more tears than laughter, I could better appreciate the humor of the striking contrast between father and his very young son during those first toddler years. The one: formal, proper, articulate, self-controlled, healthily predictable, low-key, and stable; the other: unfocused, erratic, mute, mud-covered, impulsive, and all id.

The one with strong boundaries, the other with none at all; the father: spit and polish; the son: snot and feces. The father: impeccable still at a day's end; the son: needing to be vacuumed or hosed down before he can be brought back inside after fifteen minutes of outdoor play. The vacuum cleaner and a water hose were kept at the back door. One or the other, depending on the season, formed Rob's rite of passage back into the house.

Rob was two when I threw Dr. Spock's book in the trash. It was tragic reading for me. My child behaved nothing, *nothing* at all like Dr. Spock described, in his *Baby and Child Care* except, yes, his attention span was at most seventeen seconds. I timed it often. I had been trying to follow Dr. Spock meticulously. His was at least a more forgiving book.

Years later, infant Patrick would be bathed in the family tub or kitchen sink or sometimes not at all. But for my firstborn, I bought at least one of every unnecessary item recommended on the very long list in my *First Baby Book*. That included a bathinette as big as my bathroom.

Daily, I hauled out the cumbersome but elaborate thing, filled it through a special hose that required a special adapter, and bathed Rob carefully everywhere except his face. I used only cooled, boiled water and a separate bath cloth to wash his face. *The book* said to do that.

Everything he touched was first sterilized. I had gone through two electric sterilizers by the time he was five months old. Not one other mother ever asked me how I thought babies in generations before mine might have survived without sterilizers.

He was weighed daily on the almost equally cumbersome infant scale. Actually, *the book* had suggested that I not do that, not daily. But I was breastfeeding Rob for increasingly long periods, yet he was continuing to act hungry and to cry even when I held him. I needed the reassurance that he was at least getting enough nourishment.

He was daily enveloped in a schedule of baby activities precisely as directed in *the book*. I would do all those things while he cried. And I cried because the pictures in the book are of smiling mothers and laughing babies. Presumably, those babies *liked* being tended, touched, and changed. I believe I would have been much less compulsive in the details of caring for Rob had he not cried all the time. On the other hand, in hindsight, I've asked myself, often, "What were those authors thinking?"

Rather than seeking comfort from me, at ages one and two, he seemed more to enjoy crawling into the far end of a long cardboard wardrobe box left by the moving company. Because he so obviously found it pleasurable, we kept it in his room for almost a year. He would drag his favorite blue satin blanket and crawl to the farthest end and lay there, sucking his thumb. I checked on him often and usually found his eyes wide open, although he sometimes napped. Nothing I did to love on him ever made him seem to want to love on me. But once, my husband told me that when I left our house to go shopping, sixteen-month-old Rob stood staring out the window the entire time I was gone, as if looking for me. Hearing that both thrilled me and made me sad; I thought it meant that Rob was attached to me even though he didn't act that way. But I also thought it meant, sadly, that Rob was not attached to his father. We didn't know about autism.

For a season, in Yuma, three-year-old Rob's favorite occupation was the large hole he dug in the now flowerless bed in front of our home. It was deep enough so that sitting in it, little more than his head was above the rim and his eyes were the only things about him not covered in mud. The hole, his shovels, and the water hose usually guaranteed me maybe fifteen minutes of free time, but not always.

I learned it takes less than two minutes for a three year old to bring the running water hose into the living room or less than three minutes for a four year old to melt a rubber car on an electric burner. It was astonishing to learn how much black, rubbery smoke fills a house from burning one $3 three-inch-long toy car.

Very pregnant with Patrick, I was readying to take Rob to his doctor after ten days on antibiotics. He wore a blue pin-striped suit with short pants, a white shirt, bow tie, and new shoes. I dressed him up because we weren't being invited to parties by mommies with other kids his age, so I wanted him to wear the suit before he outgrew it. He looked adorable. I admonished him repeatedly to "stay right here while mommy dresses." Minutes later, through my window, I saw him lying down in the middle of the street in the only mud puddle within miles. Miles! This is Yuma, Arizona, in 1965. Desert.

His doctor defended him: "Well, three-year-olds play in mud puddles!"

"Why then," I asked, "were five other kids ages three and four standing *beside* that puddle laughing at Robbie in it?" They could control their impulses! Why couldn't he?

I didn't burden the doctor with my most recent hurt; it was too painful to share just yet: I had given Rob another bath and dressed him in clean clothes for the doctor's visit. We stopped at the door as we entered the large, crowded waiting room of this busy, multiple-physician practice. I looked around for a seat. Impulsively, Robbie pulled his hand from mine and ran across the room past dozens of moms and children. His arms were flung wide as he called out, "Mama, Mama, Mama." He ran directly to and climbed in the ample lap of an affable, laughing African-American lady. I laughed with the whole room, but I cried on the inside. He had never called me "Mama." He had never run toward me with enthusiasm like that; he had seldom climbed in my lap and never in anyone else's.

And the memories stream: *When had he ever voluntarily come to me for love?*

CHAPTER 4

"Mom, yesterday was a pretty bad day. I don't mean to complain but you're the only person I can talk to. I feel like my engine is blown. I've been pulling a heavier load than I'm built for. All my gauges are in the red zone, I've lost all power and I'm sliding back down a steep, steep mountain, my tires are worn down and overheated. I hope tomorrow is a better day." Rob from prison.

The phone rang as I was putting newborn Patrick down for his nap: "Mrs. Bowers, this is the lifeguard at the O Club pool. Robbie is here and he's jumped in the deep end again. Do I *have* to pull him out this time?" Funny guy.

A few months after that call, Robbie had just turned four; we had recently relocated to Jacksonville, North Carolina, from the Yuma Air Base and hoped for base housing but had temporarily rented a house in town. I was very glad to be back among trees and water.

Rob was still almost completely unaware of the kinds of subtleties which for other children function as cues for how they ought to behave. He rarely, if ever, noticed any difference if I scolded, approved, laughed, or cried. He was indifferent to my shows of affection and usually to my requests. I didn't know how to teach him these things and I couldn't find a single book that even mentioned how to teach your child to love you! I read that children imitate. Rob didn't imitate much of anything I did. He imitated motors.

Toweling him after his bath on an ordinary day, I engaged him, not expecting a response, by pointing first to his eyes, next his mouth and nose, and asking him to tell me what each was. He responded: "head lights," "gas tank," "exhaust." I was stunned and excited. I started pointing at everything. When I pointed to his legs and asked what they were, he answered, "my wheels."

Curious, I pointed to his penis, "What is this?"

"My steering wheel," he stated with no humor at all. *"Well, you're definitely male,"* I thought. I'd often told him the names of his body parts, but never car parts. I was thrilled to discover that he was more "tuned in" than he seemed to be in order to make those intelligent analogies.

There were fewer long periods of silence from him as he occasionally initiated some sentences, but more often just made very accurate sounds of cars as he ran through the house. He identified our neighbors and friends not by names or faces, but by the make of car they drove. He hardly noticed humans, even children…even me. His attention was drawn to all cars and trucks, especially to broken ones, but he seemed to notice little else of the life around him.

We were in the car on our way for drive-in food for dinner. I asked him what he wanted to eat. "Oint duiner." Just one day before, I had held an intelligent conversation about food with a neighbor boy younger than Rob. Again, I asked, "I know you want dinner, honey, but what *food* would you like for dinner, a hamburger?" "Oint duiner," he grunted again and again. I thought he must surely have understood what I wanted him to do because previously, he had sometimes stated his choice of food. I was scared for him.

Robbie was also oblivious to whatever consequences I delivered for misbehavior. He did not seem to make the connection between "crime and punishment," nor did he cry about the latter. Time-out meant nothing to him. Removing him immediately from the scene didn't faze him. He didn't keep "contracts," nor try to manipulate me to return something that had just been taken away. He simply acted as though nothing mattered. Holding him to restrain him was impossible if he did not want to be held, which, painfully, was most of the time. I never found a consequence for bad behavior that bothered him or thus modified that behavior.

Living in his own world most of the time, his waking hours were by then spent almost entirely in pushing Tonka trucks that were practically his size; he ran them into whoever might be in his path. He didn't do it deliberately, nor meanly; in fact, he did so with an almost angelic expression on his face. There did not seem to be any malice intended in any of his strange behaviors; he was just not social or aware of others. If children were in his space he casually hurt them or equally casually took their things. Indeed, he treated other children like things. He didn't appear to dislike people. Rather, people were merely large objects that moved and who had learned to move a bit faster when near him.

If anything, he seemed bewildered when children and adults reacted to him in protest. He appeared to be just as unaware that any human had feelings and could be injured as he was unmindful that Tonka Trucks had no feelings and were indestructible. Tonkas were at least without protest; he seemed not to notice that difference, either.

Rob was equally impulsive about poking fingers or objects into my nose or eyes or tugging at some part of my body, as he was about removing all moving parts from anything else he could get his hands on. He seemed compelled, even into adolescence, to disassemble things in our home and elsewhere. I remained uneasy at the thought that I might faint or fall and lose consciousness and while out be disassembled by Rob!

At four, he was not yet potty-trained and might still have as many as five soft bowel movements a day. Further, he smeared his feces all over his body and everywhere else if not caught in time. Such things were not merely isolated incidents in otherwise age-appropriate behaviors. They defined my child...and they confined him. He was not to enter the happy, awe-filled world of other preschoolers.

In a seeming paradox, two weeks after the duiner incident, Rob responded heroically to my instructions in a more complex situation. Arriving home after dark in pouring rain, I accidentally locked my auto and house keys inside the car in our driveway. With me were Rob and five-month-old Patrick. Neighbors were gone and all lights were out inside and outside our house. All my doors and windows were locked shut. We were drenched and helpless. Rob was absolutely quiet, but thankfully, so was Patrick, who was getting rained on although I shielded him as well as I could. "*Who,*" I mumbled to myself, "would build a house without covered porches?" But then, who would rent such a house?

Straining hard, I managed to remove the screen and open a bathroom window that was several inches over my head. I couldn't crawl through it, but I could lift Robbie on my shoulders and have him crawl through it. We were in the back of the house; the only door that could be unlocked from the inside by just turning the handle was in the front. I had no choice but to risk having Rob alone inside the dark house and Patrick and me outside. Standing in the pouring rain, I carefully explained to Rob what I needed him to do. Then I held him up to the window and watched him disappear, his arms sliding through my hands. He had not spoken a word the entire time. I could only hope that I had impressed upon him that he must open the door.

My heart was pounding and I silently berated myself for such a stupid move as I ran, covering Patrick with my body, around to the front of the house. Rob had opened the door by the time we arrived. I hugged and praised him and thanked him profusely. He indicated no pride and acted no differently than if he had opened the door on a sunny day to go out.

Rob and Patrick were down for the night. For the past several months, my husband had been away on some far-away island with a name I couldn't spell. I was celebrating my birthday with a glass of wine and my favorite crackers and cheese on the table beside me and a new book in my lap. Having discarded Dr. Spock two years earlier because he didn't seem to write about my son, I had hoped that night to gain some reassurance from the newest one, the title of which I can no longer recall. But as I read I saw that it, too, seemed to be about everybody else's children. I tried to rip the book in two; failing that, I threw it in the trash. The next day, I pulled it back out and forced the twisted cover back in place. Perhaps he will fit by next year.

How do you train a child who disregards all rules, learns nothing by observation or mimicry, and seems to be unaware that pleasing anyone else would be of personal benefit? How do you train and discipline a child who treats restrictions, discipline, and punishment with the same detachment as he does his Christmas presents or any other event that elicits enthusiasm and excitement in another child?

How long do you spank a child who never cries when he is spanked and then repeats the same behavior again and again? How do you teach a child who rarely even looks at you, takes no pride in mastery, who, in fact, has little mastery and who therefore does not aim for such satisfaction?

How do you remove the belongings of a child as a behavioral consequence, when all of his belongings have already been removed? How do you declare a time-out for a child who can't sit still unless his environment is moving, who might with no anger, destroy the room, or who voluntarily chooses time-out anyway, because he is equally comfortable being alone?

I longed to have Rob show spontaneous affection. I needed to have those special smiles that say: "You are *my* mommy!" I lived with an aching, gnawing hunger for hugs given spontaneously, slobbery kisses like those other kids gave me, and smiling eyes seeking mine. In later years, they would come, rarely at first and then more and more often. They were diamonds in an otherwise gray world.

———◆———

"If it was my kid, I'd take him out and drown him," thus spoke Rob's new pediatrician after reading the journal I'd been keeping on his behaviors. I'd found I needed to write down each day's events because the pain from them clouded out the memories of those from each previous day. Finally, the fear and sadness from writing down the behaviors had become too heavy to continue keeping the journal. The final entry was summarized, "Something is terribly wrong with my child!"

At first I was shocked by the doctor's comment. Then I felt relief: "He gets it!" I immediately fell in love with that gruffy, scruffy, but deeply compassionate, no-nonsense man who finally agreed with me: Something was terribly wrong with my son. Silly me, I thought now that a doctor sees what I see, he'll just fix Rob.

A brain scan was attempted but of course Rob could not lie still. Sedating him was not an option because that would alter the brain activity a neurologist wanted to observe. We were referred to a major university's child diagnostic center where for five days Rob was tested and scrutinized. Finally, we were given a pronouncement delivered by the leader of the team. We were to spank him for every infraction and put him in his room in which there was to be nothing but a mattress on the floor. That's it.

Dumbfounded, more frightened than ever before, and bitterly disillusioned, I commented that I didn't think they understood that Rob didn't mind being spanked! "Then beat him," the psychiatrist replied with no emotion.

It had cost no small amount of money, time, planning and effort for us to have Rob undergo that evaluation several hundred miles from our home. My husband had made two round trips to get us there and himself back to work and then to return on Friday to pick us up and for the report. I'd had to leave my baby, Patrick, with a friend for five days, which in itself was a difficult thing to do. My husband would be going away again soon, and my heart was heavy with that sad fact. I would miss him, terribly, and I would need him even more.

We had gone to the diagnostic center with such great hopes and, as I realized sitting there, with a very desperate need for reassurance. I didn't only need reassurance that Rob would be okay in time. I needed just as much to be reassured that I was a good mother, and that Robbie's living in his own little world wasn't just because he didn't like mine.

The psychiatrist also told Rob's dad he should not act on his current military orders to be deployed because at the very *least*, a child like Rob needed both parents. But this was my husband's career, and I don't think either of us had yet fully grasped that Rob's problems would last a lifetime. His dad went to Guantanamo Bay, Cuba, and Rob went into his room, often, always unperturbed by it. The only relief I had was that he was at least safe, but it was never a comfortable thing for me.

I certainly never beat him, but he matured over the following months so that he wasn't demanding constant restriction, and I forgot about putting him in his room. I don't recall ever thinking it was effective. I never went back to the center. Now I would have confronted them, but then, I was too uncertain about my own parenting to ever challenge experts who I thought knew more than me! To be fair, socialization must occur, and, as I've said, few professionals in the field at that time understood the less profound manifestations of autism.

Rob turned five and had almost suddenly begun talking very well in the previous few months, when he so chose. He was still not sociable. Because of his constant running off, his dad very care-fully selected the house in Oceanside, California, where Rob, Patrick, and I would live for the thirteen months his dad would again be away, now in Vietnam. His father had by then been away on other Marine Corps assignments for the past thirteen or fourteen of the previous sixteen months. He was leaving again after being with us thirty days, but that while traveling across country from the east coast to California. I managed to smile on the outside at any opportunity but the feelings of mourning, dread, and loneliness were ever present. I never lost the feeling that I was grieving his death.

In typical Rob fashion, he registered no emotion about his dad's leaving and never asked about him. But he didn't need to because I talked to both boys about their dad every day so they would not forget him.

Our new home had an ample backyard surrounded by a solid six-foot-high stockade fence. It was on a safe cul-de-sac with only mountains behind.

The first week after his father left, I bought the most elaborate swing set I saw in the store. It had many moving parts and things to keep Patrick and Rob happily occupied. I could hardly wait for its delivery, believing that finally I would have some worry-free time to devote to just Patrick as well as to myself. So far, his and my quality time had been largely spent, like my gasoline budget, driving around looking for Rob. The new backyard also had a patio for Rob to drive Matchbox cars, his latest single obsession. Here, he would be content to stay and play.

The deliverymen off-loaded a half dozen very long, narrow boxes and as many broad, flat ones, with a couple of squares, too. Offering me the receipt to sign, I asked, "But where is the swing set?" The man motioned to the boxes lying on the ground in our front yard, "Right there." I stared at the boxes, then at him: "No, no, there's been a mistake," I know I sounded just the way I felt: desperate. "I bought the *large, very tall* deluxe set, with slide, glider, several swings, monkey bars…"

There were, counting all the screws, bolts, and plastic protective coatings for the ends of the screws, nine-hundred and eighty-three pieces. My hunch was that there were originally an even thousand but that Rob had maybe thrown some over the fence. I decided that was already an improvement in that a year earlier he would have just chewed them up.

In the ensuing years, I have finished my doctoral dissertation and earned a PhD. I obtained a Private Pilot License. I have cooked and hosted four course sit-down dinner parties for as many as twenty people and buffet dinners for forty or more.

I can finally spell "hors d'oeuvre" and am not intimidated by Beef Wellington. I teach university graduate students and give other presentations to professional groups. I am comfortable holding a therapy group with fifteen or so schizophrenic patients. But assembling the swing set, by myself, while reigning in toddler Patrick and wild child Rob, remains my single greatest accomplishment.

I learned to discipline the boys, at least for the week it took to assemble the swing set, with a tap on their heads, just ever so lightly, without bothering to put down the screwdriver. It didn't make them cry and wasn't intended to; it got their attention momentarily.

I appreciated the humor of Rob's yet another new pediatrician who asked me if it was possible that Rob had ever received a head injury. "I don't think so," I replied. "Do you think my disciplining him with a hammer made him this way?"

"No," he answered, "I think it would have taken a Mack Truck."

The swing set, with slides and glider, took me one week to assemble, working almost all day every day. It took Rob about a minute to climb to the top and jump over the fence, a feat he thereafter repeated any day I was not out there with him. The high fence had become a problem rather than a solution. It held me captive for sufficient time for Rob to disappear. I was discovering that every solution produced a bigger problem. Wasn't it supposed to be the other way around?

I've often been asked what it was like managing Robbie on a daily basis. I relate the following story and assure people that it was a typical day in my life with Rob, exceptional only in that we were going on a trip. We would be driving to San Francisco from our home in Oceanside. Rob and Patrick were five and two. Their father was still in Vietnam. Rob loved to ride in a car and remained very awake, but also very quiet. Pat slept.

California was in the middle of a severe drought. As a result, field mice by the thousands had fled the mountains behind our house and entered ours and our neighbor's homes in search of water and food. I had managed to purchase what must have been the last seven mousetraps left in Oceanside; it had taken as many stores to find them. I could easily have used twice that number. The migrations of the mice toward water made headlines. They caused wrecks; they wreaked further havoc in the life I had with one child in diapers, another child in chaos, and a husband in combat.

Every evening at his bedtime, Rob and I would set the traps. Every morning, he would dutifully empty them. He did so with equanimity I envied and admired. Sometimes, he would remark in his deadpan, monotone voice, "Oh, this one isn't dead yet." *Plap*! "Now it is." I flinched; he did not. Or, to himself more than to me: "…wonder where this one's eye ball is…Oh, here it is." Flinch.

He seemed to like the responsibility of the traps and liked knowing that he could handle something that made his mother uncomfortable. He was not squeamish.

The presence of the mice everywhere in my house was quite literally maddening. It did not comfort me at all to know that all my neighbors had similar unwanted guests. All my neighbors also had husbands in their homes.

I heard the mice gnawing and scratching all night. It seemed that I would only just doze off before I'd be startled awake by the snap of a trap and then another and another. On a previous night, I'd been awakened by a mouse tangled in my long hair; I assumed it had scampered up the bedspread that I folded at the foot of my bed to the floor. I didn't do that anymore but neither did I sleep anymore that night.

Mice were inside my sofa, chairs, box springs, cupboards, closets, walls, and attic. They were bold, if sluggish, so that even Patrick was able to catch a mouse and proudly show me his treasure. They ate away at all things made of leather, and our clothing was ruined. Yet, they formed the pleasant topic of more than one bedtime story as Rob and I would snuggle in his bed, with Pat asleep and the lights out, watching mice play in the patches of moonlight that splashed across his floor. He and Pat liked the mice. There was some comfort in that since getting rid of them by attrition was not working.

On this day-just-like-every-other-day, I had been awake much of the night listening to the mice, fearful to sleep. After showering, I quickly applied lotion and makeup then got the children up for breakfast. We were all three cranky.

I loaded the washer with Pat's cloth diapers and filled the kitchen sink with soapy water to wash our breakfast things. The phone rang and as I picked up the receiver, a mouse scampered up the cord. I was unnerved. At the same time I glanced at movement on the sink ledge and saw another mouse. In one, uninterrupted motion, I knocked the mouse in the water, pulled the stopper, turned on the disposal, and stood there shuddering then pretending calmness as I said "hello."

The boys were fussy, and Patrick was mad at the cat for eating his breakfast. I sent Rob to the closed garage as I finished our packing. Many things there fascinated him so I knew he would be occupied. Suddenly, from there I heard very loud popping noises as though a series of gunshots or explosions was occurring.

Rob stood stoically by the washing machine, now at an angle about three feet from its usual position. He told me very calmly that he had stuck a very large screwdriver into the motor of the washer while it was spinning.

Apparently, in being forced to a sudden stop, the washer... Actually, I have forgotten the explanation later offered by the repairman who seemed quite intrigued by the happening, but then it was neither his son nor his washer.

The essential facts were that the washer had more or less exploded and it was beyond repair. Pieces of metal were everywhere. Black rimmed holes in irregular shapes and sizes were scattered throughout the white washer exterior, but, miraculously, Rob was not hurt.

I was crankier: "Why?" I whined, "Why can I not have one day of peace? Why can you not behave for just a little while? Why is there constant turmoil in our home? Why?"

"I don't know. Can I look at the car motor?"

It always fascinated me in those days of real service at gas stations, that Rob knew how to pop the hood of my car and I did not, at least not without much fumbling. He loved looking at the engine. He popped it open, tiptoeing to just peep over into the engine compartment. I propped the hood up for him and then transferred the diapers to the dryer.

Back in the house, I heard Patrick flushing a toilet. He was not that well toilet trained. I hurried into his bathroom where he pointed at the water swirling down and said something unintelligible. Unlike his brother, Patrick showed obvious pleasure in all his accomplishments and discoveries. I saw no harm done there.

I walked to my room to put on my wedding rings from the dresser where I had left them when I applied lotion. They were missing. "Patrick? Where are mommy's rings?" Patrick took me by the hand and led me back into his bath, pointing to the toilet, just filled. "My rings," he said.

I could not reach them with my hand. The plunger didn't suck them up, although fortunately, neither did it suck up anything else.

The plumber told me to not flush the toilet. "All right, don't flush it again…" and to call him when I returned from San Francisco. I fought back tears as I led Patrick to the garage with his brother and returned to the house to get our bags and lock up.

From the garage, I heard the kind of blood curdling scream that every mother can distinguish in her own child. I identified the scream as not one of anger or frustration; but rather one of physical agony. Racing down the hall in terror, I could also tell it was Patrick.

My panic changed to momentary confusion. Both Patrick and Rob were standing there, two sets of *enormous* eyes staring at me, but with no apparent injury.

Our cat, which only moments before Patrick had chased from the kitchen because he thought it was eating his own tuna, had jumped onto the hood of the car and sat on the ledge just beneath the windshield. It is…it was a favorite perch. He could sit there just out of the kids' reach and disdain their every act. The cat's tail would sort of drift down into the engine compartment in the gap between the ledge and the opened hood.

Rob, monotone, said: "The hood closed itself."

What I saw was a cat racing on all four feet going nowhere very, very fast since he was anchored by his tail. In some ways, I can handle a child's pain better than I can handle the pain of an animal. My reasoning is that since the child and I are both verbal, I can talk to a child, soothe it, reassure it, apologize, kiss what hurts, or promise ice cream if that will help. I can't do that with an animal. I have a couple of scars on my upper lip that prove cats don't like to be kissed when they're terrified.

If my hands had not already been shaking, I would still have fumbled with the hood release. My hands were shaking badly; it had been that kind of morning. I'd started trembling when the mouse went down the disposal, it got worse when the washer exploded, worse yet when I imagined my rings under the city sewer, and worst of all when I thought Patrick had been impaled…perhaps with a very large screw driver. It was Rob who calmly reached over and popped the hood release.

In amazement, I watched the cat sail out of the garage. It was as though he had gathered so much momentum racing on the hood that he simply flew the twenty- foot distance to our sidewalk, his tail bent at a 90 degree angle. He was gone in a black streak.

"Why?" I asked again, this time in horror over the cat. "Why can I not have one minute's peace? If you do one more thing, Robbie, we are not going to San Francisco!" Of course, we were going to go and of course I had said that already this morning at least three times.

I continued to ask why they cannot behave as I plopped them in the backseat and as I buckled their seat belts. I told them how hard life is when you can never anticipate anything going right. I continued explaining that mommies are much nicer when their kids behave well. I started the engine and I jammed my foot on the accelerator to back out of the garage in a burst of energy fueled by an accumulation of fear rather than anger.

Crunch, bang! Bang! Clatter! Bang! There were dark clouds of thick dust, flying objects, and falling boards. Dead silence inside the car.

There had always been a very, very thick rope, at least three inches in diameter, dangling from the rafters of the garage, and curling onto the floor immediately in front of the car. At the end was a large, permanent knot. The rope was there when we moved in. Rob swung from it; mice scampered up it.

On that day, Rob told me when we were finally on the freeway, that he had tied the loose end of the rope to the bumper of my car. The rope was too thick for me to tie much less for him. What I imagine is that he somehow lodged the rope, with its huge knot, between the bumper and car so that rather than coming loose when I backed out, it tore down the rafters of the garage.

CHAPTER 5

"A person like me doesn't belong in prison. I should be in some other kind of place." Rob from prison.

There's this thing the baby books don't tell you: it's about the heart part of you that is so in love with your children that it is impossible to step back, step outside the box labeled "mother" so as to look at patterns of misbehaviors objectively. Objectivity would diminish the fear for their futures or grief for their trials. It's a positive thing for counselors and teachers who can do that, except with their own children. But the books don't tell you that mothering *hurts*. They don't describe how it will be that in your humanness you will in turn hurt your children: with sharp words you can't take back, with temper flare ups you can't erase, with times of selfish pursuit you can never regain and give back to them.

Looking back over earlier years as a mother allows me to see with the advantage of hind-sight vision, but it also brings the tears of regret for those decisions I made that were not always in the best interests of my children.

Some of the anger in those years, whether righteous or not, was born of my frustration that there was no real help for Rob. No professional came up with an intervention; no teacher devised a plan to strengthen his basic skills or help him better integrate into the class. Very few ever saw the loneliness in him and extended a helping hand. Grandparents kept quiet and largely absent. Only a rare friend understood the situation enough to talk with me about him. Everyone shook their heads because they had no suggestions.

The diagnostic terms tossed about by subsequent specialists during Rob's earlier years included: autistic, childhood schizophrenia, minimal brain dysfunction, brain damage, hyperkinetic, grossly unsocialized, and dyslexic. Attention Deficit Disorder and Asperger's Syndrome would come later, the former not yet a discrete diagnosis, having been previously subsumed under others.

He experienced one minor surgical procedure during his fifth year, remarkable, I then thought, only in that pain from it made him scream and shake violently. I'd never known him to have that kind of extreme reaction to anything. His pediatrician believed that Rob's enuresis was due to a stricture in his urethra, so the abnormal narrowing was corrected by inserting a device through the urethra. The screaming and violent shaking re-occurred every time he had to urinate for the next several days, something he tried to avoid, thus adding to the problem.

He also had chronic ear, eye, nose, and throat infections. Therefore, he was almost always taking antibiotics and antihistamines. Two rows of green mucous seemed permanently attached from his nostrils to his upper lip. He sneezed often and for some odd reason, he kept his mouth closed when he did; the aftermath was rather gross. Those sneezes were one of many reasons he was *persona non grata* in restaurants.

He always looked adorable, at least to me, except for the mucus. He had no outward physical signs of any disability, yet, somehow he looked different. His face was usually without expression and his attention was inward or very scattered or only on cars; his lack of impulse control seemed exacerbated by the anxiety he had developed around others once he began to acknowledge that others existed.

He couldn't just chat or tell jokes or discuss sports or anything else of interest to others. With some periods of exception, through most of childhood and adolescent years, Rob seemed almost incapable of engaging in meaningful dialogue. He might give a monologue, but his attempts at conversation led us on circuitous verbal paths while he asked a stream of endless questions without answers. Or, he interrupted and interjected into all conversations the unrelated subject of cars and then seemed unable to change the subject from cars back to whatever the rest of us had been discussing.

To a very great extent, we are each the product of those we love. When those we love struggle with disorders or handicaps or disabilities, we, too, are deeply, pervasively affected. We are forever changed. It cannot be love and be otherwise. Love respects the boundaries of others, but it lets down its own.

I've come to think of Rob as having paradoxical boundaries, in some ways, he has none. In others, his boundaries are granite casings. In both he has too often been profoundly isolated from meaningful, mutually satisfying relationships.

Sooner or later, a child has to start playing with other kids. Almost as great as the force of life itself is the force that compels a child to step into the world of others. He must separate from being only a son in order to test his discoveries that he is "a someone." He has to learn that when his "music" is rejected, he can change it and the kids will want to play with him again.

Without the sustenance of healthy relating, it is not possible to have a normal life. Ultimately, we know ourselves through others' responses to us. We learn to think, act, and speak through these reciprocal interactions.

Autistic individuals tend to have very significant impairments in social interactions. In varying degrees, depending on the individual's idiosyncratic traits, people with autism will experience rejection for their social efforts. Yet, it is as true for the socially impaired as it is for all individuals: we can only genuinely love ourselves by first knowing we are loved by others.

Parental love is an essential but insufficient force for equipping a *troubled* child to genuinely love, to recognize when someone is "playing his song," or to ultimately play in the symphony called life. A conductor and one lone cymbalist do not comprise an orchestra. Rejection is a powerful, destructive force in the heart and soul of any child.

———◆———

Rob's kindergarten picture had evoked a collage of more tangled memories of his childhood. He was grown up, yet, tapped into that evening were memories as fresh in their pain and as current in my heart as if they belonged to that day. They had been triggered by his call to me from jail to inform me of his decision to waive trial.

He was at once adult and wise in the ways that woundedness causes, yet still the lonely little boy. How very heavy-laden must be the soul of a man or woman for whom remorse and regret are daily companions, year after year after year. He who had wandered most of his life in the nature and freedom he loves will wander no more.

When, at what moment in time or humiliation or tragedy or genetic disposition or scolding, was the pivotal point in childhood when he took a different view of himself and the world? Why did his perceptions differ so drastically from those of other kids regarding themselves and their environments? What was it like inside that lonely self to be the "misfit kid" who did not act the way other kids did even though he was cute and looked normal?

There have always been many more questions about my son than there have ever been answers. What about his life was so intolerable that he felt compelled to try and flee from it in every possible way?

Rob's life in adulthood has been a circuitous, perilous, and misguided journey sometimes to inner peace and self-respect, other times to war against his conscience and self-condemnation. What in his genes or his environment or his imagination turned him to drugs and alcohol and to roaming and wandering, searching and seeking an illusive place, quiet and sane, where he would feel he belonged? Had he always been trying to escape something I couldn't see?

Whatever form his escapes have taken, they have all been finally destructive: Days turning into weeks of drug abuse then fleeing the imagined demons that chased him across states or into caves or abandoned shacks. He entered the gnarled world of psychosis through extreme abuse of LSD and methamphetamine, and attempted, with only momentary success, to drown his demons in alcohol. Always hovering around the edges of his sanity was the dim hope that he might someday also drown the greater evil he firmly believed he contained.

In the projector slides of my mind, I see him walking down endless freeways hitching rides to nowhere in particular. I think of countless times when he walked away from fiery crashes or out of locked facilities; off his ship in the navy; over cliffs; down the Grand Canyon with a jug of vodka; deliberately into on-coming traffic; along lonely roads; in the middle of summer's Death Valley; away from broken-down cars. Walking, handcuffed, away from me, again and again.

His escapes have sometimes been on hands and knees: Crawling to the far end of a cardboard box as a very young toddler; crawling directly into the surf as an infant, without flinching or wavering when the water covered his head. Crawling from multiple stab wounds on multiple occasions after being savagely attacked and robbed, or being San Diego's first victim of the then new "hate crime." Crawling, leaving bloody trails to the sides of yet another road; crawling under bunks in prison to avoid another kick in the face or groin; and crawling into dark holes under free-ways to wait out another thunderstorm or alcohol poisoning.

However otherwise ill-equipped he was to undertake his jour-ney through life, he has not been without a strange and peculiar courage. It is not the courage of defying laws, nature's or society's. That defiance is perhaps an absence of respect, although much less for the laws than for himself. Rather, Rob's courage seems to be that he continues to live in a world he regards as home to all others, but too often hostile and strange to him.

That is not to say that Rob has never fought for his life, argued against real or imagined injustice, or is never argumentative or oppositional. He holds strong opinions to which he silently clings as though changing them would cost him his identity. Indeed, it might cost him just that since autistic individuals typically lack the capacity to take in the perspective of the other person. That lack may look like stubbornness or be perceived as opinionated by another who has not spent a lifetime on the outside of society looking in.

Rob is never provocative, hostile, sarcastic, or faultfinding. In fact, the art of sarcasm is beyond him. Yet he can be belligerent when he is intoxicated and backed into a corner, and his fragile sense of self is being trampled.

Sober, he is very considerate and non-confrontational. One of the most unexpected features of his adult personality is a quiet respect for the individuality of others and their rights to hold dif-ferent opinions, as long as theirs are not forced on him.

However, he has violent, unwanted, and detested fantasies. He cannot, at will, stop repetitious thoughts so morbid and repugnant that "the worst ones *cannot* be told!" Not even to me to whom he has told and entrusted more dark secrets than I want to know.

His obsessions seem to him to be demons with wills of their own. That they come from his mind is the source of shame so intense that he thinks death is the more desirable alternative.

Always, his fantasies include his own welcome death in fiery crashes. To contain them, and contain them he must, demands that he both try to drown them and that he further barricade his emotional self from others.

"Mom," he has cried out to me, "my fantasies are like a barrier between myself and everyone else!" At thirty-three, he tearfully stated again what he had said throughout his life: "The thought of my ever actually doing harm to another person is the worst thing I can imagine!" But in the rogue images that steal into his consciousness, he does imagine such harm to others; and because he does, and because his fantasies are so morbid and reprehensible to him, he believes that he must be "evil." Being "evil," he cannot love himself and he believes no other can love him.

"But," I have pleaded at these times, "I love you!"

"You're my mother," he says dismissively, "you're supposed to love me." The demons from which he runs run with him.

I don't know when Rob stopped believing that he was like other people, or if he ever believed he was. He has had many reasons to stop trusting his instincts about how people will respond to him. I know that from a young age, barriers existed and that from behind them, he seemed to march to a drummer I could neither see nor hear.

As I searched for answers in my own mind, "why" and "how" took my thoughts back to San Luis Obispo and I did not want to be there just yet. San Luis Obispo was the end point; I still needed to follow the mental route that led Rob to that bus bench in a park-like setting in a pretty college town. Along the route is autism.

CHAPTER 6

*"Drugs came along at seventeen and solved all those problems
and temporarily destroyed my shyness and made me feel strong.
Too strong, though, and eventually brought on even greater
problems."* Robbie from prison.

Autism, I learn too late for Rob's benefit, is a pervasive developmental disorder of unknown origin although many researchers believe it is diffuse brain damage. That belief is current among some researchers now but it was also the first significant diagnosis given to Rob when he was eight and again at nine. It makes sense in that Rob's problems were so varied, as were his strengths.

Some individuals are so severely autistic or drawn into themselves, that they have almost no discernable interaction with or response to their environments. These people need total care all their lives and require one-to-one staff attention for their most basic needs.

No two autistic people are alike, but they have some traits in common. Often, they have impairments in certain basic capacities of *cognition* that the rest of us take for granted, such as knowing the difference between a mother's face and that of a stranger's. I've noted as one example for Rob the time when he called a stranger "Mama" although he had never appeared to single me out as any different from other moms in a group. He went to none, at first. Also evident is impairment in the manner in which the brain of an autistic person processes information about their environment.

Merriam-Webster's New Collegiate Dictionary defines "cognition" in part as "the act or process of knowing, including perception, awareness and judgment." It is an overly simple statement but nonetheless true that in Rob, all three of those mental functions were impacted.

The definition addresses the unusual manner in which information about their world is processed by individuals with autism. This difference includes how they interpret actions, as well as the facial and verbal expressions of others. For example, as a child, Rob didn't respond any differently to smiles than he did to frowns or expressions of fear.

That in itself is quite significant: facial and verbal expressions in one person that don't correspond in kind to the event or words spoken by another (parent, teacher and other children, as examples) trigger a variety of reactions. Those may range from anger and frustration over what seems to be a disregard for the seriousness of a matter to rejection by the other, again, because the child might *appear* to lack concern or sympathy.

I was constantly asking Rob if he'd heard or understood me, feeling frustration or irritation because he hadn't responded as I thought he should. His physician noticed it, too, but misread the signals just as everyone else did. He had Rob undergo an adenoidectomy and tonsillectomy, believing that Rob's lack of social responsiveness meant he suffered from a hearing loss because he had so many ear, nose, and throat infections.

A pattern, then, of reactions from others from what appears to be a lack of reaction in the autistic child adds to that child's confusion and lack of self-confidence in social situations. It also interferes with the child's learning social skills.

Individuals with autism typically also have selective attention. That is, they don't always respond to the entirety of an object or event, but to one part of it, as with Rob's focusing only on one part of his environment at a time. In the vast world of people, buildings, trees, activities, he only noticed cars. With a room full of toys, he spent his playtime with upended toy trucks, turning the wheels over and over. As he matured, his interests remained singular, but progressed to pushing toy trucks, then to motors only, not acknowledging other children or adults.

Their thinking is often more concrete as with Rob's logic that if he changed his name he would be like other boys with that name; or his difficulty with idiomatic language since everything was taken literally except the words he made up. "Run upstairs and get your coat," literally meant to run up them.

Having lived with an autistic person for so many years, and having worked with them professionally, I find them fascinating and to have intriguing perceptions. The difficulty is that too often, it also sets them apart. Autistic individuals vary in the extent to which they distort perceptions; and in their idiosyncratic misreading of the emotions, intentions, and attitudes in others. This is significant for learning to make friends and interact with others in a meaningful way from childhood on.

Another serious result is that their judgments will be different from non-autistics since from the outset the processing of information on which their judgments are made is different from most non-autistic people. Before I understood anything about autism, I was describing Rob's behaviors as coming from "short circuits in his brain." Despite what I now know, I still find that to be an apt description of how he often acts and perceives things, and that includes the endearing, pleasant, and sometimes brilliant, but always unique, perceptions he makes of his environment. Yet, I so often enjoy seeing things through his eyes, his perceptions of non-threatening matters are fresh and unique.

We human beings are wired to acquire all knowledge through our senses: we know what we know through what we see, hear, touch, taste, and smell. Different parts of the brain are activated as we are learning, forming complex nerve pathways in the brain. Certainly, newborn infants who will acquire enormous amounts of information in just their first year are experiencing rapid and intense neural (nerve) development and activity. For example, the very young infant touches, manipulates, and "tastes" everything in their budding processes of learning about their world. This is not random or senseless; it is purposeful behavior that helps them establish pathways in the brain for increasingly complex learning.

As discussed above, one of the most important things to be learned by all humans is how to relate to others. The processes for that begin at least shortly after birth with the image of the face of their mother or primary caretaker. Yet, research suggests that the portion of the brain of an autistic child that is activated when they are looking at their mother's face is that part in non-autistic children that is activated when they are looking at and learning about *things*, objects. If that is true, then immediately, neural *distortions* of how they will process information about other human beings are being established. I've mentioned that Rob didn't act as though I was any different from any other human; but even more applicable here is that he seemed to associate the fronts of cars with human faces, giving his facial features the names of car parts, instead.

The impairments are critical because at birth children's brains begin to perceive and organize their experiences and to process and store details of their environments. Again, this especially starts with the faces of their parents or close caregivers. We become human by being able to observe and then copy, mimic, and internalize the mannerisms, facial expressions, moods, language, and behaviors of significant people in our lives. In a very practical sense, our humanness requires that we identify with another outside ourselves. It flourishes through the vehicles of bonding, security, and love. But what happens when cars seem as "human" as humans?

There are many other aspects of autism, but the above features are those that perhaps most impact meaningful interactions with others. They will determine whether individuals can focus on the "otherness" of people or remain inside themselves. If the perceptions of their worlds are effectively altered as described in the different brain activity of people with autism, then it doesn't require a stretch of anyone's imagination to understand that so are their inner thoughts, fantasies, and informational processing. Their inner worlds will contain at least unique and different realities.

Contrast the above with how nature intended things to be. In a simple sense, additional pathways form in a baby's brain in accordance with the mutual exchanges between parent and child. The baby coos; the mother smiles. The mother smiles, the baby coos; he is learning the beginnings of social behavior and appropriate self-expression. He will add to his skills daily and soon he will have a whole set of deliberate behaviors he has learned so that he and Mom can have increasingly meaningful times together. He will use these new skills, add to them, and modify them throughout childhood as he learns how to be liked, accepted, and loved by others. The skills also help him learn from important others like peers, teachers, coaches, and youth leaders.

In another sense, then, those early interactions with the parents prepare the non-autistic child to play in the symphony comprised first of the family, later of the neighborhood, and finally of that portion of the world the child will claim as his own. To play in the orchestra, fortunately, does not require perfect ability of either parent or child. But it does require the ability, ultimately, to recognize one's own discordant notes. My Robbie may be the cutest kid, but he's also the one who claps when the others sway and the one who always seems to play *a cappella*.

Autistic children seem not to observe and process or respond to the nuances of moods, personalities, and facial expressions of others, or to always exhibit behaviors we think of as showing affection and preference for their parents. The result is that many appear to be in a world of their own where it is difficult for others, even mothers, to enter. For example, although I understood Robbie found the cardboard box comforting as child or that he often connected more with cars than people, it was difficult for me to understand why.

These differences can set them up as targets for childhood mocking and rejection because they fail to develop the essential and appropriate emotions, facial expressions, and other social interactions like their same age peers. Unable to take in the perspective of other people, many autistic children become perplexed by the significant differences they sense between themselves and others and about why people react to them as they do.

It is this, the *reactions* of others to the individual with any impairment, that are very often more hurtful to their vulnerable and developing sense of self than the specific disability. Repeated negative reactions of others finally leave deep emotional scars and painful memories for any child. Children with impairments of any kind have a more difficult time overcoming the harm; most may never fully recover from the effects of rejection, mocking, or bullying.

There is also almost always grief, guilt, and fear, ever present in the hearts of parents with an exceptional child. Those feelings are normal responses to an abnormal situation. Because they do not feel normal parents are reluctant to admit them or to reach out for comfort because of them. For many parents of children with disabilities, there comes a series of "deaths."

The first death is of our image of how our child will be; another is the death of our image of the parent we thought we would be. We mourn those losses while we're also grieving over those things the future will never hold for our child. For many who must let others play a bigger role in their child's care, there is the mourning, too, of the death of their role as parents as the primary care givers with all the joys that it should bring.

Those mourning times come again and again. They come at every challenge and stage along the way of life. They come every time we realize that our child is not going to participate in those activities and achievements enjoyed by the "normal" kids whose lives go on as nature planned. And surely too, every parent feels times of remorse about the bad consequences of wrong decisions made out of a desperate hope to somehow propel our child onto a more equal playing field.

The life of a person who is "not like everyone else" often represents only an accumulation of painful, failed efforts to be a someone to somebody. The capacity to bond with others and to give and receive esteem and love develops normally in the absence of disorders or severe disturbances in significant relationships. Bonding with others and giving and receiving affection and love are as essential to the nourishment of a human soul as is oxygen to the body that houses that soul. Where there are perceptions of being rejected instead of accepted and belonging, the pattern is set in which a child learns to devalue himself and is therefore never sure about how or whether to value others. That accumulation of painful interactions finally breaks the spirit of an individual who has struggled to live in a world where he also struggles to figure out how he belongs.

No matter that Rob has gifts and talents that he might contribute to society. If no one values the person, how can they value his works? He remains locked inside himself, still trying to say "I am," before he can get beyond that to say, "I do."

And yet some secret hope that both he and love are ultimately of value propelled him to journey also in search of them. Whatever it is, he knows love exists; he has redefined it all his life.

A product of his culture, the adult Rob now comprehends love in vague romantic terms. Yet in rare moments of more vulnerable conversations with me, he has been able to express deep, deep longings for intimacy, belonging, knowing, and being known, and in being known, for respect and acceptance. As my heart listened to the insights he stumblingly shared, I heard that his life experiences have left him better equipped to suffer than to rejoice.

Rob has sometimes sold his heart, mind, and body for acceptance and companionship. I know that because he's told me his shames. At other times, he has longed with equal fervor for simple peace in isolation. In finding that neither lasts for very long, he has courted death, fearfully uncertain that even his grave will offer solace.

Hungry, lonely, and desperate, he sometimes accepted a counterfeit affection that only left him more injured. Individuals of both genders have at times offered him "love" in exchange for his money or his drugs. Not able to discern real love, he nevertheless hoped. Each time, he closed back inside himself to lick his wounds, enveloped in a grief too deep to express and too intimate to analyze.

Whenever I have sensed Rob withdrawing, I am reminded of Poley, my family's childhood dog. There was no veterinarian in the small Oklahoma town where I grew up. An injured pet healed itself. Poley had boundless energy and abject devotion to us kids. He seemed always at once to be wherever each of us was. If not snoozing with one eye opened in observance, he was tugging us out of danger in the street, or defending us from imaginary stampedes. Having rescued us from harm's way, he would romp, chase his tail in dizzying circles around us, and yelp with the incredible joy he seemed to find in simply being alive in such a place, in such a time, in such a family.

Sometimes Poley's protective love resulted in injuries to him that one of us would have otherwise received: a car just missing us, but hitting him, or Poley, from out of nowhere, coming between one of us and another, aggressive dog.

Regardless of whatever comfortable bed would be made for him while he healed, Poley rejected it and all our help. He crawled, limped, or dragged himself to the far corner of our property and lay concealed among the sunflowers for the days or weeks it took to heal. My brother or sisters and I would take fresh food and water to him daily. I would sit hunched beside him, grieved that I could not heal him, beseeching him to get well, to feel my love, terrified that he might die. Poley didn't seem to be aware of my presence while he was deeply injured.

In time, I learned to recognize the signs of Poley's healing. The morning would come when all his food had been eaten sometime during the night. Shortly after would follow a morning when he would wag his tail and lick my hands and face instead of his own wounds. Finally, Poley was bounding again with joy, ignoring whatever residual pain there might be, disregarding his most recent limp. Poley's exuberance came not at all from any sense of how important he was but seemingly from the secure knowledge that the purpose of life was life itself.

Poley taught me unconditional, sacrificial love; he taught me that love is what we do much, much more than what we say. And he taught me that loving is always, always worth whatever pain it may bring. Poley never "learned" to avoid risking injury for our sake. He would have been indignant at the thought of doing so! He licked his own wounds and he licked ours. He only withdrew when his injuries made it impossible for him to give himself fully to us.

In direct contrast to Poley's physical ones, Rob's deepest wounds have always been rejection, exploitation, and failure. But like Poley, when he was injured, Rob dragged himself to the farthest corner away from human beings. In time, he would place ego defenses, like soiled bandages and raggedy casts, over unseen wounds and set out into the world again. Limping, seeking and searching for meaning, he was most alive when he was wooing danger and defying death, never understanding that these are substitutes.

His signs of healing came finally in those mornings when he pulled some nonsensical prank or asked a question that had no answer. But the scars remained, as visible to his mother as those from the stab wounds all over his body. Never has Rob had more than brief moments of any sense that his life has a purpose or meaning. I wish Poley had been here for Rob.

Eventually, we learn that Rob had difficulty distinguishing among the many, many impulses that flooded his mind. He was nine years old and under the care of a child psychiatrist. For him and for most autistics, learning to do the socially acceptable thing or making an appropriate comment is a tense game in which everyone else knows all the rules. The game demands that he or she immediately guess the right one out of many different vague and obscure options from which to choose.

Added to Rob's difficulties, then, and to countless others diagnosed with Attention Deficit Disorder with Hyperactivity, is the multitude of impulses that occur in a flash. Whereas most children learn before kindergarten to focus on the appropriate or acceptable act and to inhibit competing impulses, many children like Rob do not. How can such a child do the right thing, that is, initiate appropriate behavior, if he or she can neither identify the "rules" or know which among the multiple inner impulses is the one that is going to please another? Nowhere are these complex issues more glaring than in social situations outside the home.

Deep wounds are made to the fragile little self of a child who is unable to understand the rules and also unable to distinguish good from bad impulses. The child's good act might receive a scolding from a parent, punishment from a teacher, or rejection from his playground peers. Rob once deliberately missed the school bus because he'd wet his pants in class and was too embarrassed to have anyone else see, so he instead ran all the way home. The school saw this as a problem behavior; his mother did not. Very often, the parents of a child who is different must act as a buffer between their child and the institutions intended to serve them.

On another occasion, he picked all the newly bloomed flowers in a neighbor's yard to bring me a bouquet. "I just thought you'd like them, Mom!" Often, there is additional hurt and confusion because the other person attributes wrong *intentions* to the behavior. Too often a motive is defined by the bad results of an otherwise innocent act.

Modification of behavior is also a mutual occurrence between parents and child. A parent responds to his or her child's temperament to a certain extent; the child responds to the parent's moods and acts. They arrive at a rhythm in which both will play out the music of childhood.

To cope with the confusing noise of a world he didn't quite understand, Rob would in time quietly compose his own "music" while others played around him. Only later would I learn that the music he composed contained dark, tragic lyrics that no one heard in time. Eventually, the macabre lyrics and complex notes of acid rock imposed external form to his internal chaos. And he indeed found a balm for his wounds, as that music had promised, in drugs and alcohol.

Rob's discovery of drugs was quite by accident, as I now suspect is true of many young, lonely teens. His subsequent discovery that they made him feel good about himself was far headier stuff than the states of oblivion he would finally reach. Drugs dissolved his fear of people and alcohol drove away the unbidden morbid thoughts, usually.

Whatever other problems his substance abuse caused him, and no matter that other demons took the place of his own morbidity, drugs and alcohol offered him a respite from intense shame. More importantly, they turned loneliness and isolation into an adventure. He sometimes preferred the consequential rejection by society to the torments of his own inner life. In neither environment did he find peace.

Outside that altered state, Rob, in true autistic fashion, continues to largely live out other fantasies about what he believes all people to be like, except himself. All others have, it seems to him, a freedom from self-recrimination that permits them to at least dwell in peace with themselves. All other persons offer something of value to others. Others take for granted that they are equal to everyone else in at least the commonality of their humanity. Rob does not.

No other person, thirty-two-year-old Rob believed, had morbid thoughts like his. When I tried to assure him that there are many others who do, tears welled in his eyes, "Where are they?" he cried out. "If I found other people who had thoughts like mine, I would... Mom, I would *love* them! I would love them so much! I would understand them!"

Because of his fantasies and his thoughts, he saw himself as so different from others that he wondered if he was an alien. He felt like a *something*, always unwelcome and unable to communicate with anyone else beyond awkward superficiality, and always fearful lest others discover the evilness he kept within, unless he was drinking or using drugs. Then he believed he spoke and acted like everyone else.

"Mom," his voice pleading for me to understand his private agony: "I *like* myself then!"

It is often in the simplest of sentences that the most powerful messages are communicated. I had never before heard Rob say that there was any situation in which he liked himself. I had no more words of rebuttal.

Finally, in time, the alcohol abuse led to enough trauma and punishment to cause Rob to accept that he must quit drinking. To quit alcohol posed the difficult challenge of learning to live somehow with a sober self in a world where he still thought of himself as a misfit. For whom or what might he quit drinking? For himself? There was nothing of himself worth quitting for. For others? Who? With whom could he now bond sufficiently in a united goal of sobriety? How might he suddenly form attachments with people? He feared people more than death or drunkenness; he was convinced that whatever made other people tick is a part completely missing in him.

Again and again, he committed to quitting. Again and again, he relapsed. To violate his commitments was to continuously repeat the endless cycle of confronting personal failure and shame and the groping for some shred of personal dignity. Such were his struggles until incarceration for auto theft forced sobriety and sobriety forced him to find new ways of being around people, because escape and avoidance were no longer possible.

———————◆◆◆———————

As his mother, I have always grappled with my own flaws and vulnerabilities on a daily basis. Mothering isn't a profession one might change upon discovering one isn't good at it. For better or for worse, mothering is a forever thing.

Becoming a mother is an instantaneous and permanent transformation of identity. Almost overnight, and even in the middle of the night, a mother finds she cannot imagine life without her child. She learns that she loves in a way she could never have imagined and she discovers she can hurt with the same intensity. God wired mothers to do things like nurture and protect their children and to heal their broken hearts.

But Rob was broken and I could not fix him. I had fixed a thousand toys, a half-dozen bikes, and more overflowing toilets than I could remember. I had fixed all his things that could be replaced, but I couldn't mend the one thing that could not be.

Everything about Rob seems a paradox to me: He is so fragile; he is so sturdy. He has a strong sense of humor but understands almost no joke. He wants to be loved, but he distances other people. He collects things he loves and then destroys them. He can explain Einstein's Theory of Relativity but cannot spell. He wants positive recognition yet does not disclose his own many good deeds. When most terrified of prison, he steals cars. When he most wants to remain sober, he drinks. And worst of all, when he thinks hurting someone else is the worst thing imaginable, he kills another man.

Beginning in adolescence, though it would cost him further rejection and though he would pay with his freedom, telling the truth about who he is and the bad he has done became more important to Rob than acceptance from living a lie. And while it was difficult for him to say, "My name is Robert and I'm an alcoholic." It was impossible for him to say, "My name is Robert and I need a sponsor."

He has always reminded me of a line from an old Kris Kristofferson song: "He's a walking contradiction, partly truth and partly fiction." With initial poor fine motor control, he mastered things that demanded it: art and guitar. When he had the opportunity to have recognition for playing the guitar, he played the more complex songs he had not yet mastered, rather than the simpler ones he had. Perhaps such a choice illustrates in a small way some of the difficulty autistic individuals have in their judgments.

Rob has spent much of his adult life roaming the country, going without food for days, sleeping in abandoned cars and houses, or nooks and crannies, or under freeways. Such a life has had its freedom and its agonies. Though he carefully stashed his guitars or radios and his other meager possessions, rarely did even a month go by that he did not have them stolen while he slept or went inside a store. Some of those years he slept in juvenile halls, jails, or prison; even in those places he has been often permanently stripped of belongings.

On more than one occasion, he detoxed from drug overdose or alcohol poisoning, alone; more than once he hid under an overpass from heavy rain and cold, dehydrated, vomiting, and delirious. Yet, he has also found extreme adventure and powerful reasons to believe that there is a God who looks out for homeless wanderers.

On one long, meandering trip, he was freezing, hungry, and penniless in the middle of nowhere in Canada. He came upon an unlocked train car that had blankets, food, and supplies. I don't know if Rob thought to thank God for that serendipitous find, but I did. He has been confronted with multiple dangers at unexpected turns, and it has been largely through resolving the problems and surviving human treachery that he developed a peculiar self-reliance and a very high tolerance for loneliness and misery.

In between those times Rob came home for a few weeks, sometimes for many months. Sooner or later he left again. I knew that I could not be his world, nor did I want to be. I am also wired to have my child become autonomous and independent. But my most ambitious imaginings for Rob have become only that he find inner peace and self-respect.

CHAPTER 7

"I just heard a song that fits my situation pretty well, 'Mama Tried.' One of the lines in it is, 'I turned twenty-one in prison...' It makes me think of you." Rob.

Rob returned home from his first term in prison of one year; he was twenty-one. He was incarcerated for stealing and wrecking a car while intoxicated, of course. Some months passed and despite his best intentions, he began to drink and smoke marijuana again, trying his best to conceal his use from me.

The marijuana use was revealed unintentionally. We were having breakfast and I noticed that a plant on my patio I had watered a few days ago had miraculously grown taller almost overnight, taller than the description had indicated it should. I marveled at it and Rob started laughing, admitting he had stubbed out marijuana cigarettes in the pot, leaving seeds.

Sometimes over the years when his substance abuse was too destructive and overwhelming, and whatever treatment we had tried hadn't worked, I would ask him to leave. Most times he left on his own for a little while because roaming and seeking were his only means to fight off depression and to perhaps distance himself from the understanding that he ought to be gainfully employed. He found something in his lonely travels that quieted the internal chaos that he found more intolerable than danger, cold, and hunger.

In that year, he discovered that the life he had idealized while in prison still contained demands he could not meet and demons he could not escape. He got jobs and immediately lost jobs until I ran out of friends who could employ him.

In one sense, Rob's adult efforts to salvage himself and his life seemed to match the improvised "repairs" he compulsively attempted in childhood on all mechanical and electrical items in our home. He was forever disassembling anything electrical or mechanical, which, of course, especially included our small kitchen appliances…and some not so small. It was as though he sensed that in discovering how *things* worked, he would come to know how *he* functioned. He had to "know" them, and they could only be truly known by taking them completely apart.

He said that he was fixing things, even when they were not (previously) broken. But he was vastly more interested in taking them apart than he was in reassembling them. Some things, somewhat like Rob, became operational again absent the parts that lay scattered about.

He had a surprisingly good work ethic and volunteered to work longer hours each day without pay to finish his meticulous detailing of an automobile. But, at twenty-two, he still had very minimal skills and no capacity to focus and concentrate for eight full hours, nor often even four. He apparently had no way of predicting when obsessive thinking would take control and certainly no acceptable way of explaining to an employer or coworkers that it had.

That seeming moodiness and apparent "loss of motivation" further alienated him from co-workers. It was that perceived alienation that took up so much of his emotional energy and concentration. He knew he should be able to converse, make friends, and reach out; he desperately wanted to. He was still the young man who made awkward, nonsensical statements because he couldn't seem to conceive the more ordinary and appropriate ones like, "What kind of music do you like?" The more he tried to force his mind to reach out to others, the more awkward, shy, and self-conscious he became.

That seems to be the definitive disconnect between individuals with autism and those without it. I think it must be worse than being isolated with an alien from another planet with whom one is expected to relate.

He looked forward to Friday pay days so that he could buy a twelve-pack and go to the desert and find respite from almost unbearable tension. Out there, his demons were more familiar than any coworker.

In that first year back with me, he also took a mechanics course at a community college. He studied dutifully hard and took pride in being able to learn. That he could even enroll in a course of studies and sit and read were themselves so seemingly miraculous that I asked little more. However, he found it impossible to apply what he learned in any consistent manner.

Therefore, as an adult, despite a strong ability to understand everything about automobiles, he can't consistently rely only on his superior knowledge of them to make efficient repairs. Always imposing into that knowledge is some sort of mental interference. I think of it, in part, as an inability to retain multiple, sequential steps toward a goal. In having other mechanics come to repair Rob's repairs, I eventually learned a little more about how his mind worked and, as always, I found his intelligent and unique creativity amazing.

According to the other mechanics, all of whom might require hours to retrace Rob's steps, he could be brilliant and innovative. He seemed to compulsively improvise. However, he invariably created a secondary problem or omitted an essential step in his mechanical endeavors. Given all the time that he needed, Rob generally succeeded in getting a car to run. Employers did not have all that time.

Nor did car owners have the patience of the other mechanics that might marvel at Rob's creativeness. He typically succeeded in major repairs, but more often overlooked the minor things. Over the years, he would again and again drag himself home from job after job, defeated by the simplest task, such as having forgotten to replace an oil cap, rather than the luxury of pride that he had done something quite difficult such as an engine overhaul.

Under pressure of time or a critical boss, he simply ceased to function. He lost all ability to focus and lost as well the fragile confidence in himself. He was still not very good at describing what happened to his mental abilities when he perceived that he was expected to function in someone else's mode. He described it as his mind going blank. He became exhausted from the struggle to focus. He could run five miles without fatigue, but he could not struggle for ten minutes to regain focus without exhaustion and despair.

Fixing cars was Rob's one essential skill. It was an obvious area where he excelled over his parents, his brother, and most others. Failing in that required enormous adjustments of a fragile ego and limited pride. Sometimes he defended against the assault to them: "That man was mean." Sometimes he succumbed and withdrew, "I can't do anything right."

It amazed me that Rob could tolerate repeated obstacles and miscalculations in his efforts to repair something major in his own car and persist with it hour after hour before emerging with a new drivable creation. It also amazed me that he tended to turn most things about cars and life into catastrophes. If something didn't work, he assumed the very worst cause, and that is where he began his attempted repair.

He would observe that he had created another problem and pursue fixing that one and then another and another. He could disassemble and improvise for some part he lacked, and he could reconstruct parts from something else.

He might conceivably have a creation on exhibit at an art or automobile museum, but if time was critical, he could not make a living at car repair.

Failing to have something that would qualify him as a con-tributing member of society was one more "reason" he returned to alcohol. Drugs and alcohol drove him back to risk and defiance of laws and craziness in the endless cycle that defined his life.

It was a precious and familiar sight from time to time to look out and see my son bent over his hood for hours on end. Each time, my wish was that he would somehow, some day, find purpose and contentment. And almost every time I watched him, I thought again about the hundreds of attempts I had made throughout his life to make him happy, show him he was loved, and find effective solutions to his problems. Despite these and despite the many prayers and sleepless nights, I grieved that he still ended up alone with only a broken car for comfort.

CHAPTER 8

"Mom, even after a week your letters still smell good. Rob

Patrick entered our family early, by inducement, because his father had orders to the other side of the country. Rob was three years and two months of age. Patrick, thank you God, was an affectionate, loving, blue-eyed towhead who loved to cuddle and be held and sit in my lap to have books read. He gave wonderfully, slobbery kisses and exuberant hugs; his eyes lit up at the sight of his mommy or daddy. It was Patrick who first validated me as a mother. He still does.

However, I became depressed during my pregnancy with him. I was terrified that something was wrong with me as a mother. Robbie hadn't taught me how to parent. He had only taught me how to love—and how to apologize to neighbors and strangers.

I realized that kids teach their parents about parenting in many ways. Each molds the other. Rob and I seemed to be warping each other. I developed a sense of humor that mothers of more normal children sometimes considered warped. I guessed they hadn't needed the defense of humor to cover pain as often as I have.

Only if you are the parent of a disturbed child, can you appreciate that humor is a salve. If you have a special needs child, humor is an essential coping skill. It is a compensation for a reality you only wish you had. It is a saving grace. One of my favorite bumper stickers during those years, few other parents thought as funny as I: "Insanity is contagious; parents get it from their kids!"

In recalling that insanity joke, my mind naturally turns to his potty training. At sixteen, when Rob could almost comfortably talk to me about the very uncomfortable fact that he still had bowel problems, I could joke with him that it was because I had never potty trained him. Indeed, I had not.

I did everything wrong in the process that can be done wrong. It became the battle that every child-rearing book cautioned against. It was self defeating for me in every sense of the word, particularly given that Rob had three to five bowel movements a day. It was *personal* with me. I don't know what, if anything, it was to Rob. How do you determine what matters to a child who acts as though nothing matters?

Each day I searched for clues that would indicate that he was going to be all right. Immediately, it will be grasped by the reader, that choosing potty training for such proof was not the decision of a rational mind. He drank out of the unflushed toilet, waded in it, flushed Patrick's diapers down it, and put toys and other objects in it, but he pooped everywhere else.

One of Rob's first real masteries, however, was that of riding his bike without training wheels. He was five when his father bought him a bike and put training wheels on it just prior to leaving for Vietnam. Rob could not reach the pedals from the seat, so he sat on the back fender and wobbled off down the street. I was thrilled for him with that. It was normal!

Two days after his dad left, Rob began asking hourly for me to take the training wheels off. I would not. He was still unstable on the bike. He still exhibited too many risky behaviors in everything he did. I needed that one small comfort of knowing he had the training wheels.

He persisted. Finally, knowing that he could not remove them himself, I told him that when he was big enough to take them off, he could do so. I had already determined that they were on so tight that I doubted even I could remove them. I returned to the kitchen from where I could hear him in the garage.

Minutes later, there was only silence. Off he was, down the middle of the street, pumping, swerving, wobbling, but staying upright. The training wheels were scattered in pieces all over the garage. It was a triumphant time, remembered because there were so few. I smile now, remembering.

Most of Rob's triumphs have emerged from some sort of behavior that was either outside the normal for his age or from breaking a family rule. I became so desperate for him to have successes, I developed a very high tolerance for aberrant behavior. There was, however, mutual and strong bonding between Rob and cats and dogs, gerbils and white mice, ferrets and rabbits. And motors.

After infancy, with one circumstantial exception, Rob almost never cried, regardless of how much physical or emotional pain he was in. I cried for us both, almost daily. I interpreted his not crying in many ways, but it also seemed to reflect a sort of dignity I still see, despite the very undignified things he has done and has had done to him throughout his life. In any case, he had learned early to hold inside deep grief and humiliation. He acted out these feelings in other ways.

One such acting out, and an exception to his not crying, was the many times when he would gather his most treasured toys, Matchbox Cars, and smash them all with rocks. Then he would cry. He would be scolded for it, disciplined about it, and threatened because of it, and we would start over collecting others. He would have chores to do to earn the money or get a car as a reward for some desirable behavior, but every few months, he would sneak them out and smash them beyond repair.

Most handicaps place the individual outside the standards of "normalcy" that society holds. The nature of the handicap determines the strength and quality of the responses the individual receives from other people. Those responses may include indifference, pity, revulsion, and rejection. Any one of them robs the child of dignity and a sense of self-worth. They are always an additional and enormous burden with which the child and parents must somehow cope.

The birth and care of a handicapped child place incredible strain on parents. Beyond the obvious mourning and grief, they also struggle to somehow learn how to help their child and to cope with the loss of hope. The negative reactions elicited by some impaired children force parents to struggle with emotions of hostility and anger toward others, guilt, a sense of a different kind of loss, and more grief.

Already, we parents have to learn extraordinary skills in order to meet our child's needs. But we also have to grapple with our own sense of isolation from the parents of more normal children. Whatever distinguishes our child from the norm can similarly distinguish the parent. Emotional handicaps are in a category all their own.

Parents of emotionally disturbed children do not have the freedom or inherent satisfaction to simply respond lovingly to the needs of their child. We love them with no less fervor than our non-handicapped children. But our love is also a struggle to find an effective response and to identify the most pressing of seemingly too many needs and demands in any situation. Our love is also a struggle against feelings of guilt, self-doubt, and embarrassment and then more guilt for feeling embarrassed.

Always, parents live with the unending tension of anticipating the unpredictable. Always, we cope with immediate and powerful conflicting emotions and demands. Daily, our sense of adequacy as parents is further diminished by the disapproval or veiled criticism from others either toward our parenting or toward our child. Sometimes the negative reactions toward parents come just as strongly from mental health professionals as they do from naive strangers.

I don't know many mothers with autistic children, but I know a lot of mothers of children with similar behavioral and difficult-to-diagnose problems. I know these mothers vary in their capacity to love and bond. I believe that very difficult children with very unpredictable behaviors can cause some parents to distance themselves from that child for their own emotional survival. At times, parents seem to involuntarily retreat back inside some safe emotional boundary where the pain is not so intense.

Sometimes the retreats are only brief respites occurring in the office of a professional. It is as though the parent hopes that someone stronger and wiser will take charge for just that one forty-five minute hour. I've been such a parent.

Other parents present as only angry and only wanting to place blame outside themselves. I know how often anger conceals intense fear and hurt. Others seem resistive or non-compliant with recommended treatment. It is less often that parents don't want to know how to help their child. Rather, it is too often that they've already discovered that the suggestions being made don't work nor seem to address their more critical concerns.

It always seemed condescending for a professional, younger than I, sometimes unmarried and childless, to make suggestions about the care of my child, suggestions which were completely unrelated to the reality of life with Rob. There is a significant difference between textbook theory and practical applications of child rearing!

Professionals who may have spent no more than an hour with the child can too easily stereotype parents. Diagnoses and labels such as dyslexic, hyperactive, conduct-disordered, and oppo-sitional defiant communicate reams to other professionals but speak little about the inner turmoil and shattered lives of their clients.

Jackie Kennedy, the now deceased wife of former President John Kennedy, once said something to the effect that if you mess up on parenting, you've pretty much messed up on life. Deep down, I think most mothers intuitively feel that. I think, too, that within the heart of almost every mother of a disturbed child there is a battle waging in which she struggles not to blame the child or condemn herself. Now as a professional myself, and especially as such a mother, I've sometimes asked my students or those I've supervised, "What is the one thing you know about the mother of a disturbed, different child?"

Their answers run the gamut from, "She's disturbed, herself," to "She needs to learn better parenting skills." While both those may be true, my answer is this: "First of all, she is hurting deeply, and secondly, she's scared to death."

There is never, ever closure for parents of disabled children. Their child does not get well. There is no funeral for the death of hope. There is no final acceptance of a trauma followed by the rebuilding of a normal life. There is, at best, a redefining of normal in order to go on with life and with loving. And there is the struggle to understand why there is no positive result for the incredible sacrifice of effort and energy. Patience and time are necessary to finally accept that one's child is not like others in his world.

I've learned that the "different" child is no less precious to God and sometimes the greater gift to the parent. But knowing that took a long time and didn't help Rob at all.

Exactly when Rob became aware that he was "not like all the other kids," I do not know. It was not, of course, that he made some sort of matter-of-fact statement like, "Mom, I know I don't behave like everyone else." Rather, it was his remaining on the fringes of play groups, and by age six, an occasional awful sentence uttered each time with grim finality: "Nobody likes me. I don't like me, because I'm damaged." I would try each time to swoop him in my arms and reassure him otherwise, but his opinions were deeply held and deeply ingrained, as though he knew things about himself that I did not.

From hearing such remarks, I began to dimly grasp that perhaps Rob's greatest enemy was within, not outside himself. This I could not combat nor protect against. Added to that was the fact that he *couldn't* do the ordinary things that other kids did like cooperative play, read, catch a ball, or consistently control his bladder and bowels. Those are rather strong elements for the makings of a "misfit" in society. He referred to himself as damaged throughout his childhood years. Cars get damaged; kids and moms get wounded.

When you have poured into someone you love all that you are, all that you hope, all your compassion, and all of your best, what is left? What is left when you are poured out and the contents of the vessel taste like failure?

The stress associated with my efforts to meet Rob's needs took on a life of its own. I came to see that those clinicians that had warned us he would need more attention than two parents could give understood what they were talking about. I had not grasped the full implications of what it would mean for parents, alone, to try and socialize Rob. In any case, I had long forgotten their admonitions. I was still functioning more obsessively than ever as a sort of super mom, the parenting version of the Lone Ranger.

The more Rob did wrong, the harder I tried to compensate for the emotional bruises he seemed to be acquiring on a daily basis. It had been years since anyone had offered me any encouragement or suggestions. Worse, years would pass before anyone except my husband again suggested that maybe it was not that I was a bad mother, but that my son needed more than parents can possibly give.

Pediatricians were as perplexed as I but now only treated his chronic allergies. Friends studiously avoided mentioning him or his behaviors. Strangers were neither so inhibited nor so kind. Family members, who very rarely saw him since we lived two thousand miles from the closest, seemed certain that I was at fault only in that I wasn't *making* him mind! I should have, but I could not. But I was learning to parent Rob by trial and error, and he had seemingly learned to trust me.

I don't recall that Rob learned anything by trial and error, although he had many, many of both. One day he could or would not do something that every other kid his age was doing; the next day he could. No glee. No wanting to "show off." No pleasure.

Similarly, he had begun talking. Within a very few months after our "conversation" about what he wanted for dinner, Rob began speaking in paragraphs. Again, one day he hardly spoke, the next day he was speaking fluently. He instantly used very good grammar in correct tenses that were superior to most children age four. By the end of his kindergarten year, however, his grammar had regressed to that typical of his age.

He did not talk consistently. He either chattered endlessly, obsessing on one point of one interest, or reverted back to infantile and repetitious demands: "Want cookie, want cookie, want cookie, want cookie." At those times, he could not be distracted, could not be redirected, and did not accept "no." When finally he spoke in sentences, his speech was almost without inflection. He spoke in measured monotones but distinctly and correctly.

Rob's vocabulary was surprisingly extensive, not only for his young age, but considering that he had not previously used words with which he now formed sometimes complex sentences. Increasingly, as he grew older and particularly when under stress, he created new words and spoke sentences that were more nonsensical. He applied phrases or clichés out of context in ways that struck him as hilarious. The failure of others to understand his application required that he remain alone in his own world of meanings.

Initially, it was almost impossible for the rest of us to understand the similarities he found in two unrelated things. As an adult, he continues to speak in that manner at times, but his associations are more often apparent and delightful surprises. He sees a commonality in disparate things or events that few others do.

Similarly, he adopted his own peculiar use of certain symbols. The question mark is one such symbol, adopted in middle childhood and continuing on into the present. It is his Mark of Zorro, so to speak. He draws question marks in odd places as though to note to an uncaring world, that he exists, and as though to ask why of a world that has no answers for him. He scrawled them across my papers or books when he wanted to make affectionate contact. He left lipsticked question marks on my bathroom mirror or circled them at times in the middle of the newspaper.

That delights him in ways I don't quite understand; perhaps it is some passive sense of personal power.

"I realize," he explains, "that those kids who didn't like me are now my age and older and they live and drive all over the country. Instead of damaging or ruining the lives of the kids that made fun of me, I just put question marks everywhere, so they'll wonder." I smiled sadly at his illogical logic and I wondered. I wondered how it was that he got even by writing question marks and another child did so by shooting his peers.

The strength of his urge to draw question marks was revealed in the rap sheet produced on Rob as defense for him progressed on his charges of murder in the second degree. His puzzled attorney asked me what I thought was behind the hundred or more misdemeanor tickets Rob had received over the years all over the United States. They all seemed to have to do with defacing property, written in different ways in different towns and states.

At first my confusion matched his until I recalled that several of those tickets lay in drawers in his room: all were written during the times when he got caught for drawing question marks. More than once, when riding with me, Rob had me drive by a sign or lamppost where he had drawn perfect, precise question marks. The more difficult the mark's location was to reach, the more pleased with himself he was for having accomplished it.

Drawing question marks was a purposeful behavior even though its full meaning was known only to Rob. It existed from childhood on, but there were other childhood behaviors that seemed random and without purpose. I assumed that I knew what Rob liked to do by the fact that he did those things repetitiously. He'd be endlessly turning wheels, pushing toy trucks, making the sound of a car as he ran through the house and all over the outdoors. He would stand for a long time twirling about in one spot; or spend long periods flapping one hand back and forth very near his face and watching it out of the corners of his eyes.

I don't recall the sound of laughter from him as a young child. That, too, makes me sad. Yet he did not seem *unhappy* before he started school.

School was a place he went daily to face his own inadequacies without inner strength to do so. It was a confrontation of how unlike the other kids he felt himself to be. However, I saw the gains he had made: he could verbally respond to others, he had developed interests somewhat beyond self-stimulation, and had added goal-directed, rather than more aimless or destructive, activities to his daily routine. Best of all, he seemed bonded to me.

He sometimes returned affection; he shared more thoughts and ideas with me. He was rightfully proud of his elaborate, complex Lego constructions. Using only the basic pieces, he was creating gears and revolving parts with Legos long before such parts were manufactured and introduced on the market. *And he called me "Mom!"*

Still, his interests were very restricted, and he showed none in books, learning, or in modifying his behaviors to adapt to expectations. He still remained more in his own world than in the world in which the rest of us lived. But he compulsively set out daily to explore all *things* in the world.

Exploration of all things seemed to demand dismantling most. He remained so unpredictable and impulsive that he needed almost constant attention, and he still acted more like a lonely outcast than a loved little boy. Yet, he was finally establishing a piece of turf for himself in this world and in some ways, his fierce need to be a self seemed more important to him than did cooperation with peers. At least that is how I interpreted such things as his looking at them without comment when others teased him about something strange he might have done; or that of riding his bike in the street ahead of his peers as they called out to him "You're supposed to walk with us on the sidewalk."

To be more self-contained did not mean that Rob was more self-content. I thought of him as often tormented after age five. Every night at bedtime and every morning before school, I gave him pep talks about how good he was and how smart. Those talks did no good. He didn't believe he was good or smart. He seemed to be matter-of-fact about his real and imagined deficiencies. A lack of vocal inflection can be deceptive regarding a person's true feelings. In hindsight, I believe that Rob became very depressed about not being accepted by peers and about not understanding why that might be so.

He would share his day's activities because I prodded him to do so. They were filled with what I regarded as only hurts and humiliations, but he cited them with no apparent self-pity. He hadn't known the answers at school, he had been placed in time-out, "Johnny" had made fun of him, "Suzie" wouldn't play, "Joey" had made everyone laugh at him, "Billy" had taken his things. Nobody chose him for their team. The "big kids" had hit him. And so it went, the routine events of a child who accepted as fact that nobody liked him.

I would try to help him cope in some way that did not always place him as the one at fault. He would not be read to, but he would listen to stories I made up if for no other reason than to postpone bedtime. I made up stories in which he was a good kid, or a hero, or knew the answers. He listened quietly, never once commenting on anything I said. I did not know if he heard them. He had no insight about why his behavior alienated other kids. I had no explanation for why the kids retaliated with such vengeance.

The time came when survival of his own ego demanded that he defend himself by rejecting those who rejected him. His kindergarten teacher remained in that group.

I knew it was the practice of his teacher every morning to ask the children the date. If it was a particular holiday, then that became her theme of the day. Beginning October 1st, I introduced a plan I was sure would cause her to change her mind about him and see that Rob was lovable and bright.

Two or three times a day, I talked to Rob about Columbus Day. I showed him on the calendar, told him all about Columbus, the names of his boats, and why it is a special day. Beginning October 10th, I took him through the drill: "When your teacher asks what day it is....."

Columbus Day arrived. I could not be any more excited if Rob had the lead in the school play. I asked him the date over breakfast; he gave me his brief spiel. He answered my questions. He was brilliant. He trudged off down the sidewalk, dodging bikes of older boys who tried to run him down. I thought, "Here's a boy with a mission today!"

At eleven-forty in the morning, Rob entered the house as he did every day. No greeting. No eye contact. The usual. I initiated, "Hi, sweetie, how was school?"

"Fine." It was always fine immediately after school, regardless of whatever had happened.

"Uh, did your teacher ask what day it is?"

"Yes." Silence. I waited. Intolerable silence.

"Did you tell her?"

"No."

"Why Rob?"

"She has a calendar right on her desk; she *knows* what day it is." To this day, Rob retains that simple, concrete logic that one does not need to discuss the obvious.

There are several difficulties associated with that logic. First, he typically and mistakenly assumes that people share his perceptions. Second, it prevents all small talk or normal conversation. Third, Rob's logic does not always correspond to that of others. Sometimes, on matters of the intellect, his might be superior, but his lack of social deftness will already have caused most listeners to disregard his opinion.

Preparing to enter kindergarten, Rob changed his name at age five from Robert to "John."

"Why 'John'?" I asked.

"Because Johns are good boys."

His school principal happened by when I was registering Rob for school and good naturedly agreed to Rob's unofficial name change saying, "If he wants to be called John, then that's what it will be!"

His teacher, however, refused to allow him to call himself John. "Robert is a perfectly good name!" Later in that same year his kindergarten teacher stunned me, "Mrs. Bowers, I love you, but I want you to know, I hate Robert!" She had "loved" me because I was already entrenched in my practice of compensating for Rob's different behaviors by being, or trying to be, the best room mother, babysitter, neighbor, and PTA member. At least I was proof that behavior modification works! Rob was, of course, an exception to the rule. I believed I could make up for Rob's lack of conforming.

Late into his kindergarten year, his teacher died of cancer after a brief sick leave. I dreaded telling Rob about it; I was afraid his imagining her dead would disturb him. I wasn't even sure he knew what death or dying meant. I said simply that she had died, and that I was sorry. He said nothing so I asked if he was upset about it.

"No. She didn't like me and I didn't like her; I'm glad she died." While I was disconcerted by his deadpan remarks, I admitted to myself that I had never liked her either and had come to almost detest her after her comment about Rob.

His kindergarten teacher was not the first nor the last person in his life to react negatively to Rob's non-conformity. Those who cared enough to understand him, outside the family, were few. I can still count their number on one hand. I can also still count them as best friends some forty years later.

I have found that those people who saw and appreciated the humor in the many awkward situations he created or had compassion where no humor could be found are all very special people! One of these was his paternal grandmother.

"I love to go to Grandma's and Granddad's!" They lived in Florida. We had been mostly living on the west coast by then, so our visits there were usually only once or twice a year.

"What do you like best about visiting them?" I asked when he was seven.

"Because Grandma always goes, 'Oh Robbie' all over me!" She showered him and Patrick with unconditional love and kept any complaints to herself. I loved to go visit them, too. It was the only other home where I could be reasonably relaxed with Rob, without excusing his behaviors. Somehow, his grandma and granddad seemed to acknowledge some genetic responsibility for whatever they saw in him of concern.

CHAPTER 9

"Nobody will to talk to me, I guess it's because something's wrong with me. I don't know what it is. Is my brain damaged or something? I try not to care. I'm glad I have good memories of home." Rob from prison.

"Mom, Mom," a breathless but monotone eight-year-old Rob announced with finality: "I just figured out why I'm not like the other kids. God meant for me to be on a different planet. I wasn't supposed to come to earth." Ouch! Who told him he wasn't like other kids?

He always *knew*.

Thus, Rob was sent to a special school where there were other kids like him. And so the kids would like him, his behaviors became worse. They regressed to those of a more impaired autistic child who was also isolated and rejected. Ralph became the second real friend eight-year-old Rob had ever had.

His first had been another seven-year-old named Heidi. She had blond curls, sea-blue eyes, and a freckled nose. She was normal, adventurous, and self-confident. He adored her. But we left the Aleutian Island, Adak, Alaska, and Heidi remained behind. He spoke about and missed her for years. She can never know how precious was the gift of a first childhood friendship she gave to a lonely, little boy. He laughed with her.

We left Adak on what is referred to in the military as a humanitarian transfer. A child psychiatrist had been flown over to the island for the purpose of examining Rob. As this was prior to the 1975 law requiring, in part, that public schools provide an education for every child, regardless of their needs, we were advised to enter him in a private, specialized school and we chose one in San Diego where Rob met Ralph.

Within three months of starting the private school, Rob's sympathetic teachers called in secret, eliciting promises not to disclose that they had contacted us. They wanted us to know that Rob was not being helped, and that our medical insurance company was being exploited because he was not receiving any of the special training we were told he was getting. We were shocked and acutely disappointed.

So, back Rob went to public school into third grade before the concept and guidelines for mainstreaming had been developed. Lacking a choice, we hoped that since he had shown evidence of imitating behavior, he could do well around normal kids. We hoped he would mimic their behaviors as he had mimicked the regressed behaviors of the neurologically handicapped. He seemed excited; at least, he talked about it in the sort of way he talked about other positive events. It signified to him that he was perhaps normal after all, like other kids, good kids.

For the first time in eight years, Rob got himself up and dressed for school without prodding. He wanted to go. He was on his best behavior ever, for about three months. Soon he began wetting the bed again after not doing so for the past year.

He lost all interest in school. He became isolated more and more when at home. I was accustomed to his periods of regression to a less effective way of functioning, so while I was scared and worried, I didn't think to look for an unusual cause. Gone was the short-lived excitement over being like everyone else.

Months later, I learned the cause for his regression and succeeded, with the help of other parents, in getting his tenured teacher fired for the very real cruelty she had inflicted on him and a few other children who came to school with injuries. Rob had not spoken of it. It took the parents of other children in the same class to let us know. They did so because their own children were beginning to act out and wanting to stay home from school; they kept talking about how mean their teacher was to a boy named Robbie.

That initial period of time in public school was an episode in Rob's life like isolated others before and after. There seemed to be narrow windows of normalcy in which he made some gains and demonstrated unexpectedly advanced development that gave us hope.

The windows of hope never remained open. They were always shuttered by some disaster that seemed to remind him and us parents that trying and hope were for other kids, not for our little boy who lived in a world where he didn't belong.

We still did not have a working diagnosis for him. He had been tested and retested, but nothing was ever conclusive. On one IQ test, the Stanford-Binet, for example, his score was 86. Months later, on another, the Wechsler, it was a superior 128. There were very broad gaps between his performance and verbal scores. Those inconsistencies remained. Every new concept of training, reading, correcting hand-eye coordination was tried, with no significant results. I don't think he understood success.

<hr />

At six, Rob could correctly identify anything on a topographical map. He could retrace directions to anyplace we had ever been without missing a turn or a highway change. I grew to depend upon him to get me anywhere I needed to go because my own sense of direction was as poor as his was precise. If he said I should turn, I turned against my own strong sense that I should go straight, but he would be right. That represented another skill that was better than his mother's, but he took no delight in it.

At age seven he wrote his first letter as a class project. I held his note to Santa Claus in front of a mirror, turned it upside down and read it in the reflection. Only his printed name at the bottom had no reversed letters and was right side up.

Again, I read it with the same familiar paradoxical emotions: thrilled that he had actually printed something legible (if upside down and backwards) and sad that another disability was now apparent. Months went by before he wrote again. He didn't read at all, but he had memorized his first grade reader and in doing so tricked both his mother and his teacher into believing he could read when he had to. His grandfather sent a telegram stating: "Dear Robbie, when you can read this, I will send you any model you want. Love, Granddad." I kept it for years, but it was lost before Rob taught himself to read.

In working with him at eight and nine, I observed that his typical alphabet letters looked like chicken scratch. I would tell him to make an A, show him how to do it, then have him draw the letter, but his letter in no way resembled an A, yet he seemed to think it did.

He was then so intently applying himself to these lessons that his apparent lack of progress overwhelmed me. I would set aside the materials and go some place to cry. He was just a trusting, naive little boy wanting desperately to be like all the other kids, believing anything I suggested would make him be like them, yet having no notion of why or how he was not.

At eight, he was just beginning to grasp the rudiments of phonetic reading. He had been working with an optometrist who discovered that his eyes wandered and therefore prevented his maintaining focus on any one line of reading material. The man liked and sympathized with Rob and went out of his way to help him as much as possible. He would often phone to tell me how impressed he was with how rapidly Rob caught on to the use of all technical gadgetry in his office. Apparently, Rob's focus wandered all over the page so that he picked up words randomly from many lines that resulted only in garbled sentences.

One of the first complete sentences he ever read stated: "Robbie is retarded." It was written in yellow paint in large block letters on the street in front of our house. He saw it before I did.

I can still hear him slowly pronounce the words, focusing only on each syllable rather than the content; the whole family sat in shocked silence inside the car. He finally grasped the meaning and he sat silent. It was the first time I'd ever heard him voluntarily read aloud. At that moment, I wished he hadn't learned.

He didn't understand retarded; he just knew it was the "worst thing to be in the whole world" because he had been so often so derisively called that word. He first hung his head and then with as much dignity as he could muster, got silently out of the car, and walked stiffly in the house, head high, knowing that the kids who had written it were watching from their yards. I cried; he did not, at least not outwardly

In yet another paradox, as Rob grew older, he excelled in drawing and sketching. His drawings contain minute detail and perspective and require time and patience. He omits nothing and remembers everything in hindsight about wherever we have lived. His sketched exteriors of our former homes include precise placement and reproduction of details such as faucets, air vents, and sidewalk cracks. Things that I had hardly noticed when I lived in each were as important to him as the structure itself.

When Rob was eight, I entered psychoanalysis. Sigmund Freud had been my hero since I first read about psychoanalytic theories at age fourteen. I had whimsically selected that from a long list of topics for an assigned research paper. While my classmates explored such worlds as rockets, astronomy, or anthropology, I delved into the mysteries of the mind.

Everything about the subject fascinated me. Before that research, I had wanted to be a medical doctor when I grew up.

Afterward, I wanted to be a psychologist. It was a logical choice for a girl who had spent her first twelve years crying over and bringing home every wounded animal and every bird that had been shot with a BB gun.

Psychology was perhaps a wiser choice than medicine considering that for most of the animals I tried to heal, I ended up singing *Amazing Grace* over their graves. Wilted in spirit, I buried each in the ever-expanding pet cemetery in the otherwise empty lot behind our house.

Psychology was an ironic choice for a girl who would be the mother of a disturbed child and a condemning one for the student who then believed that parents alone determined life's outcome for their children. I went back to college to find answers about Rob and entered analysis to find answers about his mother.

Adherents of psychoanalytic theory hold that one can never be an effective therapist until one first thoroughly knows oneself. Nowhere else does one learn about oneself so intimately and completely as on an analyst's couch. And so it was that I entered analysis to know myself, to know my son, and ultimately, I hoped, to know my future clients.

Analysis is not counseling. Although it is psychotherapeutic, it is much more than psychotherapy. It takes more time to learn to be a patient of analysis than most people ever spend in any other form of therapy. Analysis can only begin after one has learned to let go of one's own sense of self and as many of one's even normal defenses as is humanly possible.

In analysis, the patient lies there, in my case, staring at a ceiling, and monologues for forty-five to fifty minutes. It struck me that behavior appropriate to analysis was very similar to the behavior found in Robbie to be so inappropriate! The patient tells the ceiling whatever comes to mind without monitoring, selecting, or inhibiting his or her thoughts. What the patient inhibits is often more revealing that what he or she discloses (and much more interesting, as well). It became surprising that Dr. Robbins learned his patient so well he was eventually able to articulate for me what I'd inhibited myself from saying.

I did that four days a week for three and a half years, interrupted by a nine-month military-ordered move out of town before returning and resuming. Otherwise, I never missed an appointment; I very rarely rescheduled. I was a therapist's dream, if only in that respect.

I also recognized another similarity between my analyst and Rob. Both typically remained silent after I had poured out some acutely painful observation. I used to joke that "Dr. Robbins made his usual monthly comment today; he said, 'Hmm'."

As analysis progressed, I learned much from Dr. Robbins's interpretations of my mental meanderings. I didn't just learn about myself; I learned about the intricacies of human minds everywhere, at least according to the Freudians or neo-Freudians. In those hours, I learned more about the workings of the subconscious mind than I learned all together through nine years of college.

Very rarely in that first year or two does an analyst valuate or validate, at least not aloud to his patient. Analysis is not for wimps (like the one I was when I naively entered it) who seek support for their neurotic tendencies. It is a subtle yet brutal process that cuts like a finely sharpened scalpel through layer after layer after layer of this thing we call "self." It is like removing, one at a time, all the tissue-thin layers of an onion-like life, complete with tears.

It was, then, all the more precious that Dr. Robbins made a validating statement to me about two years into my analysis. He had been aware of Rob's history before I came to him for my own therapy, so he had more information than just the self-pitying wailings of a harassed mother and college student. I had, of course, spent many sessions over the two years free-associating about Rob and my own guilt that I was failing him.

In one such session, I was immersed again in the misery of my earlier fears that Rob would "only be a vegetable" when he grew up. Dr. Robbins's response was one of those studiously casual and very rare remarks that touch a wilted spirit and give it life again. "Has it not occurred to you," he asked, "that Robbie may very well have been only a vegetable except for your love?"

Ah! It is intensely satisfying to one's heart to know and be known; but it is a transformation of the soul to be truly *known* and to be accepted and respected. Dr. Robbins knew all of my demons. He knew the very worst about me. He knew more about me than my mother or my husband or myself. Despite all he knew, and because of all he knew, he found me worthy as a person and as a mother.

One of my concerns in analysis at this point had to do with Rob's reactions to our many military disruptions in his life. Why, I wondered, had it taken me so long to see that most of Rob's worst behaviors occurred within the three-month period immediately following a major change in his life! I did not, I'm sure, because change was both frequent and inevitable in our military life style, and because Rob always grew excited about a pending move. He had few attachments in the neighborhoods where we lived after Heidi.

Those attachments he did have were to an occasional adult friend of the family and especially to our cat. When it came time to move, he had already known so much ridicule, bullying, and "being made fun of" by the other children he was ready to leave. He had explored or taken apart everything of interest in that neighborhood. Our pets did not reject or condemn him. The cat would always move with us. It would sometimes fly in luxury while the rest of us drove in searing heat across the country in summer, but we kept a cat.

Moving on, I think then meant to him a hope of a fresh start. It would be a change that would temporarily jolt him from constant boredom. At least he spoke of ways and things he might do differently. But he spoke of those things in a rhythm of a neighborhood to which he was at least familiar. He knew who to avoid and who might be tolerant of his differentness.

Rob's impulsiveness and unsettling behaviors increased for about the first six months following each relocation. The behaviors typically established his reputation in the new neighborhood as odd, but he made eventual developmental gains forced on him by the demands of the new environment. However, we didn't look upon the increase in Rob's subtle disturbances as a direct result of the moves.

The setbacks following each move almost always served as new crises that had to be addressed. Crises invariably spawned others. We would necessarily be so caught up in dealing with his problems that we could little attend to the gains. It seems callous now to realize that we expected gains; we expected him to "act his age."

We reacted to Rob's adverse responses to change by creating other changes: a new play group where he was left out, a new project that went unfinished, a new kind of activity he could not master, new doctors and worst of all, new schools.

Today, Patrick is a schoolteacher. I have a special place in my heart for teachers, and of course, I think his students are fortunate to have him. I know that the vast majority of teachers are well-intended. I respect them because they contribute so much to molding good character and preparing our youth for adulthood. I respect them too, because I have learned that they often need to compensate for inadequacies in a child's upbringing or lack of nurturance in his or her own home.

However, it seemed that Rob was assigned the few on each end of the bell curve of patience. After his bad experience with his kindergarten teacher, his first grade teacher had delighted in him and consequently he responded well to her. I do not doubt that some of his teachers felt as frustrated and helpless in their efforts to help and motivate or to even understand Rob as I did. With only vague behavioral descriptions but no diagnoses, and therefore no recommendations for teaching him, we were all at a loss. One thing remained consistent, though, regardless of failed efforts to motivate him: all teachers regarded him as sweet-natured.

Rob started fourth grade in a new state, on a new military base, and at his fifth school. After a month or so, I began daily receiving a complaining phone call from the principal. The initial complaints were about behaviors that I thought were at most only minimally bothersome and not even unusual in any other child. I'd gone all the way through secondary school with kids who got away with doing far stranger things and thought little of it.

With Rob, I'd lived through big things like a fire in the house, his near drowning, chewing glass, exploding washers, dismantling of televisions, radios, and a generator. Rob had lived through being the recipient of hostile acts, but never, ever as the initiator of hostility toward other people. He had also been too shy in groups to be regarded as disruptive in class.

His behaviors at this new school, at a shy and immature ten, included impulsively grabbing a handful of gravel just outside the upstairs window and throwing it on the school roof and accidentally touching his teacher's breast. She had pulled him in her lap to comfort him. She told me, with tears in her eyes over the whole matter, that she had impulsively held him because she grieved for him.

"Why, then," I asked through my own tears, "did you report that to the principal, if you regarded it as a totally innocent and accidental thing?" She reported it because she had been instructed by the principal to report *every* thing Robert Bowers did that was in any way "out of line." That dictate had been given after the school received the confidential psychological and academic reports on Rob, one month after the start of the school year.

This particular school was among those at the top, statewide, in scholastic performance. It was a unique school in that those students attending were the sons and daughters of some of the military's finest higher-ranking officers. These were personnel selected for Command and Staff College, the Marine Corps equivalent of graduate school. They were bright and superior in intellect, achievement, accomplishments, and self-discipline, so were most of their children. Also among them were some of the best and brightest from other countries that are allies of the United States. It was a school that most parents would have paid high tuitions to have their child enrolled, not only for the high academic standards but also for the wonderful international flavor and influence on the social and extracurricular activities.

It was a school where second grader Patrick, with straight A's, enthusiastically pored over a research paper that demanded at least three external sources, and where he voluntarily included extra information. After submitting his paper, he was sent back to first grade for a week, his first real humiliation, in order to have those first graders teach him to write more legibly. That the content of his paper was superior seemed of no importance. Neither did his self-respect, apparently.

When I insisted that his teacher bring him back into class, she responded by moving his desk out of the rows with the other children and placing it next to hers. Again, I wanted to know why she was singling out an ideal student who had no discipline problems or classroom disruptions. She told me that she had read Robbie's records and had "absolutely no intention of having his brother ever become like that!"

Rob's reports were confidential. Actually, nothing in them indicated that he could be expected to be a classroom disruption; he hadn't been. I had talked with the principal when I enrolled Rob, and related his history of rejection and particularly pointed out the bad experience he had had with a previous teacher in his last class.

The principal had nodded in what I thought was understanding and commented that Rob should be given a fresh start. Of course I didn't realize he meant *somewhere else*. He volunteered to withhold the reports on him when they arrived, stating that they should be kept confidential. Certainly, Patrick's teacher had no need for them and should not have had access to them.

I came to also understand that the school staff saw that Rob was "different" and they treated him as such. He fulfilled their expectations less in what he did than how he was: unmotivated for class work, awkward, sweet, but now beginning to clown in order to compensate for his failures in friendship and academia. I appreciated the new addition of clowning! That seemed to be a personal gain for him over the withdrawing.

Complaints about what he did were easier to articulate and measure but lesser in intensity than would have been the more ill-defined complaints about what he was: shy, distractible, immature, cute, nice, sweet? I don't know what words those teachers and staff might have used had they tried to know him and to help draw him out. This school had absolutely no intention of accommodating a student who would lower their academic ratings.

Of all our bad years, this one was becoming our worst ever. Rob no longer offered even minimal participation in school. He told me, before his teary-eyed teacher agreed that it was true, that "all the teachers and the principal get me in trouble." Within weeks after his reports were made known, all I was told was that he began refusing to remove his coat at school; instead, he would stand by a window that looked out at our house and repeat over and over, "I want to go home." He was sent home almost daily. He did not return in triumph but in defeat.

At home, Rob wandered the windowless attic of our apartment building all night long, refusing to have lights on. He would talk almost enthusiastically at breakfast about his night-time experiences but could not explain why he preferred the dark. He would join the family in the evenings until bedtime, but he went to the attic to sleep instead of his own room. It was not unlike his preference for the long wardrobe box as a baby.

At first he sneaked up there, lying awake downstairs in his room until after his dad and I had gone to bed. He pleaded, explaining that he felt better up there. With a heavy heart, I finally made a bed for him in the attic and allowed him to take some of his things up. He welcomed visits but preferred that space to his own room after bedtime.

Rob reacted to being picked on with awkward, senseless responses that failed to earn him the respect he so needed. He still had no real friends. His brother had many of all ages. It was rare for Rob to be chosen to be on someone's side, because he would not likely have been paying attention when the rules were explained. Patrick became "captain" every chance he could and often picked his brother. Pat sometimes had to agonize over such a decision; it might result in the loss of the game or a playmate.

Rob was still under the weekly care of a child psychiatrist. By then, I had no sense that I was contributing anything positive to his situation except to just be there for him, but I understood his behaviors less and less.

He was prescribed the anti-psychotic medication, Mellaril, halfway through this year, with some remarkable improvement in his mood and behavior at home but not sufficient to combat all that was happening in school or within himself. He also, at ten, entered puberty. It was one more grossly humiliating development for him. He said it made him even more of a freak than he already was.

Patrick, at seven, disagreed. He would beg Rob to show him his underarm hair. Reluctantly, Rob would finally lift an arm, knowing that he at least would not be ridiculed here. "Oh, I wish it was me," Patrick wailed. "Boy, so do I!" Rob answered despairingly.

Patrick, almost three years younger, would actually model appropriate social behaviors for Rob. He had also early on taught Rob some skills, such as how to tie his shoes, and had fought many a verbal and sometimes physical war defending his older brother from the taunts of other kids. Rob could boast, however, that he had taught Patrick to tell time.

The day came when Rob told Patrick, after a particularly humiliating neighborhood "war," that he no longer wanted him to fight his fights. As with any other pronouncement coming from Rob, it was said in a flat, emotionless way, but it was declared firmly.

Rob had arrived at that decision, again, by some unknown process. He never learned to fight (even when prison later demanded it of him), but he no longer let Patrick come to his defense. Nor did he ever become coordinated enough to win any prison fight. It became sufficient satisfaction to him and no small amount of pride that he at least always stood his ground and did not allow himself to give in or give up. He stood until he was sometimes battered flat, but he counted himself a winner if he had resisted the other's assault.

Given Rob's courage in childish defense of himself from a group of taunting opponents, the assaults on him, and his tolerance for pain, I was surprised he didn't develop hostility or a chip on his shoulder. Certainly, if any kid does, he had every reason to act out in anger. He shamefully thought of himself as too cowardly. I didn't think so. He showed remarkable courage at times, even when he faced known physical pain. I felt that he didn't fight because he did not believe he had a self worth fighting for.

Along with his refusing to have Patrick defend him, there had been other subtle indications that Rob was making developmental gains which he did not entirely abandon, even though he was very depressed. He was assuming his position as older brother in any way he could.

As Rob began arguing against his brother's opinion on things or correcting him on a matter, Patrick entered what I termed his "displacement period." He had functioned all his life as Rob's "big" brother, although three years younger. Now, for a time, he had no familiar role; it had been usurped by its rightful owner.

The brothers worked that out in their own ways. Patrick found his own niche, and with it, greater autonomy from Rob. As Rob grew increasingly miserable with himself, he sometimes took his rage out on Patrick. But they remained very loyal and rarely tattled on each other. That two more opposite personalities could co-exist in relative harmony was a blessing I did not take lightly. Robbie was not an easy brother.

CHAPTER 10

"Mom, when you sell my lonely truck, will you be sure to sell it to someone who will love and appreciate it?" Rob from prison.

Like connecting dots in a child's puzzle, I think about the significant meanings automobiles have held for him since infancy and a picture starts to form. As mentioned above, Rob mimicked the sound of an automobile engine constantly. He did for forty years, which is to say that he still does, though not as often, I suspect prison guards and other inmates frown upon it. Yet, it was always a pleasing indication to me that he was in a happy mood. He also went from crawling to running with little walking in between. So there he was, running everywhere when walking was more appropriate, more controllable. Running and making the humming sounds of car engines.

He learned, however, to stop running over people. To avoid that, he had to squeal out the sound of tires as he braked and make deft turns just in the nick of time. The older he got, the better driver he became. At least I didn't have to dodge anymore.

He grew to be so sophisticated as a motor vehicle that he could mimic different kinds of cars and trucks in different gears. It was automatic (the behavior, not the transmissions).

When he was seventeen, running in the house, making the sounds of a race car, I asked him to stop and reminded him, jokingly, that he was no longer a car. He paused in thought, and commented wistfully, "I know I'm not, but I wish I still was."

I think of Rob's relationships with cars. First was his believing that he was a car. Later came his strong preference for only cars as toys and his intense attachment to them. Despite his pleasure in having them operate, he constantly disassembled them; then he began lining them up and deliberately smashing his very favorites.

His other early acts of vandalism were minor but were also done against cars. Damaged cars and damaged model cars had to be condemned. It was never enough to simply discard the pieces of a model car that he had accidentally botched in construction. Instead, they had to be at least smashed. For a while, he would sneakily burn them.

Much later, he was driving cars so deliberately dangerously that he wrecked over ten cars, most of which he had stolen, all of which were at least twenty years old. He strongly preferred cars of 1962 through 1967 vintage, those cars that were produced from his birth through age five. I pondered often whether or not his fascination with cars had its origin in our endless driving while he was a baby because the movement and sound of the car soothed him when nothing else did. I also pondered whether or not his choice to be a mechanic contained some hope of "fixing himself." Yet, even that image of himself was reduced as he grew up: "Mechanics are opportunistic predators!" he would later say.

Rob has walked away from wrecks in which his cars turned over or had their chassis ripped apart or rolled down sides of mountains. As noted earlier, it was with unusual insight, that he matter-of-factly shared with me on one occasion that a part of him wanted to kill the "bad Robert."

I believe he has greater insight than I into his reasoning. I'm sure it reflects his struggles with his private demons and the disturbed thoughts that, when he drank, roared as loudly as any engine from a muscle car. I can make no other sense of it. I don't do abstract thinking very well where Rob is concerned. I don't want to. I want to be just his mother.

The failures and humiliations were finally more than ten-year-old Rob could cope with and too powerful to be balanced by just his family. His psychiatrist recommended residential placement.

———◆◆◆———

His father and I had said good-bye to Rob, leaving him in a residential school. The only person that had ever consistently been there for him had just abandoned him. I was inconsolable. I was a wretched, miserable mother who had done the worst thing a mother can possibly do!

Mile after mile on the drive home I sobbed, to the acute discomfort of my husband who, perhaps rightfully, thought that placing Rob would also be the best for my own well-being. Certainly, Patrick and I both needed a break. Again, his father would be to leaving to go overseas. It would be Patrick and me for another thirteen months.

Until it came down to actually leaving Rob behind, I had at least taken comfort in the thought of time to return to college and time just for Patrick. Along with my constant grief about Rob was a constant nagging worry that Patrick was not getting as much of my attention as Rob. I compared the amount of time and energy I devoted to each and knew that Rob received much, much more. Rob's behaviors, failings, lack of friends, and his many trials demanded so much more.

Letting go of the care of my son, putting his welfare, his hopes, and his very life in the hands of strangers, defied description. It was the antithesis of the maternal instinct. It was a gut-wrenching ripping apart of the very idea of mother.

Up to this point, I'd had ten years of discovering that no one came nearly as close to caring about him as much as I. No one else knew the meaning, if not the causes, of his subtle moods, the strange words he used or the habits that seemed to make no sense. No one else had ever given him comfort. No one else had ever loved him unconditionally. Now, I was failing him. I had apparently failed him so badly that strangers were left to do what I could not.

My grief was underscored by what I thought was a nonchalant way the staff at Rob's residential school treated our parting. They were unaware of the wrenching that was occurring between my heart and my sensibility.

I remembered the long distance call I'd made from Virginia across the United States to speak with the director of the school to which we were to send Rob. I described my son's behaviors and our concerns. The stranger on the other end of the line assured me that most of their children were just like Robbie. *Imagine! There are others like him!* I remember thinking. There was something comforting in that. That was actually terrific news. They knew what to do to fix him!

From the very beginning, Rob was involved in the decision to go away to a residential treatment program. He wanted to go. He hated public school; he loved adventure. I felt a ping of sorrow that he didn't express concern about being away from his family, but then when had he?

However, in hindsight, I realized that it had not occurred to him until we were saying a final good-bye that he would be left behind. Through tear-filled eyes I saw his shocked, hurt expression change to what seemed like resolved acceptance of yet another rejection with which he must cope by himself. I thought I saw desperation in that last look in his eyes. Did he see the love in mine?

Very rarely does anything replace the love of a parent. This parent needed help. Less, I finally realized, because I was inadequate as a parent but because relying only on parents was inadequate to meet the intense, diverse, and paradoxical needs of our child.

At the parents' meetings held at Rob's program, I met many fine parents whose love for their similarly difficult child was as great as mine for Rob. Most of us were making severe financial and personal sacrifices to place our child there. There were children whose parents never came at all.

There are very few truly sweet memories about Rob that are not also riddled with pain for him. Most of the sweet ones are from the monthly weekend visits with him during the eighteen months he was in residential school. We explored beautiful Santa Barbara, had conversations about normal things, laughed and held hands, waded in streams, walked through parks, and inevitably shopped for models and music. He seemed to love just being loved and to show for the first time, ever, that his mother was special to him.

I heard new kinds of things from him: "You are the best mother in the whole world!" "This has been the best day of my life!" And "Let me order."

That last remark was almost the best: We were welcome in a restaurant! Rob in coat and tie, eleven years old, was clearly enchanting our waitress, being sociable and appropriate and ordering a meal for his mother. Other diners at nearby tables smiled at us. Sometimes diners stopped by our table and remarked about how charming Rob was. No one glared at us or asked to move to another table. They liked Robbie! In those sweet, lost moments, the pain seemed very behind us now and very worthwhile. They did not last.

He learned to write, if not to spell, and wrote heart-wrenching letters about how much he missed his home and family. Patrick and I had moved back to California while Rob and his dad were away. San Diego had become more like home to us; and Rob would not feel that he was a continent apart. In his letters, he apologized for "wrongdoings" that I had long forgotten and promised to be good when he came back home to stay. He was afraid that his ten-year-old cousin, who had come to spend the summer with us, had replaced him in the family. He was reassured with each concern that he was special and much missed.

There were very welcome changes in his behaviors and there were those other changes: I saw that he was becoming manipulative. He learned fastest how to manipulate my guilt. Things. He wanted things. Mom would mail him gifts, tapes, and models that he requested, because Mom felt guilty that she was not otherwise there for him.

Over the phone, I consoled him and later had a private phone conversation with whatever staff member Rob persuaded me had mistreated or misunderstood him. All staff had been through this kind of maneuvering before; they handled my concerns with skill and tact, but they remained resolute. They were in control; I was not.

The staff had known identical experiences with countless children and their overly attached mothers. I had not. This was my first experience and I was naive. I was not the mother of countless children; I was the mother of the most important one!

In time, I learned too. I learned to trust the staff and to realize that they cared about my son. I learned that collective minds are more effective than the mind of one mother who sometimes operated as much from her own needs as from her son's. In time, Rob, with the help of the medication, Mellaril, became much less impervious to discipline than he had once been.

On home visits when he initiated some negative behavior, he monitored himself. From Rob's mouth came delightful phrases like "That was inappropriate behavior, wasn't it?" He knew what "exploit" meant! He volunteered: "I'm being manipulative, aren't I?"

He participated in more of our home life than he ever had. He liked the same music. He would sometimes sit through movies with his brother and me. He could sometimes converse instead of monologue, and his monologues were beginning to expand beyond cars. They now included planes.

Rob flew home for regular visits. At ten and eleven, he flew unaccompanied, changing planes in the complex Los Angeles

International Airport. On each return flight, he carried back a model to be assembled at school. He acquired at least one of every possible plane in which he might ever conceivably fly.

He became a seasoned traveler. After each flight in, he repeated word for word the instructions of the flight attendants on each plane. He pointed out imaginary exits, oxygen mask instructions, and described the engines in sophisticated detail. These were pleasant monologues spoken with confidence and a newly discovered delight in being genuinely entertaining. He became discerning about planes and knew each kind intimately; increasingly he accumulated detailed facts about the wars and battles some of them had flown in. "How did you learn all that?" I marveled.

"I saw it on the model instructions." At first, he saw; later, he read the instructions. Rob taught himself to read almost entirely from the instructions on model planes.

Although I knew I was being manipulated into buying him more stuff than he would have received at home, I tolerated the manipulation for the sheer joy of seeing him express pleasure and appreciation, just another trade-off. He was more human, more normal.

For the first time since his birth, I enjoyed him without an overriding sense of grief and worry. It was becoming comfortable to relinquish to his treatment team the behavior modification techniques, and the teaching and enforcing of boundaries and rules, and to enjoy for a season the real pleasure in being his mother. His behaviors were still different but for this short time something very new had entered his life: acceptance by other kids, and fun; and into my life: hope.

A significant advantage to Rob of living among a group of peers with a multi-disciplined treatment team is that there were other children like him. Most of his peers had similar problems and were given similar consequences. The vocabulary of their behavior applied more or less equally to all. He was not singled out. His behavior did not stand out as glaringly different from that of the other kids. They all got to just be kids and to thrive in similar social groups from which they had formerly each been excluded. They also required several staff in attendance, not just two parents.

There, also, when someone came to play, Rob was included. There were no more doorbells being rung by kids Rob's age who came to play with his brother instead. There was no more laughing because he couldn't read well since many of them could not and he was improving more and more. Rules of equality and inclusion replaced those of inferiority and exclusion that he had known in countless neighborhoods and playgrounds.

For reasons I was never told, Rob made a suicide attempt early in residential treatment program. He kept a scrawled journal of countless heartbreaks, and was, for a time, nightly molested by another boy. Those things he did not write about to me. It was others who handled those and who did not inform me of them until they were over. They were never quite finished.

It wasn't until my regular monthly weekend, three weeks after Rob had deliberately run in front of a car, that I learned of it. I remembered how I'd grabbed the chair arms, tears filling my eyes, but crying inwardly, imagining the desperation behind such an act. I felt sorry for myself, too. I had not been there to comfort him. I tried to discuss it with him all weekend. In hindsight, I realize he acted coy with me, at the time it was as though the reason had vanished. He was in good spirits and had made strides. Staff assured me they had handled it appropriately. It was years later that he told me about the molestation.

Those incidents reflect the other side of residential or any specialized group treatment: a significant disadvantage to Rob's living among a group of kids like him was that many were much worse off. There were children there who had been severely traumatized by abuse. There were kids whose behaviors seemed motivated only by hatred and rage. Eventually, he not only learned desirable behaviors, he picked up a few undesirable ones as well, though they were passive. Another trade-off.

At no time in his young life, did Rob manifest the kind of out of control behavior I've since seen in other children. He did not have many temper tantrums or overt hostility or deliberate defiance toward his parents or any authority figure. He was sweet-natured. He was innocent and child-like. Even the staff of the residential treatment program remarked about his sweet nature. Because he was those things, he was placed with the eight- to ten-year-old children, instead of the ten- to twelve-year group.

Rob's graduation from the school coincided with the decision by his insurance company to no longer partially fund his attending. After eighteen months, he returned home and to public school. He was an immediate target for every act of cruelty that any junior high school kid can devise.

CHAPTER 11

"Mom, I go back to Devereux so I can remember that once upon a time I was a leader and had respect."

It took Rob twenty years to be able to talk about his return to public school and what he still regards as "the worst time of my life." His school day hours were relentless in their pain and stress. Going off to school every day was, for him, going into enemy territory, alone.

Each day, I later learn, started with apprehension and dread, knowing that enemies with tactics he once again could not understand would soon surround him. His training in good social interactions at residential school had not prepared him for what he met in junior high, but his parents didn't know that. He had no comrades and no effective "weapon." He could find no shield from taunts and demeaning pranks. The school years for most seventh graders often represent a time in which their worst fears surface. Rob was the scapegoat on whom his peers projected those fears.

With no counselors constantly in attendance to process every event, no one to intervene in any injustice or to insist on fair play and forgiveness and patience, Rob became again a tormented recluse. He lost the gains he had made in the residential treatment program. He lost the zest, confidence, and social skills he had acquired. He grew irritable. He became isolated and secretive. He tried in clumsy ways to retaliate against perceived cruelty that he could only hint at to me.

There are no effective means for even very emotionally stable youths to cope with such intensive and pervasive rejection. Rob's only means of coping was to develop vivid imaginings of retaliation and engage in minor vandalism of cars or bravado boasts about acts he only wished he had committed. He could not physically confront his tormentors. They were many; he was one. More and more he grew to think of himself as a coward because he would not defend himself with fists.

The social skills he had learned and used effectively in residential school, only resulted in his being mocked in public school, that, and an increase in the very pressures he tried to relieve. His verbal confrontations against injustice included words he had learned that communicated precisely and effectively. "You're inappropriate..." is not the way public school seventh graders register complaints to each other. Rob's vocabulary only further set him apart. Another child might have been able to deflect pranks into opportunities to win friends and gain respect. Rob never grasped such nuances. Doing so required more confidence than he possessed and a kind of mental flexibility in relating that was beyond his understanding.

If he could not be accepted, he would at least be rejected for something tangible. If he could not be liked for trying to be nice, he would be admired for risk taking. This he did in odd ways, no open defiance against teachers, no classroom disturbances, but instead, in after school attention seeking from his peers in immature and awkward attempts to "be a somebody."

In residential school, he was so like the other kids that he became a leader by the end of his eighteen months. He could even boast of ways in which he was superior to his peers. He became "king of the dorm" there.

He became "a worm" in public school. He forgot how he had once longed to be back home and began to long to return to the only place outside his home where he was accepted. Years later, on many occasions, several in stolen cars, Rob would return from wherever he was in the United States to park and look out upon the California campus of his former residential school. With prodding, he would finally explain such compulsivity. "I go back to remember that there was a time when I was respected and a leader."

Even within his home, Rob was daily confronted with his own inadequacies. He would return from school at the end of each day filled with hurt and frustration that he quietly turned inward, concealing his emotions. I would try to engage him in conversation about his day, but he gave short, routine answers and escaped to his room as soon as possible to work on models. He did not then have the ability to either recognize or verbalize his pain, yet his family was highly verbal. He acted out his hurt, which only further distanced him from us.

Rob usually enjoyed the same family TV shows the rest of us liked and would join us for those. He did not, however, enjoy games or most family activities, particularly those that required concentration or suggested competition. He said they were "boring." He was also awkward and uncoordinated, while his dad and younger brother were just the opposite. He could not have participated in sports even if anyone had picked him to be on their team.

Earlier efforts by his father to teach him to play ball ultimately ended only in reinforcing for Rob how inadequate he felt. If the ball was thrown slowly, right to his front, at chest height, he was as likely as not to reach up to his left or too low and to his right. He never caught the ball. He never reached where it actually was.

He enjoyed most going camping with his father and brother. These outings remain fond memories for him, and he still repeats wisdom given him by his father during their campfire chats. But aside from those activities, he tended to isolate or to seek more and more outrageous behaviors that created turmoil for the rest of us.

Patrick often admired some of Rob's exploits at twelve and thirteen for their sheer audacity, as when Rob and another kid discovered the keys left in two bull dozers at a construction site near our home and drove them, into each other. Patrick also admired Rob's courage to stand alone, silently, without defending himself while other kids berated him. Nonetheless, Pat was embarrassed by most of Rob's behaviors during those years. Rob tried at times to bully him, but I think he also realized that he had best not totally alienate the only kid in the world who accepted him.

He required so much discipline, "being talked to," and intense concern because of each day's strange behaviors that even his home could not always be for him a respite or a place to heal. He had no motivation to achieve, to learn new skills, or even to work to earn money for more models. He was encouraged to mow lawns, but his seasonal allergies were so severe that he sneezed almost without stopping. I didn't know if it was the allergic reaction or the depression that kept him away from the lawn mower, but he was scolded for being "lazy."

Rob had also regressed into obsessive automobile talk and open, compulsive masturbation when most disturbed. We did not then know this was common in autistic youths. Patrick was outraged that Rob would not even close his bedroom door or conceal this behavior.

Rob was by now very disturbed and I was at a complete loss as to what to do. Recalling that he had functioned at a much higher level the previous two years made it harder to watch his regressive behaviors. I felt defeated and helpless with nowhere to turn for help. There were no Individual Education Plans, no school help, and counselors hardly knew what to say to him. He was not a problem in the schoolroom and he did not talk to teachers or counselors.

Also, perhaps to try and participate in the family, he developed his own sense of humor, but it was making nonsensical and silly remarks that were funny only to him. His habit of assigning phrases or unusual words for most routine activities and objects became more pronounced and intrusive. He asked more and more nonsensical questions for which there were no answers. He interrupted constantly with something, usually about cars, that would be totally unrelated to the on-going conversation.

Rob also spent increasing amounts of time in building models or listening to music alone in his room. His daily habit after school was to have a brief chat and a snack and then to isolate. He could tolerate no discussion about his day or school work. In hindsight, I wonder that he did not become truant. There were repeated episodes of awkward behavior in misguided efforts to get any "positive" attention at all. He made two friends briefly.

When Patrick or his father or I referred to our friends, we meant close, enduring friendships with people whom we shared much of our lives. Rob's reference to friends included almost anyone who would make even small talk about cars with him on more than one or two occasions. For a while, one such friend attached himself loosely to Rob. He was an unhappy child with an unhappy home life. A second friend seemed, like Patrick, to initially admire Rob's defiant exploits against decorum. In a short time, this friend abandoned him. "Jeff de-friended me," said Rob, in yet another play on words.

As life worsened for him, so did his secretive behavior. He stole things from stores, usually model glue. He vandalized more than even we knew, I'm sure. As always, targets for his vandalism were cars. To his credit, they were usually abandoned wrecks. He did not commit extreme vandalism; his acts were pushing the cars some distance. He received his worst spanking for putting objects or sugar in people's gas tanks. There was no indication that he was hostile toward the owner of the car; most he did not know.

As Rob became more argumentative with his brother and more secretively resistive to household rules, our creativity in designing effective consequences was taxed beyond its limits. Previously, discipline had been only incidental to otherwise affectionate or supportive treatment toward him, although even that seemed to just be taken for granted. However, in his entering adolescence, nothing was effective against his repeated breaking of household rules. We were facing our toughest challenge in coping with Rob as a teen, because the direst of consequences very rarely modified his behavior and the challenges increasingly demanded more sacrifice and energy from me, with diminishing returns. Today, parents of troubled teens more often complain of drug abuse or sexual activity or angry defiance. Relative to those, Rob's behaviors were in one sense minor. Yet, they reflected the more serious inner conflicts and destructive self talk, which unlike his more rebellious peers, he would never merely outgrow.

Life with Rob had taught me many, many things. One of those was to speak less impulsively or off-handedly and to be as precise with him as possible. I learned to say exactly what I meant and to do exactly what I said I would do. It got harder and harder. I learned to alert him to the consequences of any of his predictable behaviors. One carefully designed consequence remains in my memory with a searing pain. It hurts as much today, thirty years later, as it did then.

Rob was very skilled at building models. It was by then his only source of pleasure, pride, satisfaction, and productive endeavor. It was also the major source of much knowledge, as each model contained a legend about its place in history. His model building was strongly supported by the entire family. By age thirteen, he was an artistic expert and had long since progressed to extremely complex models, with equally extreme costs.

His more complex and tediously constructed airplanes hung from his ceiling, in varying heights in order to accommodate them all. He liked showing them off and we made sure that visitors to our home got a tour of his room, with appropriate, accompanying praise.

Rob's naive parents learned late about glue sniffing from public concern. I don't think Rob ever deliberately sniffed it. The media informed us and therefore presented us with a dilemma. Rob *had* to build models; that could not be curtailed. He just could no longer build them in his room where there was inadequate ventilation. His dad built a workbench in the garage for Rob's crafts. Rob avoided using it. Repeatedly, despite threats, pleas, ultimatums, and a hiatus in buying him models, he would not use the garage workbench. He would not use it despite repeated promises to use it.

Of course glue sniffing presented a new source of guilt for me. I had allowed him to use the toxic glue to build models, in his room, since he was six years old! We did attempt to switch to the safe glue, but Rob demonstrated to us that it was highly inferior. The models did not hold together. The delicate, precise constructions that best reflected his skill level were particular problems with the less effective, safer cement. Besides, he stole the toxic glue from stores if we did not buy it for him.

To use the better glue was the reward for also using his garage work place. He broke that promise. He became a "closet model builder;" literally, in his closet, he'd work late into the night after the rest of the family had gone to bed.

I sat him down and explained very, very carefully what would happen if he ever built models in his closet again. I began, once again, to explain to him about responsibility, trust, accountability, and consequences. I told him firmly, kindly, with no intimidation, that if he ever built them there again I would destroy every one of his models.

I pointed out that the power and control were in his hands, not mine. I went on to carefully relate how he had the power to keep his models by obeying the rules that accompanied that privilege. Then I asked him to explain back to me what I had said. I determined that he fully understood both the consequences and the fact that he was in control of them. He agreed.

A few days later, his father and I left for the afternoon. Ten minutes away, I remembered something I needed at the house, so we returned. I'm not sure why I stopped by Rob's room, perhaps to just explain why I was back. He was working on a model in his closet. His face paled when he saw me at his door.

With his father waiting in the driveway, unaware, I pulled all the models down from Rob's ceiling, dropping them into a heap on the floor. I was crying, but otherwise wordless, except to comment that he had given me no choice. He fought back tears as he lay on his bed and watched me in silence. I stomped the pile of models into rubble.

I did not even have the luxury of losing control and stomping in anger. The force of will required to destroy his models was something alien to me. I cannot yet identify from where it came, except that it came from a love that demanded extraordinary denial of all that love seemed to be.

I was not angry. I was more frightened and heartbroken than I had ever been in my life. I had exhibited my very best parenting skills with him and they had produced nothing. Those models were not replaceable *things*; they were my son's heart and soul. They represented the best he knew to do and all he had to offer to society to show he was of value. They were the only positive "I am" he had.

My heart and hopes were also in that pile and in as many pieces. His sneakiness in disobeying after my careful boundary setting was most alarming to me.

Having to destroy his treasures was one of the most painful things I have ever done in my life. I would give anything if I had not returned home that day. Rob did not even become angry with me. I wish he had. I wish he could have.

Through psychoanalysis, I had learned to speedily cut through the chaff and identify and verbalize my truest, deepest emotions. Yet, when I returned to my husband waiting in the car, I could not speak at all for a very long time. I could not even move to adjust my position in the car seat. I felt wooden and heavy, like something dead. I could not then and I cannot now assign words to the terrible and primitive hurt that engulfed me that afternoon so long ago...only yesterday, still.

My husband received orders to Japan, and I announced my intention to get a divorce. Again, in hindsight, that was a reckless decision. It felt more comfortable to divorce and therefore know he was never coming back, then to grieve a loss, though temporary, that always felt like a death.

However, my own inability to tolerate the long separations was secondary to my decision. Primary was my inability to tolerate any longer the splitting in two of my heart. I had watched the almost complete deterioration of a relationship between Rob and his dad. I felt constantly pulled by powerful emotional attachments in opposite directions by each. Neither of them exerted that force on me; I did it to myself.

Father and son did not war. No one waged war in our home, although I roared on many occasions. They could not communicate. In the five-day workweek, preceding my announcement that I wanted a divorce, I watched the same scene acted out as my husband came home each evening.

Joshua, our collie, Patrick, Rob, and I would go to the door to greet my husband when we heard his car pulling in the driveway. Beaming, my husband would smile warmly at Pat and me and pat Joshua on the head. Rob stood silently by, unnoticed, staring up at his dad's face. It was the hungriest expression I had ever seen. His dad would place his things in the hall closet and join me in the kitchen.

Quietly, without a word, Rob who had been rejected all day, would turn and go back to his room until I called him to join us for dinner. In unusual quietness, he would eat, and then return to his room. For that week, his dad did not address anything to Rob or respond to his minimal comments.

I don't recall if Rob had done something over the previous weekend that had been particularly alarming, probably he had. Perhaps his father was too weary of the stress of Rob's increasingly disturbed behaviors; we all were. Nothing overtly happened and that was the problem. I did not think that his father was deliberately ignoring him. I simply knew that he was not deliberately reaching out to him, nor even aware of the longing on Rob's face.

It cannot be said that Rob and his dad did not share happy times, or that he did not have good times with his brother or with me during this worsening period. The good times were too few to offset the oppressive atmosphere of tension that surrounded Rob. He seemed always to be getting into some kind of trouble and he was failing in school.

Still, it was not Rob's overt behaviors that concerned me nearly as much as his depression and secret inner life. Had he been able to talk about it, I think things would have been different. Perhaps he was too ashamed or frightened.

From within Rob's world, almost anything was likely to pop out of his mouth but rarely did his comments invite a natural or comfortable conversation. Further, the fact that he communicated in this quirky, idiosyncratic way instead of one more appropriate was so disturbing to his family that we grew weary from trying to coach him to talk more directly. It was common that his efforts to make conversation, which, incidentally, included always interrupting an on-going conversation, were to ask questions like, "Mom, what would you do if this house suddenly turned upside down?" "Mom, what if you found a train running down the middle of the highway?" Or, "Mom, what would you do if you woke up and discovered our backyard was caved in?"

For endless months, I tried to give a realistic response to his questions and to try and help him reframe or rethink questions that were more appropriate. He didn't change and I grew too saddened by them to continue to consistently offer specific answers to his awkward questions. My fear for him and his future too often morphed into anger. Less because of what he'd actually said or done than with my own impotence, I more often felt tense and apprehensive about what each day would bring. I yelled at him and at Patrick more and more. I am sure they saw it only as anger, but under my shame at having yelled was a pervasive fear that colored my perceptions and an overwhelming sense of helplessness.

The one topic that dominated all Rob's monologues was an endless elaborate presentation about cars. Day after day, month after month for several years, we heard about little else but cars. No matter how kind our intentions, our patience wore out from trying to either make a response to Rob's nonsensical questions or to teach him to ask more appropriate ones. Following one more such monologue, I once again exclaimed to him that he must stop his monologues on only cars, he must ask people about their feelings, and he must simply ask people questions about themselves, instead of his doing all the talking.

He sat in silence for a minute and I knew I'd hurt his feelings. Finally, he spoke: "Mom, how would you *feel* if a motor landed on the top of our house?"

Rarely was there even that much apparent effort in his responses to our efforts on his behalf to improve anything. In dressing, Rob would first pull on a pair of pants. If he happened to get the zipper in back, he left them that way. No amount of arguing would get him to dress more acceptably. If he wore socks at all, he put on the first two he pulled out of his drawer. He more often wore mismatched socks than matched. Dressed for the day, he might have a shirt on inside out, cut-offs on backward, mismatched socks as well as shoes and the latter always left untied. He was impervious to my pleadings to correct his dress.

In earlier years, I had insisted that he dress again. By age twelve, he was actually worse than before, except I think he always wore his pants with the zipper in front. I hoped that public ridicule would force him to pay more attention, so I stopped making him correct his clothing. It did not.

He was accustomed, not comfortable, not insensitive, not impervious, but accustomed to public ridicule. It just did not modify his behavior. His attitude toward such social graces seemed to be that they were silly. It shouldn't matter how a person dressed; it was nobody's business. People should not dislike him because of the way he dressed.

Perhaps he could tell himself he was not liked because of his outward appearance rather than his inward being. Perhaps his "nobody cares" meant "nobody cares about me enough to care about how I dress."

My husband and I seldom quarreled about anything except Rob. Our tension because of him mounted until it required intense steeling of our minds to bring up any matter relating to him. I saw my husband as more often detached than involved with Rob. He saw me as a formidable barrier between Rob and his own efforts to discipline him.

I had little defense for Rob except that he had no friends, no achievements, and no acceptance. He had no normal, essential activities for a kid his age. The world outside our home was enemy territory for him; inside should at least be safe. I argued, therefore, that his family had to meet his needs and that we had to extend ourselves to do so, regardless of the effort. His father argued, in effect, that discipline from us was a necessary consequence to Rob's nonconformity. We were both right.

Rob's dad was the oldest by six years of only two sons. He was one of two grandsons. He was taught that the "birds sang for him" and truly, I think they did. He was a practically perfect child who grew up surrounded by a loving, supportive, even adoring family. I don't think there had ever been anything he couldn't do, except maybe dance the twist.

I had grown up without a father. Even before he had been killed, he was not involved with his children. From that void, I idealized what daddy meant. "Daddy" was everything good and strong and loving and superhuman. Mothers disciplined; daddies embraced and made right everything wrong in the world.

In the homes of my childhood friends, I could chatter with their mothers over after-school snacks, but I was excruciatingly shy with their fathers from whom I desperately wanted affection. I was the only one of my friends who did not have a father in the home. I ached with envy every time I saw one hug or play with his child. To be excluded from that love sent me home much more preoccupied with the wonderful mystery of "daddy" than with the afternoon of play.

I knew, as a mother, that the expectations of my husband's role as a father were molded by my own childhood needs. His and my relationship was appropriately husband and wife. But the part of me that identified with Rob needed his dad to love Rob more than to discipline. I knew my mother's love was hardy and could withstand the risks of disciplining, frustration, and even yelling. A father's love was precious and fragile. It could die.

Though divorce is ultimately a very selfish act, I chose it finally, believing that I would at least provide a home for Rob where he would not know rejection. In all of his dad's absences, I had read his letters to me, pretending they were written to Rob and Pat, in which their father expressed all the things I supposed a daddy said to sons. I could do it again. I rationalized that Pat would not be more affected by divorce since his dad was going to be absent from him anyway while in Japan for the year.

Rob has never accused his father of rejecting him. He simply believes he is not worthy of his dad's full acceptance. He believes that his own actions have not warranted respect or approval from his dad or any man. He can express surprisingly insightful perceptions about his dad: he respects him and knows he loves him. His memories of his childhood times with his father are largely positive. Now that Rob can articulate his feelings and his experiences of life, he holds himself responsible for any awkwardness in their relationship. He states that he is the dark side of his dad; I don't know what he means by that.

CHAPTER 12

"Mom, I feel so sorry for all I have done to you." From prison.

The boys and I relocated to another city after the divorce. It was the summer Elvis Presley died. Elvis's music had always been one strong reminder that I was also a person with passions and frivolity. His death heightened my sense of loss as if the one who gave voice to the exuberance of my youth had now taken it away. I had grown up with Elvis's music, his songs expressed for me so much of what I was as a young woman, and later a wife and mother. Every love song defined passion and devotion; every song of loneliness was straight from my heart's own experience. Although he hadn't made the original recording of it, "I'm So Lonesome I Could Cry," as sung by Elvis, reminded me of those long months of loneliness while my husband was away on military orders. His "American Trilogy" caused my heart to beat hard with pride and patriotism. "How Great Thou Art" humbled me before a perfect God, reminding me he existed even when I was too self absorbed to turn to him. I played those songs over and over. They spoke of the transcendence of eternal values. Then, suddenly, Elvis was dead, my marriage was dead, and I felt for a while as though every emotion that made me human had died, too.

It was a new kind of world we entered, but not a better one. Patrick had just finished sixth grade; Rob was entering ninth. I had just completed my master's degree in psychology. Other than an internship, it would be my first time since I had become a mother to work full-time as the sole breadwinner.

My now-former husband left for Japan where he would ultimately remain for three years. We had lived together in mostly kindness and consideration for over a year after agreeing to divorce. We had waited until all of us had completed current life goals.

I bought a house with no job and therefore no assurance that I would be able to make the mortgage payments. I had a kitchen newly filled with groceries and $911 left when I received a job offer. I then had to immediately pay the employment agency $900. We had eleven dollars to last two weeks until my first paycheck. I had no credit card.

We managed. I packed our lunches, drove nowhere else except to work and we stayed home all three weekends. It was glorious when I got that first check, but it was on a Friday after the banks closed. I'd stuck it in my jacket pocket at work, forgot about it, and ended up laundering the jacket the next day. The check practically dissolved in the washer; leaving a tight wad of lint in that pocket. The largest piece I could retrieve showed the decimal followed by the amount of the change, but no dollar amount.

Monday morning, this new counselor very sheepishly asked that a new check be issued. The organization's paychecks required two signatures. One of the critical signatories was climbing the steps to a departing plane at the airport when I caught up with him. He good-naturedly signed the check there on the spot. The boys and I went out to dinner that night.

Life as a single parent was disastrous. Rob had expressed hopes for another new beginning and announced that he would now be the man of the house. I took him at his word, but he did not even know how to be just a boy. He tried to make friends and joined Boy Scouts for a time. I recall ironing his scout uniform. I was newly divorced, broke, lonely, and thinking it was all worth it because he was fitting in and going to be all right now. In scouting, he would have companionship and good leadership. It was never necessary to iron another. He dropped out.

It was senseless of me to expect Rob to be happy or to conform to group expectations. He never understood what they were. He was miserable alone because of his depression and emotional disturbances. He was miserable in school because it required relating and focusing attention, and he was too shy to ask to sit with anyone during lunch. Now that I was working, he didn't even have me to greet him after school. Day after day, he had no companionship, no productive endeavor, and no hope. He looked forward to nothing, achieved nothing, his grades were average. I had only brought him into a worse time.

As I looked back over those years, I realize that I felt, as his mother, almost as impotent and helpless as Rob. I had lost hope that there was any professional help for him. It is as though I clung to one irrational and foolish hope that somehow Rob would grow out of his problems one day. I could hope for that, because I did see gains in his intellectual functioning, though not his schoolwork. I had to believe that they would be matched by emotional growth. They could not be because he lacked any previous level or plateau where he had achieved emotional stability on which to build further strengths.

He desperately needed friends or a passion that could absorb his energy and attention, but he had neither. Movies provided his primary outlets. He saw *Star Wars* eighteen times. He could not even play video games like his brother. Every slight interest Rob showed in anything, I tried to develop in him. I was afraid for his future. So far, there was nothing about him that offered any hope that he would ever learn a trade or have a normal life.

He grew silently angry at a world where everyone else had friends, laughter, successes, and goals. As always, he sought solace among cars. I eventually learned that he was sneaking out of the house late at night and wandering around used and junk car lots blocks from our residential area. If he vandalized, it was not sufficient to attract anyone's attention. I would not learn for several years about his morbid fantasies and the contribution they were making to his self-loathing during those years.

Rob made one significant social change. He began trying to dress the way other kids did. That seemed huge to me. It was the time of disco music and *Saturday Night Fever*. For the first time, Rob wanted to pick out his own clothes, *Saturday Night Fever* clothes. He would only wear the polyester fitted shirts with the wide collars and wide pants. Although he didn't attempt disco dancing, that became his favorite music for awhile. He trimmed his underarm hair, voluntarily showered, and shaved a widow's peak from his forehead. These were giant gains, actually, and signs that he identified with his age group. His efforts attracted no girls and still, he made no friends.

In the loneliness and frustrations of a friendless fifteen year old that was again failing at his own goals, he became hostile in his defiance with me for the first time. It frightened us both. It was the first time I grasped that he would not, dared not, submit his will to mine.

I briefly considered having him go live with his dad in Japan. His dad agreed to take him. Rob surprised me by not wanting to go and I backed out. I imagined what might happen to him if he vandalized in Japan. If he alienated his father, he might not then have even nurturance. He was still "my" son, and for all his problems, I loved him and loved having him with me. I just did not love his misery. I have wished many times that I had sent him to his dad!

Nothing seemed to give Rob much pleasure except taking things apart. I let him fix even our televisions and stereos just to keep him occupied in some way pleasant to him. Most of them ended up in the trash. I now know that when we moved away on our own, I moved into a world of denial to a large extent, hoping rather than believing that Rob would be all right. I grasped for anything that would give him a sense of accomplishment.

If riding his bike without training wheels was a triumph for Rob, getting his driver's license ranked up there with winning a gold medal! It had been a treasured goal for years. I taught him to drive. I started when he was thirteen years old so that I could be certain that he would be competent by sixteen.

The first time I ever allowed him to drive much further than our driveway, I foolishly permitted him to take a winding mountain road at sunset. The road had guardrails on the passenger side, beneath which were steep declines. I had never before noticed how fragile the guardrails seemed. But then I had never before been so close to them.

I had survived thirteen years of Rob's very high-risk behaviors. I was long past worrying so much that he would be physically hurt. Having also survived his indiscriminate dismantling phase, I no longer worried about my own physical well-being around him. Sitting beside Rob while he drove after dark back down a winding mountain road was the first time I had ever seriously considered my own mortality.

The mountain rose on Rob's side of the car. It fell on mine. Steeply. I suppose he drove in such a way to make sure he did not hit the side of the mountain he was nearest. He drove so that he remained less than inches from the guard rail, and therefore from our death. I sat in absolute silence for the entire forty-five-minute drive. I was not about to diminish Rob's confidence by my own lack of it. "If we perish, we perish," I decided. Rob was also silent, but he was elated. It was perhaps the most prolonged period of extreme tension I had ever endured.

My jaws were clamped together so tightly to keep from protesting that they hurt, but I could not seem to relax them or the grip I maintained on the armrest. Mercifully, we safely reached the bottom of the mountain. With a pretended calmness, I finally praised his driving and very, very casually, asked him to stop at the 7-11 store on the corner near our house. "Why?"

"Uh, Rob, I'm going to get some vodka…and a lemon."

"Mom! You want a *drink*?"

"No, Rob, I *need* a drink!" I think I fully understood addiction at that moment. It is a condition that develops secondary to teaching your child to drive.

CHAPTER 13

"Mom! Cars do too have feelings!" Rob at ages 21, 27, and 32.

In ways I do not understand, his compulsive and morbid thoughts and fantasies symbolize for Rob his intense struggle between his own perceived good and evil. Cars embody that struggle. He believed he was a car as a young child; he wished he "still was one" as an adolescent. He expresses his deepest feelings metaphorically as a car engine. He draws cars when he is most bored. His greatest sense of freedom is driving his own car. His worst anger or hurt is projected onto cars. Until he stabbed the man, it was never onto the people who hurt or rejected him.

Cars have feelings and are sensitive to rejection. They have needs and want to feel appreciated. Cars love their owners if they feel loved by them. One never gives up on a car, never abandons it, and never ignores it for very long. I supposed that if anyone ought to know these things about cars, it was Rob who had "been" a car for so long.

More than one letter or phone call from jail stated, "Would you please go start my car so it won't get lonely?" He interviews potential owners of various cars he will trade with as much concern as devoted parents who are interviewing potential nannies.

If cars are his means to his own self-destruction, it is because they embody his "evil." Shortly before he stabbed the man, something strange happened. He sold a car for a pittance, leaving him without transportation. "I realized that cars have caused me trouble all my life." There are enough car stories to fill a whole other book on Rob.

One of the stories took place when he was fifteen. Before he was licensed and before I had regarded him as a good enough driver to cope with city traffic, Rob snuck out of our house in the middle of the night and drove my car eighteen hundred miles away. His doing such a thing was shocking and uncharacteristic. Regardless of his hidden inner world, he had outwardly seemed utterly incapable of doing such a thing. The care and thought he put into his plan were frightening in their deliberation.

He had planned it meticulously; he had overlooked no detail, except costs. Afterward, I imagined him lying in bed at night planning his escape after having spent all the previous evenings acting as though nothing out of the ordinary was going on.

He had exchanged my license plate with one from another car; loaded food and whatever of his belongings that he could sell or trade for gasoline, and took his bedding. He did all this in the middle of the night, creeping in and out of our front door, then departing with less than two dollars in his pocket. He left a note for me and for his brother, apologizing, telling me not to worry, that he would be all right, and that he knew that the man I was dating would loan me a car and take care of me. He'd said nothing about where he was going.

When he was arrested after what had been, for me, a nightmarish week, we flew to Florida to drive him back home. My car frame had been damaged but it was drivable. In the interim, I had arranged for him to start counseling immediately upon his return. Arriving back home, I took him straight to the counselor who in that first session obtained a commitment from Rob that he would call him the next time he felt like running away.

"I didn't run *away*." "I ran *to…*" He paused.

"To what?" I'd asked.

"To find *myself*, Mom." His words seemed solemn and wistful.

Our return trip home had even been fun. (I have struggled all of Rob's life to determine whether my inability to remain angry with him is a weakness or strength.) With unusual inflection, he could barely suppress his excitement and self-pride that he had done something as incredible as driving a car by himself across state lines. He spoke with a maturity and confidence I'd never seen in him before. The confidence was derived from an almost giddy sense that he had succeeded at something that had required a resourcefulness he did not know he had. Nor did I.

In fact, in listening to his saga, beneath my grief over what he had done, I marveled at the intelligence and problem-solving abilities that he had shown. His trip was no ordinary, relatively uneventful journey. This over-protected kid had put himself in highly dangerous circumstances again and again.

His resourcefulness was equally matched by poor judgment that repeatedly demanded that he solve problems very unusual to him. So it was a tale of a long series of events originated by bad judgment but escaped through clever thinking. He had traveled eighteen hundred miles on $1.86 and peanut butter sandwiches. He had stolen gas, exhilarated by getting away with it, exhilarated by a sense of accomplishing something so huge.

The night we returned home, feeling silly about doing so, I stayed out on the sofa, awake all night, just in case Rob decided to run away again. *Of course he won't!* I argued with myself.

He did. He crawled out his window. He did not take my car this time, but he was gone for another two or three weeks. Along with intense fear for his safety, I felt horribly violated and betrayed.

I could not have comprehended the more hideous violation and betrayal that Rob experienced during this second sojourn from home. My worst nightmares of what might befall him were, with the exception of his death, relatively benign. I thought he would suffer more mockery, starvation, injury, or illness. I was afraid he would commit other crimes in efforts to survive and would go to jail.

Rob was hitchhiking, hungry, and broke, in Florida and was given a ride by what he thought was a very nice family man. The stranger showered Rob with compliments: for his courage, intelligence, and good looks. Compliments from anyone outside his family were very rare, but craved, particularly from any authority figure. The man offered him a meal and night's rest in his family's home. There, in the presence and with the participation of his wife, the man molested and raped Rob all night long. Rob could not tell me this for years.

"I was lured into their guestroom by him and his wife. I thought it would be where I could finally sleep; I hadn't slept for days. When they started doing things to me, I kept telling them 'I don't want this' but they just kept on. They would not let me leave, even after it was over the next morning. They offered me anything I'd want if I would stay; they even offered me a car to drive. I could not stay. I just remember being glad it was finally over. It was no different from the kinds of crap I'd experienced all my life, only this time it was physical."

I am his mother. I cannot write about that without deep rage and grief. Rape is a hideous thing done to a person's sense of self, spirit, and soul, even more than an assault on the body. Rob understood well that being used in that way was equivalent to the emotional violations he had experienced all his life. But he understands now no better than he did then, how to distinguish between seducement and genuine attraction.

He left that house and stole a truck to escape from town. He had not, he said, regarded taking my car as stealing it, because it was *our* car, and I had access to another one to drive. So, to escape his rapists, he stole his first vehicle.

The truck became mired in mud and he could not get away in time. The police arrested him, phoned me, refused to hold him as I asked, and released him back on the streets the same day. No one knew what he had endured the night before. He was just a kid who had run away from home, polite to the police, always polite and cooperative with adults. The pattern of running continued.

Police departments from all over the United States called, notifying me that my son was in custody. I would either go get him or arrange for him to be flown home. Sometimes he would have been either immediately released or escaped by the time I arrived. "Why did you release him?" I always demanded to know.

"It isn't against the law to run away from home."

"Then why did you retain him long enough to call me?"

"Ma'am, most people want to know where their kids are." Finally, I quit going after him or arranging for transportation. I was in despair, but I never considered rape.

I begged judges and police all over the country to incarcerate him instead of releasing him to me. I knew he needed a very painful consequence to this activity and I was afraid that natural consequences would be disastrous.

"What kind of a mother are you?" asked one chief of police in response to my request. I didn't know anymore what kind of a mother I was. Like my son, I felt damaged.

I needed for Patrick to be away from Rob's insanity and the upheaval it was causing. I needed for him to be in an emotionally safe place. His dad was willing to have him join him in Japan. Patrick, at age twelve, would be flying alone from Dallas to San Diego where he would spend a few days with friends and then on to Los Angeles, Honolulu, and Tokyo.

It was his first time to fly alone, although his status was on the computer of every airline he would fly and assistance was to be available at every airport. He stood looking small and helpless in the enormous airport, apprehensive about what lay ahead in maneuvering his journey to Japan. "Oh," he wailed, "where's Rob when I need him?"

Where indeed was Rob? I didn't know. I had finally succeeded in arranging for him to be taken to Dallas Juvenile Hall on the condition that I transport him back, from Louisiana this time. A friend flew him into Dallas. I had tricked him into thinking he was simply coming home with me, knowing he would leave again if he knew he was about to be arrested.

We were met, as planned, by police officers at the airport. What I had not planned and what shocked me was that they said nothing to him; they just clamped on handcuffs and hustled him away. I had not realized it would be so brutal or cold or sudden. I was stricken. It summoned the horrible emotions of having left him in residential school and of stomping all of his models into pieces.

He looked back at me over his right shoulder, long blond hair and pale blue eyes and a sweet expression on his face that I couldn't understand.

That look is another framed snapshot that hangs on the walls of my mind. I would better have understood anger from him than that meek acceptance. He just said softly, "Bye, Mom," and he walked away from me, hands cuffed behind his back. He was five feet seven inches tall and weighed a hundred and ten pounds. His slight frame had always made him seem younger than his years and had been one more sense of inadequacy for him.

Funny how everybody else's child in juvenile hall is just a scruffy, punk kid, but your own is handsome, sensitive, and sweet. I did not think that Rob belonged there, I just hadn't yet found a place where he did belong, and I could not have him running wild while I searched for that magical place.

I did not have to grieve long about my son's captivity. Rob escaped from juvenile hall three days after he arrived. He escaped barefoot and wearing only a swimsuit. He drove out of Dallas in the first vehicle he found with keys in it: a heavy-duty water truck, used by Dallas County to dampen roads that were being repaired. It had standard, multiple gears, but Rob had only driven an automatic transmission.

The truck also had a full tank of gas and a full load of water, apparently in readiness for the next day's work. Both were near empty within a few miles. "You know, Mom, you can't get far on a full tank of gas in second gear!"

In his efforts to figure out the complex gear system, he had accidentally activated the lever that controlled the outflow of the water. He, who is new to the city and has only driven out of Dallas himself one time, now drives out again. He departs from an unknown point of origin within the city, in a strange truck in second gear, barefoot, mostly naked, off-loading water along the way, and does not get stopped. A second major triumph!

Most of us have grown up receiving sufficient approval and rewards for overcoming difficult challenges by our own acts and efforts. We've earned enough recognition for successes and personal value to have a reasonably positive sense of self and a sufficiently positive acceptance of the rights and rules of others in society.

People whose "social intelligence" has developed appropriately and whose cognitive abilities pretty much work like those of other folks and whose bodies have always been under their own control have usually acquired the prerequisites for being a normal, productive person. They've developed a sense of belonging, are aware of a sense of purpose to their lives, and have a sufficient degree of self-esteem, self-trust, and empathy for others. Most of us take those qualities in ourselves for granted; some of us thank God for them.

Two opposing, predominant, driving needs in Rob were to have a self he could respect and trust and to annihilate the self he could not. At an age when his peers were striving to establish their identity through competition, communication, and identification with their own group, Rob was still struggling to determine in what ways he was human. There was no group with whom he could identify. There was no friend who could commiserate with him about his failures. No friend, period.

If Rob's escape from juvenile hall, identical in every other detail, had been from an enemy camp, across an alien city in a nation at war with his country, it would have been heralded as an act of courage and a resourceful will of survival. He would have come home a hero.

Yet, in a very real sense, Rob's escape was from an enemy camp in a world that had been mostly hostile to him. In escaping, he had succeeded in triumphing over every symbol of hostility and rejection he had ever known. It mattered little to him that he had done so as a juvenile delinquent; that is only what he was to the enemy. To himself, he was a somebody who had defied all odds, succeeded against impossible opposition, and proven some powerful sense of worthiness to himself. He was fifteen years old.

It would never again hurt quite so much that the world seemed against him, for he was somewhat less against himself. He would never quite so much distrust his own impulses for they had led him to victory. So far, there had not been prison and the further defilement of spirit and soul that occurred there for him. Nor, so far, had there been hellish demons whose mocking faces replaced the insolent expressions of overworked enforcers of the law. He had not yet discovered drugs or alcohol, but he was about to do that.

For another season, until he was thrust beyond this boy-adolescent stage into manhood, he would bask in his memories that he had broken some chains of inadequacy. For a season, he would overlook that he had broken the law to do so.

There followed a series of similar episodes, which are for me only murky, ugly splashes of pain. The only memory that stands out clearly before Rob returned home "a new man" at sixteen was a visit to him in an Arizona facility for delinquent youths. I don't recall how he got there.

The memory stands out for two reasons. One, it was the first time I had ever heard him spontaneously read aloud, other than the yellow painted sentence in our street eight years before. That one, stating: "Robbie is retarded," was hardly motivational. Our visit was ending and he walked me to my rental car, his arm around my waist, and sat inside behind the steering wheel.

I sat in the backseat behind him while he checked out the rental car. He pulled the visor down and without self-consciousness or faltering mistakes, read aloud the instructions printed on it for fuel consumption and tire pressure. Tears welled in my eyes; that was a *real* triumph!

Second, I remember the visit because of the quiet and genuine show of love for me that seemed to flow from Rob. He was not awkward or puppet-like. He held my hand or kept his arm comfortably around my waist and maintained eye contact when he spoke. I had seen little of that since he was in residential school. I could overlook the circumstances that had gone before; he had again made qualitative leaps forward.

Love renews itself every day. Love does not look backward in regret; it looks forward in hope.

Some months later, Rob came home from Arizona and Patrick from Japan. Both started a new school; both had new experiences about which to boast and grieve. They were no longer little boys at thirteen and sixteen. I was less and less the most significant influence and my approval was less critical than was that of their peers. That is how nature meant it to be.

Patrick stepped into adolescence with some awareness that necessary to maturity was the process of letting go of the security of childhood. For a while, he wanted both. But he had maneuvered the stages of boyhood with sufficient success to arrive at this one with an adequate sense of his own place in it. He had enough skills and confidence to cooperate with his peers in the business of learning to carve out his trail toward mature adulthood and love.

When Rob had first gained an awareness of others, his remarks about himself often reflected a sense that he was too different from other humans to be included as an equal. That perceived differentness had been devastating, for he also realized that he needed approval and recognition from others more than he understood how to get them. Having then learned, although from defiant acts, that he might be a self with interesting things to say, he returned to trying to be a social self.

Back in the real world, he was still just a little odd. He never mastered small talk or initiating relationships. He had no common interests or experiences of any other ninth grader, no knowledge of ball players, no consistent schooling. He was older than most of his peers. Essentially, he had no peers. One cannot compete with others in the age-old struggle to be if one does not recognize one's own commonality among others.

If I felt that his repetitious, compulsive behaviors were attempts to solve deeply rooted psychological problems, others did not. I was regarded by many of those significant to both Rob and me as making excuses for him. I looked at *why* he behaved the way he did; society, as it must, looked at *what* he did. I sought causes for his acts; society looked at the effects.

All his life I have struggled with my own conflicts. I, too, am a member of and share the values with the same society that does not condone the kinds of destructive acts I'd seen in my son. And I am a member of the human race where mothers love their kids, no matter what. Disassembling the why was the only way I had of relieving the tension created by the what. Seeing that he was again struggling to find self-respect and purpose, I was scared that his fading confidence seemed only to derive from aberrant or unlawful behaviors.

CHAPTER 14

"But here I wonder how long I will have to go up, when will the 'what goes up must come down' rule apply for me?"

I gave much thought to my decision, finally, to get Rob a car. There was no teenager in our neighborhood who, licensed or not, did not either have their own car or free access to one of their parents' cars. I hoped that a car would break down his barriers of isolation, psychologically if not socially. If he could not have friends, then he could at least have the one thing that most compensated for that lack.

I bought him a dream, late-model, one-owner, low-mileage, red Ford Ranchero, in perfect running condition. Although it was a belated sixteenth birthday present, I bought it before he was licensed because I knew it would be sold if I waited. He was studying for his driver's license exam but not allowed to drive off our long road until he passed. Still, he was thrilled and loved puttering over the car. He hummed and smiled and became absorbed again in something outside himself. A few weeks later, the perfectly performing, flawless transmission had been completely disassembled.

"Mom!" He stood on the living room carpet beaming at me. His hair and clothes dripped greenish liquid that refracted the sunlight from the windows behind. He seemed outlined in a halo. He extended to me a hubcap piled high with small white plastic pieces in assorted shapes. They reminded me of the pieces that formed a plastic reproduction of a human brain I had once disassembled in a physiological psychology class.

"Did you know that an automatic transmission looked like this?" He asked the question with an expression of reverent awe that I had reserved for the occasion when I might finally get to dissect a real brain.

I suppose that his image of a transmission had been rather like mine: that it was a thing of greater mass with gears, wheels, and pulleys. Instead, much to my distress and his delight, an automatic transmission is a myriad of tiny pieces, pieces that were at that moment spilled and rolled out onto the driveway, in corners of the garage and into the grass, only some of which filled the hubcap.

What an odd pair we are, I remember thinking. *The mother naively believing she can discern the soul from a brain; the son believing he has done so from the transmission of a car.*

For the next many days, he reconstructed the transmission, without benefit of manual or advice. As he had disregarded the laws broken by a previous triumph, he now disregarded the fact that he could only drive in reverse. He had succeeded! Never mind the losses, he had won the war! It took several more days to get the car to again go forward. He then had second, third, and fourth, but no first and no reverse. It still did not matter. He had accomplished a very personal, very satisfying feat.

Both Patrick and Rob were dropping hints that every other kid in our small town Texas neighborhood drove without driver's licenses. They did. Mine, I declared, would not. They did.

All of my decisions regarding Rob have always been made after giving considerable thought to the deficiencies, failures, and loneliness of his life. Driving was a natural progression of his adolescence when little else about his life seemed to be. Having and driving a car leveled the field a tiny bit and showed the adolescent community that he might be more like them than not. It was a very special thing to him to get to do what the other kids his age did and drive to the drive-in theater. That was my rationale, anyway. I finally yielded to both their pleadings and allowed Rob to drive them the ten-mile distance straight up the highway to the theater.

I knew that every other unlicensed kid drove to that theater and that the local police overlooked it. More desperately than ever, I wanted Rob to be able to demonstrate he could be trusted. As always, I stretched limits to have that happen.

I gave them my usual talk about responsibility, accountability, trust, and consequences. The points remained ever the same through the years, if the content varied, as they grow older. Off they went to a double-feature movie of racing, trick driving, and all other automobile high action.

All would go well, I assured myself. I was awake, expecting them home at the calculated time of midnight. At twelve-thirty, I decided the movies were longer than I had thought and reassured myself that there was absolutely nothing in the world that could have gone wrong. Even if I might not totally trust Rob, I could definitely trust Patrick.

At one o'clock in the morning, the local police called. They had my sons in custody. "Is this the mother of Robert Bowers?"

"Ma'am," the voice drawled on, "I almost killed your little boy." That is not exactly what he meant to say, but it was enough to cause me to fly to the police station in robe, slippers, and no makeup.

The scenario was given to me in fragments. Rob had just carefully entered the return highway after the movies when Patrick taunted him that he could not drive as good as the Hollywood heroes they had just seen. There are two things you just don't mess with: Texas and a kid's only pride!

Shortly after Rob captured Patrick's attention, he caught that of the off-duty policeman who, with his family, had also seen the same movies. From his private car, the man radioed ahead for backup. In his report, he stated that Rob had run him off the road while apparently attempting a U-turn in the middle of the lane.

Patrick reported to me that Rob had pulled the emergency brake in an attempt to duplicate the one hundred and eighty degree turn seen in the movie. "Really, Mom, he did a good job!"

Two police cars gave chase on what would otherwise have been a very boring night. They chased with flashing lights for several miles as Rob tried to outrun them, despite Patrick's increasingly loud pleas that he stop. Finally, he pulled over and both boys bailed out of the car before being ordered to do so. It was that move that almost got Patrick shot.

"Mom," explained Patrick, in an obvious attempt to salvage the situation, "I knew exactly what to do. I jumped out of that car, put my hands on the hood, and spread my legs, just like I've seen on TV!"

The local policeman whose gun was pointed at Patrick controlled his initial nervous impulse to shoot a "prisoner trying to escape," when he saw he was just a kid. "My finger was on the trigger, ma'am, on the trigger! I was shaking so hard I almost pulled it unintentionally!"

Robbie said nothing in the police station. Returning home with me, he could only explain that he had been so scared that he would go back to juvenile hall, he couldn't think of anything else to do but to try to outrun the police.

I could not focus my attention on the police as they reported the incredible number of counts on which they cited Rob. I lost track of them all. He was told to expect the tickets in the mail within three working days and to appear in court one week from that night's date. I signed papers and they were released to me to go home, where I collapsed in tears. I was back at square one with Rob.

Five days later one ticket arrived. Rob was charged with driving without a driver's license. I waited in apprehension, not sure of what his citations would mean for his future. No others had arrived by the time I drove him to town to go before the judge.

The judge was immediately the kindest, wisest, most dignified man I'd ever encountered. He was a gentleman; his legal stature was obviously secondary to that fact. He stood for me when we approached his desk. He was African-American.

A black man had risen to the level of judge in a small town not known for liberalism or racial tolerance! I felt I should be standing in his presence, instead. I could only imagine that he'd had to work harder and think smarter to achieve that judgeship. His desk was piled high with thick law books opened wide, at angles, so that he could refer to them readily.

I was prepared for the worst and I told him so. I also explained, first, that I had allowed Rob to drive without the license and, second, although Rob was expecting a lot of tickets, only one had arrived. But, I added, I hoped we could settle them all at that time because I was going to hang him as soon as I paid his fines.

"Well," the judge said, seeming to take a full minute to say just that word and motioning to his law books, "the law allows me quite a lot of leeway in calling things the way I see them." He paused a moment and then continued: "The way I see them, Robert is sixteen years old. Now, I thought to myself, what would I do if I were sixteen and driving my car after a movie about a bunch of stunt drivers, and I look up and see a lot of flashing lights coming at me. Why, I would do just what Robert did! I'd be scared! I'd see if I couldn't outrun those suckers! Now, of course, I wouldn't do that at my age. If I did I would deserve to have all these books thrown at me. So, no, no, Robert is not going to receive any more tickets in the mail."

Gesturing toward his opened books, he talked on, "Now I looked and looked through these, but I could not find any way to get around the law that he was driving without a license. Now I did look, because I know that every kid in town drives without a license from about age twelve, but that being the law, I do have to fine him for that. But I am not going to fine him for exercising the judgment of a sixteen-year-old. No, that would not be right to expect a kid to have judgment beyond his years."

I did not want to leave the presence of that remarkable man. He felt safe and good and so very decent. I was yearning as I imagined Rob in his way must also be to have an adult man in authority treat him with respect and understanding. I committed his talk to memory because I was almost spellbound by him, and I have repeated it again and again, wanting people to appreciate that there are judges who understand the spirit rather than only the letter of the law.

As I recall part of it here, I am back in his paneled office, gazing through tears into the kindest eyes I had ever seen. I am as aware now, as I was then, that the wise old man had transcended the ordinary plane on which most of us dwell.

Frankly, I had mixed emotions about Rob's getting off so easily; but his release from potential bondage was secondary to me at that moment. I felt my own bonds had been loosened a little with the man's remark that Rob was exercising the judgment of a sixteen-year-old. So rarely had anyone dismissed Rob's behaviors as appropriate to his age.

I continued with what had been tentative plans to have Rob leave the next day to go down to the Texas coast and work in the oil fields for the summer. Friends would watch over him. The decision had finally come about when it appeared that he would owe many hundreds of dollars in fines. He was to work hard to pay them off.

Letting him go had been a scary thought for me, but it still seemed like a better idea than him being isolated at home all summer. He would be forced into some discipline, have the potential to gain some self-pride, and prepare for a livelihood in a lucrative field that required more skill with things than with people. He would be with simpler people who, I reasoned, would not judge him by his social abilities but only by his already demonstrated ability to work very hard. It didn't work out as planned; it never ever has.

For all of Rob's exploits, he remained basically gentle and naive. He strived for approval wherever he thought he had half a chance of getting it. He had seemed to find that he liked approval from worthy efforts of work, at least until he began making too many mistakes. He always seemed more vulnerable to what men expected of him than to what I might expect.

His concentration problems and low tolerance for working under the stress of speed and coordination continued to plague him. He was placed with experienced crews so that he could train, but their experience also meant they were much faster than he. His youthful innocence was emphasized by his apparent shyness. That innocence apparently challenged the good-natured, but insensitive, field hands in ways that only a company of men might understand. One of those challenges was to make a man of Rob.

A boy becomes a man, according to these males, when he has had a sexual experience with a female and when he has gotten drunk. The woman, herself, does not matter; only her gender does. The one they chose for Rob was the local oil field prostitute. The experience did not make a man of him; it further traumatized him. Less than a year had gone by since the couple had sexually assaulted him. More than a year would pass before he could tell me why he had run away from the oil field.

The men had encouraged him to join them in a drinking spree and then on to the home of the prostitute, telling him along the way what was expected of him. The woman, in Rob's words, "was the ugliest, smelliest, filthiest, fattest lady I have ever seen!" He found her disgusting and repugnant.

He found himself in an impossible quandary. He did not have the maturity or confidence to refuse to go along with the scheme. He desperately wanted the respect and camaraderie of these muscular, swaggering males. He told me he had been repelled, terrified, embarrassed, and deeply ashamed. Still, he took it upon their word that this was somehow what he was supposed to do to be a man. He had not even been granted privacy. They not only insisted that he perform, but that he do so in their presence.

That failed, humiliating experience, disgusting in its absence of any dignity, devoid even of lust, would leave another ugly mark on him. When he told me about it, and about his earlier molestation, he was mature enough to realize that each had been a cruel thing done to him, but the shame still burned. His shame, as perhaps only men can understand, was primarily that he had been unable to perform. He solemnly concluded to me, "Therefore, I'm asexual, I'm sure."

By the time Rob told me that story, he had already told me of countless other tragic experiences that, it seemed to me, had one common theme throughout—his willingness to endure deprivation, humiliation, prison, and risk of life just to be accepted by men. He did not know how to do that. He often just assumed that the requirements expected of him by assorted gatherings of drunken men were what a man is supposed to do.

There were many times when his dependency on others for survival or a perceived obligation to strangers who had given him rides or aid placed him in conflicts with which he had too little experience to cope. The fear of sitting among people who would ridicule him if he did not comply was greater than whatever other risk might be involved. Being mocked as a coward if he didn't go along with them was too painful. It would take ten more years before he was no longer willing to violate his own conscience, rather than risk rejection and ridicule by refusing to go along with someone else's exploitation of his personal fears and private longings.

To have the respect and companionship that might signal he was a man worthy of inclusion would take him into the depths of degradation again and again. He had never found it among men whom society seemed to respect; he would only minimally find it among those it did not. Never had he found sufficient self-respect to choose his own group.

From the Texas coast, he traveled all over the United States. I learned his whereabouts from occasional phone calls home, just to "check in," and more phone calls from police in the identical pattern as before. It was not against the law to run away.

Sometimes I would learn that he had been arrested for some misdemeanor: vagrancy, stealing food, or jay walking. Mostly he survived by picking up odd jobs, being picked up by hitchhikers, and often being taken to their homes. For many months, when he was sixteen and seventeen, it was phone calls or citations for misdemeanors sent by mail that chronicled his misguided, unguided, journey to his self.

He also adopted an alias. The name on some of the tickets or warrants sent to my address seemed familiar, but it was not Rob's. The physical description was his. I was dismayed when he told me that his alias was the name of his roommate from residential school. "Rob! How could you do that? Don't you realize you have jeopardized him?"

No, he didn't think he had harmed the boy since it was a very common name and he had no other address or identification that related the name to the actual person. It was Rob's own private and immensely satisfying way of revenge. The kid had molested him and been his only tormentor while in the residential school.

Sometimes the phone calls were to inform me that he had been in a wreck. In one, he had rolled a car down a mountain near his former residential school in California. It had been stolen from a used car lot. Every car Rob stole was from a used car lot. His concrete logic was "But those cars don't belong to any*body*!"

He still bears the scars from the only injuries he sustained: multiple parallel cuts across his rib cage from the ignition key board he had taken out of the office of the lot.

I've always believed that he has a host of protective angels hovering over him. They are no doubt, bruised and challenged, but they are there on the job and a very good job they do!

CHAPTER 15

"I am doing pushups now, mainly to drive sorrow from me."

A call from the Los Angeles branch of the California Highway Patrol supported my belief in Rob's goodness despite those of his behaviors to the contrary. The question, "Are you the mother of Robert Bowers?" as always, instantly plunged me into a mixture of fear, dread, and grief. "Just once," I had remarked on more than one occasion, "I would like to say 'Yes I am,' with pride instead of fear and grief!"

The patrolman was calling to report that Rob had been involved in a wreck. This time, and this, miraculously, was the only time ever, another car was involved. The other driver had sustained minor injuries and was taken to the hospital. Rob had fled the scene, but he was also apparently injured since there was blood all over the inside of his car.

The officer actually chuckled as he told me that Rob had phoned 9-1-1 from a pay phone and reported the wreck and his belief that the other driver had been injured. "Ma'am," the officer remarked, "I believe this is a first for me, that a driver reports himself and volunteers the information." Rob gave the location of the accident and he gave them my name, assuring them that his insurance would cover the expenses and that I would have the necessary information. He refused, however, to tell them his location. He fled with only a broken nose. It would be broken many more times.

Again, it was years later before Rob told me the rest of the story. He had been drinking "some" wine and driving. He had cut too closely in front of another driver as he changed lanes. The driver became enraged and threatening. Rob had tried to outrun him, could not, and instead pulled into a gas station where he thought he would have protection. The other driver pulled into the station and stormed out of his car, carrying a baseball bat.

Scared, Rob then sped out of the driveway, back onto the streets, and into the path of another car. The car crashed into his, spinning it around. He got out and fled on foot.

"I had to run away from the man with the bat, but I couldn't sleep for a lot of nights and even when I could, I woke up from bad dreams about causing a wreck. I was so afraid that there had been children in that car; I couldn't go on until I found out. I was at least glad I had insurance to pay the driver's expenses."

Christmas of his seventeenth year, he was home again, trying again. He was heavily into music: heavy metal and acid rock music with satanic and hostile lyrics. Again, it was a trade-off. I detested the lyrics and was afraid it would warp him even more. He shrugged it off, "Of course I know the words are bad, but the music is my music; it tells about *me*."

He had instantly gravitated to acid rock. I saw that his intense interest in music gave him pride, pleasure, and something to talk about besides cars or how he had escaped the police. To encourage him in music, to help him find a niche in life, to give him something expressive and productive to do and something to offer the world, I bought him an electric guitar and amplifier for Christmas.

He hadn't asked for them. It hadn't occurred to him that he might actually make music. He was thrilled. It was not often but always expensive, that something could thrill him. He spent the rest of Christmas and the next two weeks holed up in his room teaching himself to play the guitar.

At seventeen, though very restricted in his activities and social skills, he had an excellent vocabulary, if an odd way of arranging his words. He had a broad range of factual knowledge, though he lacked a sort of ordinary social sense. He could survive on the streets but not in a classroom or an apartment. He had no skills and no one but family to listen to his play on words, answer his still nonsensical questions, or smile at him running his engine throughout the house.

It is not normal or healthy for anyone to live the way Rob did or to live with Rob as he was. As much as I loved him, it was a strain to try and make normal conversation. It was painful to hear his embarrassed rationalizations about why he had no friends. I could not rest at night knowing he was awake.

He had not yet really opened up to me about the detested inner life and shameful obsessive thoughts that hounded him if he could not dispel them with something intensely distracting. He believed that as his mother I should have been able to know his thoughts and imaginings.

He later said he had given me lots of clues. I had long ago lost the ability, I think, to discern such clues from him for several reasons. First, I remained frustrated that Rob seemed always to expect me to intuitively understand even his most nonsensical comments and silent moods. When I examine my frustration, I realize that I also had a deeply held conviction that a good mother *ought* to intuitively understand her child's nonverbal communications. Surely that must often be a difficulty in the hearts and relationships between parents and troubled children.

The fantasies, which he called demons, were still occurring in his seventeenth year, but he had not yet been able to tell me about them overtly. When he later did, he explained that they had begun at age eight. In hindsight, I realize that age coincided with the time when his behaviors became qualitatively worse. "I believe my demons come from another life."

"Mom, I can't tell you some of the worst, I don't like talking about those, but they contain things that no eight-year-old could possibly have known. Horrible things about...death...that's why I think they're from another life." And he shut down again.

Rob seemed compelled to tell me, eventually, about all his worst shames. Sooner or later, I would be told things that were very painful to hear, especially knowing I remained unable to fix him.

He still cannot tell me about the inner life of his eight-year-old self. He had apparently tried to communicate these with his actions in middle childhood. I had missed his point. Who ever thinks their child has macabre secret fantasies and unwanted images going on behind their innocent faces?

He had always seemed to expect that I would understand his cryptic messages, physical symbols of inner frustrations, colloquialisms, and strange use of words. An often repeated and increasingly exasperated phrase of my own was: "Rob, I can't read your mind. You have to tell me straight out!"

I lived in tension never knowing if he might vandalize a car or get in some other serious trouble. But the greatest burden was my own continuing sense of helplessness at seeing his misery. It was an obvious strain on him to try to contain his impulses and to live within the boundaries of normalcy. It saddened me that he avoided most family interests, except for travel or skiing.

While others in our ski party stood in lines for the lifts, seventeen-year-old Rob took lessons on his first ever trip to a ski resort. He had been lost somewhere during the previous year's ski trip when Patrick and I had learned. He was scheduled to have a full day's lesson. By eleven, he struck out on his own.

As everyone except Rob sat at lunch overlooking the slopes, one of our friends called our attention, in amazement, to the skier who was flying down the expert slope at breakneck speed, going over rather than around the moguls. "Naw," I decided. "It couldn't be! He's not that coordinated!"

It was Rob and he loved skiing. It was high-speed, thrilling, risky, challenging, freedom, and isolation from people, yet doing what normal people do. It was mastery, if one was not a stickler for style, which of course he was not. "See Rob," I commented that night to a very exhilarated master of the expert slopes, "Sports *can* be fun!"

"Sports?" He asked in shock, "Skiing is a *sport?*" A success, indeed, he'd found a sport he could handle and even go faster than most. Patrick had the style and grace; Robbie had the speed and daring. Mom had none of the four.

He had come so far in so many ways that it truly seemed that Rob could achieve a life for himself if his intelligence and drives could be channeled. If he had nothing in common with other seventeen-year-olds, perhaps he could find commonality among similarly technical-minded older students.

I paid the six-month tuition required in advance and off he went to a technical school in a town about one hundred and fifty miles away, but I took away his car. He had passed the entrance exams because of his mechanical abilities; he would have a trade and normalcy. He might even excel there, given his compulsive urge to design, improve, and improvise. I felt cautious hope. There were always grounds for hope when he passed exams.

He would live in a dorm where he would never get to know his dorm mates, but they would contribute to his training— rather than learning computer aided design, machine making or mechanics, he would only master making LSD in the school lab. Rob discovered drugs, at seventeen. He had been hearing about them for years. All he had heard had only made them sound attractive.

His first use of drugs had been an isolated incident in public school months earlier. A classmate had described "speed" in glowing terms, then sold Rob one pill for fifty cents. He carried the pill in his sock all that day and hid it in his bureau drawer at home for about two weeks.

"One Monday morning I woke up in my usual dread, 'Oh no,' I thought, 'not another day of school.' Then I remembered the pill and thought, 'why not?'"

"I was a straight-A student for a day! I blew my teachers' minds! They had no idea I was actually that smart! Then it ended, and the next day, I was just back to being shy and stupid."

Maybe, just maybe, had he told me about being a "straight-A student for a day" I might have been able to reorder my thinking and realize that his discovery about his improved attention was more significant than the means of that discovery. Maybe I would have understood that another kind of medication might have been the solution. But Rob could not risk getting in trouble for using drugs, so he did not tell me about that incident until years later.

His making and then immediate use of LSD was in such large amounts over so many consecutive days, it should have resulted in his death. Under the influence of it, he left the technical school in about six weeks running from demons whose descriptions he provided me with later. They were mocking, shrieking, and condemning ghouls. And yet he followed their dictates. He ran from something worse than any reality he had ever known, but still he continued to use LSD. Running, alone, into predatory company; living in holes, shacks, other people's beds, ditches, and under freeways.

He had long since sold or lost his guitar and amplifier and everything else of value that he had owned. That pattern would be repeated off and on for many more years, although he grieved the loss each time.

There was a singular advantage to his losing his belongings: there was always something to get him for Christmas and birthdays. The one treasure that he rarely lost was something that no one wanted to steal from him—all the letters from home. He still has most of them.

There were no letters from home written to holes in caves or the shack he burned down in order to kill the devil. There were many written to him in prison, but he would not go there yet. He was then still a minor, still protected from disclosure under that protective veil.

Every time Rob came home, he came to stay, but he could not stay. Boredom, in the absence of intense stimulation, translated into depression. He didn't like conversations, so not even meal times were very pleasant for him. The purpose of a meal was to eat and then leave the table. He was always miserable if he was required to stay.

More hopeless than ever, he agreed to try Job Corps. His meek and well-intended agreement to try any approach I suggested eventually just added to my sorrow. I grew to feel that I was forever leading an innocent lamb, regardless of his waywardness, to some new form of slaughter.

Job Corps meant another new wardrobe and another flight and settling into another dorm and another hope. Job Corps should have appealed to him. This one was out in the hill country in Texas; he loved nature. He talked more and more about the solace he found in nature. He much preferred desert, the more barren the better, but any remote place was better than cities.

There were other drugs at Job Corps and other youths who hadn't found a self they could live with. He bonded with none, but he accepted their drugs and finally, again, fled alone. "It reminded me that I was always much more afraid of kids my age than I was of adults."

Each time Rob failed to honor a commitment, he avoided communicating with me for many weeks. Once he had again contacted me, he stayed in frequent touch and would return home, happy to be there for a while but would in time become restless again. I stayed alert all the time for any possible niche where he would find meaning and purpose.

CHAPTER 16

"I would like the chance to take an auto mechanics course again when I get out. I don't remember failing so much, as with the Navy, if only I had the chance to do it over again." Rob from prison.

Given his background, I cannot imagine why I ever thought that Rob might be accepted into the military. In my adolescence when boys were still drafted and police sometimes sent wayward youth to grow up in the service, the military seemed to solve a lot of social problems. Desperate circumstances called for desperate acts. There was absolutely nothing in his history that the military would find attractive. Against his being accepted by the military were, his age, his drug abuse, the record of juvenile delinquency, lack of high school education, and lack of social comfort.

Yet it was from that lack that he turned to the Navy. I don't recall the reason he gave for not choosing his father's Marine Corps. Maybe it was his own personal fear that he could not compete with his dad.

Against all those absolutely impossible odds, Rob was accepted into the Navy. I initiated the contact with the recruiter and I did all the footwork for him. I also held my breath while they ran a police check on him. Clean. Nothing. Angels?

The last remaining thing, I could not do. Rob would need to pass the Armed Services Vocational Aptitude Battery (ASVAB) himself. He would have to make above average scores to compensate for his age and lack of education.

He made the cutoff! It was one of the most exciting things that had ever happened to him from my perspective. His scores also indicated a corresponding, above-average intelligence. I had not doubted that he was intelligent; I simply doubted that he would ever make use of it in any focused, productive manner.

He was pleased. He acted as though he felt redeemed. It was a very satisfying thing for him. I sat beside him in front of the recruiter's desk as he signed the papers to join the Navy. On the wall behind the desk was a plaque with a golden shovel. The recruiter told me it was an award for having exceeded his quota of recruits. I privately felt I had just earned my own golden shovel.

As I drove Rob the seventy-mile trip to put him on the transport from Dallas to the Great Lakes Naval Station, I was melancholy yet more hopeful than I had been in years. I pondered all I thought that this would mean for him. I hoped again that he could learn a trade, but more than that, to gain pride and self-respect. I was silent about my apprehension that he might not complete boot camp, given his history. But, it was by far the best potential for a future, for success and becoming disciplined that he'd had since perhaps residential school.

I searched for words to say to my son, sensing that it would be the last time that he would be a boy. I was saying good-bye again, having said it so many, many sad and tragic times. I wanted to somehow convey something important to him, this one final time. I told him how much I loved him, how much I would miss him, and how proud I was that he had straightened out his life. But there was something more I wanted to say and I was not even sure what that was. I groped.

"Rob, of course I know we can't start all over in life, but if we could, what is it you would have me do differently?"

"Mom!" He interrupted: "Mom, don't you ever, ever blame yourself for anything I have done wrong! Every bad thing I've ever done is my own fault; every good thing in me is because of you! You're the best mother I've ever had!"

I choked back tears and could only think of something silly to say so that I wouldn't start sobbing, "Rob, I am the *only* mother you've ever had!"

"Oh! You know what I mean; you're the best mother I've ever *seen!* I've seen lots of mothers; you're the best by far!" I was not, but his comments assuaged for a while the guilt I carried around. He continued to recount memories that he treasured, and his appreciation that I had always stood by him, "when every other mother would have given up a long time ago!"

He offered mature, insightful understanding. It was the first time Rob had ever appraised me as a mother or verbalized any appreciation for my love and parenting. It is another captured moment on my mental film. His words were spring rain on the thirsty garden of my heart.

As is now so typical of Rob, he communicated his awareness, in an elegant simplicity, of complex matters to which he had always seemed oblivious. Having been validated by the United States Navy as a worthy man, he could now validate me as a mother. For the first time since he was ten years old and at residential school, we were a normal mother and son setting out on a normal journey. For the first time in seventeen years, this one did not emerge from a crisis.

I wish Rob's story could end there. I wish I could say that the rest of his life was uneventful at least in terms of extremes.

I wish, too, that I had never written him a dozen times that no matter what day he graduated from boot camp I would fly out for the ceremony. Who schedules a boot camp graduation on New Year's Eve? Who else but Rob would wait until two days before to notify me of that date?

I left out-of-state house guests sleeping at my home, as I repeated the two-hour drive to the Dallas airport that I had made the previous day to pick them up. I drove to catch a seven a.m. plane for Chicago. The door of the plane was closing as I ran down the ramp yelling, "Wait!"

In Chicago, I rented a car and found my way, without Rob to guide me, to Great Lakes Naval Station. It was freezing cold; I was dressed as though I expected valet parking. There was ankle-deep dirty slush through which I had to tread in high heel shoes for what felt like a mile. He would graduate before a crowd of a thousand, it seemed, and I thought I must be the last parent to arrive; anyway, mine was the last of a thousand parked cars. I thought also that Rob is right: I *am* the best mother he ever had!

I felt very sorry for the young Navy men who were standing at parade rest in ankle-deep icy slush, at equal distances of about thirty feet all along the base. They were freezing, but seemed proud, well-trained, tough, and red-nosed. I offered an encouraging smile to the few who made eye contact; I guessed they were trained to stare straight ahead. My thought was that Rob would do just fine with that requirement. The freezing men were there to direct all of us untrained parents to a parking space and the hangar where the ceremony would take place.

Parents and loved ones (*Does the Navy think they're mutually exclusive?*) were assigned bleachers directly behind the marked-off section where our young men would march in formation before us. I found my seat as the music started. I had momentary pleasant memories of past times like this day when I'd been married to Rob's dad. Ah, but today, it was *my* son out there marching! I knew there was a sappy grin on my face, but it seemed to match those on every other parent's.

I stared into the sea of seamen, searching every face again and again. I began to feel ashamed that I could not identify my own son and vowed I would never tell him that I could not single him out. On the other hand, I marveled that I could not; it had to mean that at last he was marching to the same drummer as everyone else!

At the end of the ceremony, every Navy man ran to the arms of his parent or loved one. I sat and I stared. I was scared and I wanted to cry; it was all painfully familiar. Rob was not among them.

Rob was red-nosed, freezing, standing in slush directing all the return traffic and he could not leave his post until every last parent was gone, (save one). Disappointed, I waited and waited, and wondered if he had been given the honor of directing traffic because he still marched to his own drum.

Hours passed before we could connect. Hours while all other parents were visiting and dining with their sons and loved ones. I'd had nothing to eat all day except breakfast on the plane and a Coke at the base.

We had fifteen minutes to talk before I had to leave to catch my return flight. I first drove him to the hotel where he anticipated getting drunk with his fellow graduates to finally celebrate his rite of passage into the company of men. I had the vague sense that he was as excited about the opportunity to drink as about having completed boot camp.

However, there was also the sense that he had really become a man. There was an air of confidence in him. He had earned membership into a valued group. I observed the respectful formality of his interactions with his superiors. I was pleased with his commitment to rules, regulations, and boundaries.

I drove back to the Chicago airport, turned in my rental car, took a tram to my gate, and flew back to Dallas. Rob would follow me a month or so later for his first military leave.

My car was out of gas and I could find no open gas stations on that late New Year's Eve. I ran out of gas in the parking lot of the supper club where I was meeting my invited guests. It was twenty minutes before the New Year. I have guardian angels of my own.

Rob had spent his pay to buy me a gold locket with a tiny diamond in the middle. It was sent by certified mail and I could see from the cost that he had been exploited by a jeweler just off-base who charged usury prices. I wondered if he would ever lose his naiveté. I hoped not. I loved the winsome sweetness of him that always belied the secrets that lurked within.

After ten days of leave in Texas, Rob's orders were that he report to his newly assigned ship in Maryland. He was very proper, spit and polish. I basked in the long awaited miraculous transformation of my son. He had his orders and he obeyed. I drove him back to the airport. It was a good, good feeling to say good-bye in this sweet way.

Perhaps if Rob had not been reared the son of a military officer, he would not have been so unintimidated by the events that followed. He arrived at his destination from the Maryland airport by cab, to the dock where his ship was not.

The ship was scheduled to be there and his orders had required that he go to that specific dock. The ship, as it turned out, had not even left Cuba to return to the states. No one had notified Rob, who was on legitimate leave, of the change. Of all the men in the Navy, how typical that this would happen to Rob!

Could there be any other cab driver with such trust in his fellow man as the one who connected with Rob? I do not recall how Rob convinced this man to do so, or how afterward, he also convinced the various hotels in which he stayed, to bill the Navy. The cab fare was astronomical. Rob had the man drive him up and down the coast of Maryland looking for the ship.

He stayed in commercial hotels and somehow got himself flown over to the original destination of his ship, as his modified orders now read. He arrived in Cuba to learn that the ship had left there just prior to Rob's arrival. He flew back to the states and in a few days, he located the ship back in Maryland and finally took his post on board. Of course I didn't know at the time that all this was going on, but to learn after the fact how well he handled that situation astonished me.

Rob was quite confident about his decisions. His logic was that it was the "Navy's fault," so what else was he to do but find his ship, eat, sleep at night, and carry on! He wasn't a homeless vagrant anymore; he was a Navy man! He didn't have to sleep in the alleys behind hotels anymore. Apparently, the Navy agreed with Rob, at least up to that point.

The Navy disagreed with Rob when he later jumped ship and went AWOL for five months. "I could not stand the boredom." My experience in the past with his boredom told me that his anxiety and internal noise were exacerbated to intolerable levels by being in such close quarters with other people for a prolonged period. I did not know his whereabouts until he was arrested in Texas.

Only Rob could have such an eventful military career in such a short time: Upon his arrest, Rob was first flown to Philadelphia and then flown to his ship now in the Mediterranean. Along the way, he managed to find ways to get off the flights to at least touch ground in Rota, Spain, and Sicily and Naples, Italy. Finally, he went before the captain for the fifteen minutes it took to be given a general discharge. He was not a misfit to the Navy; he just didn't fit.

He was then flown back to Philadelphia and given a bus ticket home to me. He had rejected the Navy, not the other way around. He could survive boot camp with sufficient success, but he could not survive whatever he felt he faced onboard the ship.

I don't know what happened to cause him to jump ship. Perhaps it was because at that time, he was not yet able to connect his intense discomfort with being in such close quarters with others as a ship required. He could not admit that he could not urinate nor have a bowel movement when others are present and in a position to observe him. He was extraordinarily self-conscious about using the toilet. He believed that difficulty was more shameful than jumping ship.

A letter he had written to me before he split contained only positive feelings about himself, including the following: "Lately I've been thoroughly enjoying the Navy and the lust of life I had been so long without. I used to be a loser, now I am a complete winner, a new intensely enjoyable high which I have never felt before. The only time I was ever near this feeling was when after weeks of studying and trying to figure it out, I finally got my Ranchero to back out of that lonely driveway."

He continued on to describe his newfound sense of self-respect, then to apologize repeatedly for "everything I have ever put you through." It was a long letter in which he again showed more insight about his regrettable behaviors and the realization that with his focus on something worthwhile. "I now have something to live for."

And then he was gone.

Five months after he jumped ship, he returned home, but did not stay long; he liked himself even less for this failure. As he was to say many more times, "Mom, something is wrong with me, I get so bored that I can't stand it any longer and I have to leave. Then I miss what I have left and wish I hadn't." He had not yet been forced to examine that boredom and his own inner conflicts. He still mostly acted out the feelings he had stuffed away all his life. His acts defined who he was and he did not much like the man. Autistic individuals process information from people and their surroundings differently and, as a result, their judgment is correspondingly impaired.

Home was less and less a place where he belonged. It was a place where he was loved, in whatever abstract way he perceived love, but it was not a place where he had much in common with those inside the house that sheltered him. Home was the place where a maturing Rob more and more confronted the self he would never be. His family lived out the standards of a society of which Rob only lived outside. He did not like looking through the frosted window at a hearth where he could not be warmed. His brother and I welcomed him, but even that welcome was hurtful.

He perceived that he had let us down again and again and felt that his own experiences had no common frame of reference with ours. He had discovered that he liked himself most when he was drunk, even if he had to be drunk alone, along lonely roads in blowing winds. He was more like the wind than like the roads he traveled.

CHAPTER 17

"I am living in a bizarre and mind-boggling world here. I feel like I'm dying. I went way too far. I should have never ended up here." From prison.

I had thought that I had seen the most tragic human condition from my experiences with the severely mentally ill. Among those were individuals who fit along a continuum of humankind from the most crazed to the most manipulative personality disordered. I had seen nothing in any of them that was as seamy and depraved as the people Rob too frequently encountered in the travels on which he again embarked.

There are human beings so predatory and so devoid of conscience that they literally consume the mind, body, and soul of all who fall victim to their prey. Their victims are people like Rob: lacking an integrated sense of self, vulnerable, lonely, chemically-dependent, naive, desperate, hungry, and ashamed.

Above all, their victims are very, very ashamed. Ashamed of who they are, what they are, and what they think they cannot do. Ashamed even that they continue to do the things they most despise and ashamed that they can only find companionship among people they least respect. Shame creates a victim for predators. It is a constant companion of the person who knows he is inadequate in all ways that society respects. Shame is all you gain when you have failed to even have an honorable failure.

Rob and those like him are prey for predators who have forgotten both guilt and shame. Such people gorge on some tender good in the hearts of their prey and then leave them behind to become emotional fodder for social scavengers. They seek power as proof that they have an importance, but it is bondage of those who think they have none. I first discovered such people through Rob, and later professionally, because many of the victims become patients in psychiatric or drug and alcohol treatment facilities.

Rob has been offered and accepted food in exchange for perverse favors, sexual and otherwise; cold and exhausted, he has accepted rides from people who promised comfort for sex. He would tell me later, "I close my eyes, and my mind takes me away from that person; they can use my body, but they can't use my mind." But they could warp and distort that mind and drive it further and further from dignity and promise.

In sleeting rain, he has accepted rides from people who then would exploit his need and might, as in one very typical occasion, have him off-load their entire truck cargo and then mockingly drive away, abandoning him still hungry, still in the rain. He has accepted shelter from drug dealers who used him as a front, feeding him the drugs to command his loyalty and dependence upon them. In time, he would escape that bondage only to enter some other.

For a time, he lived in a commune that he believed to be a religious organization that pan-handled for food for the needy. It had some title with "god" included. He was proud. He phoned to tell me he had the job and that it was for a good reason. He got to keep ten percent of his earnings as pay. To me it stunk of a scam, and in a few long-distance phone calls, I learned there was no such recognized organization.

It took weeks for him to grasp that this "religious" group was simply another form of exploitation. When he realized that, he left, taking that day's collections. No, he defended, he had not stolen from people who were innocent victims; he had stolen from the organization that expected the full $25 he had gathered that day.

It was always a matter of personal honor that persisted throughout his wanderings that he never asked for handouts. He asked for real work, for something of himself to give in exchange for necessities. He has stolen food when he has been very hungry and could find no work. In an awkward twist of dignity, he will give his body before he will beg.

In fragmented talks to me about loneliness and love, he revealed that it was his heart that he wanted to give but did not know how. Besides, he found no one among the transient groups with whom he had things in common who was lovable. Nor did he find any who were any more capable of loving than he was. He had never had a loving experience or an affectionate sexual one.

He had never had tenderness from any woman except his mother and grandmother. He had never initiated kissing a woman until he was thirty-two years old, when a stranger on the beach toyed with his vulnerabilities.

"Woman" on her pedestal was too far removed from his reality for him to ever hold in aspiration, much less his arms. It was a thrilling, remembered occurrence to have a pretty girl smile at him or strike up a conversation. Rarely had he ever found the courage to initiate contact with any girl, pretty or not. He had only hoped and dreamed and longed and been very willingly vulnerable to those who came on to him.

Exploitation of his needs was the predominant theme of all the stories recounted to me over the years from early adolescence through his mid-twenties. Those experiences formed the structure of the self that emerged from the rubble of a life spent in shame. The image of the kind of woman whose love he would want, profoundly contradicted the image he held of himself as utterly unworthy of her.

I struggle to recall those stories he has told, without emotion, of the things he has done and had done to him. My mind will not permit me to remember. They are like scenes from horror movies that I would walk out on if I somehow found myself in such a theater. Rob has seen mankind in ways I cannot even imagine. He offers no excuses, as I have done for him. "Mom," he says so matter-of-fact, "that's just who I am."

"No!" I want to scream, but I keep my voice level. "That is not who you are; that is who you only believe yourself to be!" And I tell him again about the person he is to me. I have to do this carefully, for if I reject the bad that he believes he is and has done, then he will perceive that I do not really know or accept him for who he is. If he thinks I do not know him, he cannot trust that I truly love him. In that respect, he is no different from his mother or anyone else. Nonetheless, as an adult, it is not his mother's love he seeks.

There were also, along the way, decent people who gave Rob rides, shelter, food, odd jobs, advice, and comfort. In their decency to him, they kept alive some sense of his own dignity. Over a sandwich and a glass of milk in some stranger's kitchen, he could look out upon their lawn he had just mowed, or the room he had just painted, and talk man-to-man about the weather or the car in the driveway. He would gain some sense of affection from playing with the cats of strangers. But, he could not tarry too long in decency for his demons mocked the hypocrisy.

It was only a little less hellish to him to take that first look again at mother, dad, or brother than to look in the eyes of the demons that lived inside his mind. His belief that he had disappointed us or failed to live up to our expectations mirrored his own standards more than any we might have held for him. He is a little better now at discerning between the two than he was as a child.

———◆———

"I have a death wish," was his casually offered, but deeply believed explanation for everything he did that was dangerous. It was also the reason he failed at some hopeful endeavor, and the reason he risked his life again and again. It was the reason he wrecked cars or used suicidal quantities of alcohol and drugs.

"But you also have a 'life wish,' Rob," I urged. "Look at how you concern yourself with being clean even in the worst conditions and how you stay in shape, try to eat healthily." I cited every positive compulsion of his that came to mind to try and convince him that a healthy part of him wanted to live. I pointed out his talent in music and art, his grasp of difficult, complex scientific theories. I intended to compel him to grasp that part of himself that kept striving, no matter how else he failed.

"Mom," he told me patiently as though I seemed not to understand even the most basic elements of his being, "I want to be a handsome corpse. I think I'm probably too old to be a good-looking one. That really bothers me because if I'm an ugly corpse it will mean I've been defeated." Here he smiled wistfully and added a touch of humor for my benefit, "But one does not want to be found dead in dirty underwear!" His smile faded. "I do *not* want you to be sad for me when I die. I want you to be happy to know that I am free!"

His words tore into me like sharp claws. So many of the tightly held hopes for him seemed ripped open and exposed as lies; and the knowledge I didn't want to face hung there: his life was mostly lived with a sense of tragedy and sorrow and with so much abject loneliness that only in being viewed at his funeral could he imagine anyone else really caring for him. I groped helplessly for words, knowing, too, that my words for him had rarely been more than bandaids. But his to me caused open wounds.

There has never been a place or a circumstance where Rob can dwell in peace with himself. Always he looks outward through some window of his mind where there might be solace and purpose; perhaps they are to be found only in death.

I have looked too many times through clouded jail windows that framed his face. I have pounded against scarred barriers that kept me from offering any comfort in touch. Almost as often as the windows of Rob's own mental closures were those from the jail or prison visiting rooms all over the country.

Nearly as lacking in dignity as life inside jails and prison walls are the visiting areas for those outside them. Again, parents and loved ones congregate. But here, they gather in an embarrassed lack of privacy and strained and frustrated longings, dulled by hopelessness and despair.

There are pregnant wives with runny-nosed children in stair-stepped ages; awkward friends and brothers who laugh self-consciously, aware at some inner level of the contradiction between humor and prisoner. Mothers and lovers try with their eyes and fumbling words to communicate what cannot be spoken outright for fear that their man will be seen by guards and fellow inmates, as a wimp. Those very things that most need to be heard and expressed must be stifled.

I studied, through the eyes of love, the twenty-year-old Robbie, whose own gaze was courageous, steady, and gentle. To me, he was handsome, sweet, fragile, and still innocent in a child-like way.

How he was in a cell or in the congregations of other prisoners, I only knew from his letters. But the gentleness I saw was more than only a reflection of his gratitude for my visitation and my loyalty. It seemed born of his acceptance that life is storms and gales, and that spring showers are mere illusions.

He made no excuses; he stole a car and he was caught. He would repeatedly take cars that did not belong to him, while very, very intoxicated.

As I looked at him, I knew his worst. I knew that he had broken laws, abused drugs, exploited, stolen, vandalized, run away, quit, defied authority. I knew that his efforts then to joke about his present circumstances and make light of his treatment were intended to comfort his mother. Although it hurt terribly, I accepted the fact of what he had done and I did not so much pity him for being in prison as I pitied him for having gotten there.

And I pitied myself because the institution to which I must go to visit my son was a prison instead of a college or the military.

Always, as I looked at him, I also knew his best. I knew that he was tenderhearted, brokenhearted, kind, funny, generous, hardworking, courageous, and scared. I knew that he called women "ladies" in respect for their status; that he enjoyed doing manly things for his mother; that he was patient and tolerant with helpless people and animals and very respectful of an individual's rights to his own opinion. I knew of many times he had shared his last dollar with a hungry hitchhiker; given away my blankets to homeless people; brought dirty people home to shower, given them a meal, and then a ride to some shelter.

I had seen more tears in his eyes for the plight of others than I had for his own. I had seen his detestation of the obscene and his efforts to gain respect from men he found decent. Most often, I had seen his slumped shoulders when that respect was not returned. I had seen his prideful, stiff posture when he'd created some mental logic that helped him rise above the withholding of respect or a welcome.

Despite all I knew about him, I saw his innocence. It was an innocence that seemed to derive from abject trust in me and in all others whom he saw as decent. "Quality people" was his term for those who contrasted sharply with his view of himself and others like him. "I have a quality mother and brother," he wrote on the outside of one envelope mailed to us from prison.

In time as he matured, he grew to trust his own observations of certain people more than mine. He believed me to be incredibly naive about and in need of his protection from exploiters and phony charm. Yet he continued to fall prey to such people if they treated him at all with apparent affection and respect.

As he matured, I came to marvel at how accurately he could often perceive the truer character of anyone from whom he was detached, which, of course, was almost everyone. He seemed well-trained to look beneath a social mask; faces had never given many clues to him, anyway. Prison forcibly removes such masks, but he had also been opening hoods and examining the inner workings of things all his life.

He trusted me to maneuver him through the complexities and most intimidating world of social culture. That, he could not disassemble. His simple trust in me has often been the most frightening of all, for I will let him down many times.

Repeated cycles of failure and wandering the country made his being in prison otherwise almost a relief to me. There was no safe place where he belonged, although it seemed he had so often set out in search of such a place. If he belonged anywhere, that place was out there where survival and death were equal challenges.

In prison, I at least knew where he was. In his wanderings, I could only trace his journey through occasional phone calls, many from concerned strangers. Most were kind enough to just want me to know that they had extended some help to Rob and he had told them my name and number. Such people saw the good in him that I knew. Such gestures from kind men and women were precious gifts that kept my hope alive no less than they did for Rob.

Many calls were alarming, but Rob, himself, rarely called when he was in trouble or need. He resolved those problems himself, or endured the suffering until they passed, seeming to want only to report to me when he was in any way stable. At no time in all those years of wandering did he ever ask me for money or help.

On one occasion, I received a call from the director of a drug detoxification center in Dallas. It was only a coincidence that this man, with his experience, had come in contact with Rob. He had seen him wandering along a road seeming disoriented and too weak from an obvious lack of food and water to be left on his own.

The man told me that Rob had not acted like he was on drugs, so he took him to an emergency room in Dallas. He also told me he did not want me to be alarmed, but that he felt Rob had been close to death before he discovered him. But Rob was getting medical attention now and this kind man would keep me informed.

This stranger had gone to considerable and persistent trouble to find me, so I knew I could trust that he had Rob's welfare truly at heart. He had not been able to get any rational information from Rob but found my name and former Texas address and phone number on a soiled scrap of paper in his pocket. I had just returned to California and was staying with friends until escrow closed on my house.

I never learned how he tracked me down, but he remains in my mind and in my teachings a wonderful example of how it is necessary to go that extra mile to help someone in need. We don't stop when we meet an obstacle; we find a way around it. There is always a way. There is always prayer to a God for whom nothing is impossible. That was a praying man.

He also impressed upon me his genuine desire to have Rob come stay at his center, once he was released from the emergency room, and that he would keep me informed. I phoned the emergency room for a report on Rob's status and notified his father in Florida.

I had made certain that the hospital personnel understood that I would be responsible for the bill and that I did not want him released until he was truly stable. I had had too many experiences of Rob's vagrancy status resulting in only minimal medical attention and no respect.

I also obtained the commitment from hospital staff that they would call me when he was being released. The gentleman who had rescued Rob had also asked that the staff inform him when Rob was to be released and he would come get him. I continued to phone about every two hours. Finally, I was allowed to speak with Rob. "Mom," he whispered, as though trying to not be detected, "Mom, is this really you?"

"Mom, Granddaddy is in the bed next to me. He's trying to climb out of bed but the nurses won't let him. I think they're trying to kill him; they're sticking needles in him." Rob was hallucinating and paranoid. He kept asking for my reassurance that he was safe. He was dehydrated and had not eaten, they assumed, for several days. There were only minimal traces of drugs in his system; nothing indicated recent use.

In my next call, I learned that Rob had been released back on the streets. I had not been notified; the gentleman who would give him shelter had not been called. Rather, the hospital had discussed the discharge with his dad in Florida who knew none of the other circumstances or the possibility for treatment. "Did you at least feed him?" I wanted to know.

"Lady," snapped the doctor who had been attending Rob, "we are an emergency room, not a hotel!" A few months later, he ended up in the prison where I first experienced visiting him only through a cloudy window.

"When I get out, Mom, I promise to never get drunk again, I've learned my lesson. Getting drunk is what makes me steal a car; when I'm drunk, I don't think about how bad it is. When I'm drunk, I don't think at all."

Rob matured a lot in this prison sentence of over a year, which up to then had been the longest period of incarceration. With no escape from them, he'd been forced to sort out his own thoughts. With no escape from people, he'd been forced to find ways to live with them.

He asked for the opportunity to come home and start a new life. He intended to get a job and as soon as possible move out on his own. He believed that he had indeed learned his lesson about drugs and alcohol and realized he could never use them again. He wanted to fulfill those dreams that had made prison tolerable. Behind cell walls, he could fantasize about getting a job, living in his own place, having friends. Dreams were all he had.

Following this, I spent many months driving him all over San Diego and sitting out front while he applied for job after job after job. He applied for each with little concept of what he might have to offer. With each rejection, he reduced that offering to less and less. He did not even get hired as a dishwasher.

In the free world, he found he was as shy and awkward with people as he had ever been. He had no skills and minimal labor experience. Finally, he enrolled in and finished a mechanics course at City College and proudly lugged around the $1,200 in new tools I bought him. He had to have his own in order to get a job, but he still was not hired. Folks don't want to hire odd men with a prison record.

———————◆◆◆———————

When Rob had been home a few months, Patrick asked to talk with me.

He expressed his anguish about all of Rob's problems. He said he thought he was "schizophrenic or something." He was now observing Rob from the mature perspective of an independent, young adult.

Rob was manifesting the same symptoms as he had throughout his life, but they were more severe. His prison-time hopes were not materializing, and he was being rejected as an adult. He was confused by the fast-paced world of the city: computers, banks, tight schedules; those societal demands the rest of us adapt to yet from which we also need occasional respites. Look at the parking lots of bars at 5:30 p.m.

The more he matured, the more obvious his inappropriate acts became each time he regressed. The more obvious were his gains and intelligence, the more striking were his regressions and the bizarre attitudes he often expressed. He seemed to share little in common with others in terms of world views, cultural expectations, or social skills, and had no sense of self-efficacy.

A painful truth began to emerge: in some ways, he felt safest and best when he was incarcerated in some place that provided structure and boundaries he could not cross. That truth did not come to his consciousness, just mine. For all his misery and fear while incarcerated and despite all his longings to be free, he was more normal behind bars, he was less frantic once he adapted.

Trusting also in Patrick's maturity, Rob hoped his brother could understand his inner turmoil. As always, his lack of vocal inflection or personal disclosure of his emotions belied the intensity of his inner disturbance. I took him to a psychologist for testing and treatment and for neuropsychological testing.

Their findings indeed indicated significant neurological impairments as well as deep psychological disturbances. Rob liked and trusted the psychologist but again left town before any real work in therapy had begun. From later prison cells, when he would write some rarely expressed inner conflict, he would ask me to also tell his doctor about those things.

Added to the realization of Rob's very disturbed thinking were his eccentric behaviors that Pat could no longer shrug off as "that's just Rob." He had again tried to become Rob's friend and mentor, but Rob was more resistive than ever to exposing himself to social failure. He found normal life too boring. In truth, he didn't understand normal life. He seemed to perceive a vast chasm between himself and his family. He would particularly resist as mentor, a younger brother whom he felt he ought to be guiding instead.

Patrick's initial determination to help Rob achieve a normal life became weakened in repeated defeat. He had included him on outings with friends, where Rob invariably embarrassed him, or at least elicited the even more uncomfortable emotion of pity. Rob needed to be drunk to feel equal and comfortable, which made everyone else uncomfortable.

Patrick and I both understood that Rob's acute discomfort was greatest where he was expected to act normal around young people whom he had perceived as laughing at him all his life, never laughing with him. They were people who had grown up in the alien world of campuses, not the familiar prison yards.

Yet we could not provide the individual and almost constant attention Rob seemed to need in order to keep him from withdrawing, using drugs, or becoming intolerably depressed. I couldn't be sure how he had finally coped in prison having to be around large numbers of strange men. He had written often of the terror and despair that were his constant and often only companions there. However, the expectations of him from other inmates seemed now to be less threatening than were those of males his age who were going forward with their lives: careers, relationships, hope, and a future.

A positive result of Patrick's and my long talk, and other similar ones that followed, was a processing of his feelings about growing up as Rob's brother. He admitted that he had always been aware that Rob got more attention than he. However, he went on to say that he had now come to see that Rob had always required more attention and that it was "not that Rob was more loved, just more weird, Mom!"

No one can live with a disturbed person, particularly a loved one, and not be affected in ways both good and bad. The siblings of a disturbed child also pay a price. Whether that price is too costly, I cannot say, for I do firmly believe that we are also finally enriched when our loved ones cause us to overcome our own personality obstacles and stretch and grow.

Patrick's relative normalcy, so strikingly in contrast to his brother's aberrance, made no unusual demands on me. With him, I did not have to struggle to carve new trails in uncharted territory. The strained exception was always that of balancing Patrick's needs with those more extreme of Rob's. The lost sheep is the one you go in search to find. The wounded one gets the extra morsel if only in hope to promote healing.

It was otherwise comforting to me to have had that talk with Patrick, and equally as comforting to now have him as an ally. I had always felt very alone in coping with Rob, indeed often alone in even finding acknowledgement that he had problems beyond bad conduct.

Patrick loved his brother and accepted the fact of his difficulties with no condemnation or rejection. Together, we pondered how to make Rob be all right. But Patrick had his own rightful life to live and his own challenges to meet. We hoped that helping impose on Rob an external structure of work, school, Alcoholics Anonymous, and hobbies would be fulfilling.

We could hope for an ultimate normalcy because there were times when Rob seemed not only completely normal, but exceptionally bright and together. One of those times was an occasion when a friend of mine spent three and a half hours in deep conversation with Rob about advanced technological concepts. My friend was an electrical engineer managing an advanced research department. He had a gentle, respectful, accepting attitude with Rob and treated him as an equal.

After many months, Rob had still not regarded himself as anyone in whom my friend would really be interested. He would offer polite, casual greetings, minimal conversation, and then withdraw to his room. On this particular evening, I would be leaving the two of them alone while I went to an evening class. From the kitchen, where I was making sandwiches and beverages as an enticement for my friend to stay awhile with Rob, I could hear the remarkable conversation between them.

They were discussing, as equals, such topics as advanced applications of physics, technical aspects of space travel, and potential for improvements in Radar and Doppler systems. Rob had read about these things in prison and had, it seemed, grasped the essential concepts.

Further, he was apparently able to apply them creatively in this conversation to possibilities of new products. I stayed out of view as long as possible, enjoying and very impressed by this aspect of Rob I had never known. In the presence of a respected man, who respected his mind, he was holding his own.

The next day, I phoned to thank my friend for having entertained Rob so well the night before. He insisted that it was he who had enjoyed himself at least as much as Rob and told me how long he had stayed after I left. He assured me that the conversation they had was identical to the sorts he had with his educated engineers. "He'd make a helluva good engineer!"

Rob didn't think so. He would read about and retain these topics only when the confinement of prison left him no other option. Formalized schooling to achieve any one of them as a discipline was incomprehensible to him; schools were places where he'd been made to feel most inadequate and rejected. Besides, being such a "somebody" as an engineer was outside his fatalistic view of himself.

I appealed to several friends who employed manual labor and through them Rob obtained work, for a time. I was afraid that he was too intelligent, and too easily bored, to feel gratified by such menial work, but instead he expressed satisfaction about doing a good job and earning money. He occasionally picked up odd jobs on car repairs of Patrick's friends until that became too awkward.

In one last effort, he went to work at an assembly-line job with a boss who was sympathetic to his circumstances. The man was also a friend of mine and volunteered to give Rob the time and space he needed to adapt. He was trying hard to live a normal life, but, of course, his brother and I were his only friends. We were both in school and studying nights so had minimal time to give Rob companionship.

On his first payday, Rob and Patrick were to go to a movie. I was in a doctoral program, studying for an exam. Patrick lived in an apartment he shared with friends; they were going to meet at a cafe. I could not explain the feeling of anxiety that surrounded me all evening.

I was imagining the worst and could not quiet my intense anxiety. I found myself up out of my chair again and again, literally pacing the floor and wringing my hands.

Rob was not yet late; there were no grounds for the uncharacteristic anxiety that grew so strong I finally gave up on studying and went to bed at 11:00 p.m., lying there in agitated sleeplessness. At midnight, I heard a Life Flight helicopter flying overhead toward the medical center near my home. I sat upright in bed and said aloud to the empty room, "That's Robbie!"

Again I scolded myself into rational thought. The Life Flight helicopters flew over my house several nights a week; they were stationed at the medical center. I made myself lie back down and began a spontaneous prayer for Rob's safety. I repeated the prayer over and over like a wind-up toy that has no volition of its own.

At two-thirty in the morning, the voice over the phone asked, "Are you the mother of Robert Bowers?" It was the chaplain from a local hospital telling me that Rob had been brought in by Life Flight; and following an interminable pause, "He's going to live."

I was always startled by the kinds of opening remarks strangers used to report to me some serious circumstance in which Rob was involved. Whatever they were, the words never seemed to be appropriate, although I usually felt the callers had carefully chosen them to be least alarming as possible.

"He's going to live," ranked down there only one degree of fright above "He's dead," particularly when pronounced after a maddeningly long pause. I instantly interpreted those words to mean, "He's maimed, brain-dead, will be a vegetable for the rest of his life, but he is going to live."

"Yes, yes, I knew the way to the hospital, yes, I had gasoline, no, I did not need anyone to drive me, and yes I would be all right, thank you very, very much!" I was halfway to the medical center before realizing that the man had given the name of another hospital, twenty miles away.

The helicopter I had heard two and a half hours earlier was indeed the one returning empty to the center after having flown Rob to the hospital closest to the scene of his one car accident. He had wrecked his own car by running it into the side of a mountain.

The force was so great that his chest had broken off the steering wheel and his forehead had slammed through the barrier of the wheel into and shattered the windshield. The engine compartment of the car had been ripped from the chassis. A passerby called an ambulance. The Emergency Medical Team called for Life Flight when Rob's heart stopped en route to the hospital.

He walked out of the hospital with me the next day, very, very sore, but with only a broken arm, a sutured gash across his jaw and a purple goose egg on his forehead. The fracture was severe and would, we were told, probably take nine months to heal. Rob was in a cast from armpit to fingertips.

One month later, we went back to have the cast changed. X-rays were taken and revealed no indication that a break had ever occurred. His doctor could not believe his eyes. The arm was again X-rayed, and the original ones retrieved. The fracture was grossly apparent on those X-rays taken the night of the accident. I wondered how his guardian angels had fared.

A contrite Rob, unable to work, kept a low profile for the four weeks his arm was in a cast. He had lost his job, of course, unable to do assembling with one hand. He apologized for the loss of his car but denied he had been drunk or suicidal. "I *did* hit the side of the mountain, deliberately."

He explained that he had been holding a kitten in one arm, driving the mountain road with the other. He realized he took a curve too fast and made a choice to hit the side rather than roll down. "I knew I could protect the kitten if I hit the mountain but not if I went over the edge." He grieved more for having left the uninjured cat stranded at the scene than losing his car. The wrecked car had been a second one he had purchased for very little money a few weeks earlier. He had restored it to running condition. It was totaled now, but he still had the truck I had bought him for Christmas that year.

CHAPTER 18

"Thank you for sticking with me all these years. I am so lucky to have you for my mother. I love you very, very, very much. I see a lot of people here whose family has abandoned them. It's bad." Rob, 2010.

I left Rob at home while I flew back to Texas for a week of combined consultation work and visits with friends. Patrick would check on him and provide some companionship.

The night before I was to return home after a rare week free of worry, a San Diego friend phoned me in Texas. He called to alert me that Rob had been arrested for drunk driving.

I lay sleepless in Texas, trying most of the night to force my mind to create some plan or some effective way to confront him. I could think of nothing more to say to him that had not already been said a thousand times. I had run completely out of wisdom that might intervene in his destructive pattern; there seemed to be no more programs that had not already been tried.

In despair, I prayed: "God, there is nothing at all between Rob and me except a plane flight tomorrow. Please, please give me a seatmate who will give me some wisdom, some new approach with Rob, please!" I repeated that again and again throughout the rest of the sleepless night.

On the ride to the airport, I let my friend chatter, not even listening to her. I felt an urgency to stay in communication with the only power I knew who could provide help. I continued to repeat silently all the way, "Please, God, give me a seatmate on the plane who will give me words of wisdom!"

I boarded early, having asked for a rear seat, and examined face after face of everyone coming down the aisle of the plane. *Are you the one? You? This man looks wise.* He passed my row.

My seatmate was an un-bathed, greasy-haired woman. She wore a cheap, wrinkled, and stained cotton dress that looked several sizes too small and had a button missing. She would not stop talking.

I turned my face away from her to both hide my tears and to be deliberately rude so that she would stop talking and let me wallow in self-pity. Staring out my window, I murmured, "God, that's not fair!" He had failed me in what might have been my most desperate prayer ever.

The woman talked on and on, without pause. I tried every near-polite way I knew to have her stop, but she would not. Finally, I tuned her in instead of out, ashamed of my rudeness, though she had not seemed to notice.

Her story became compelling. She was on her way to San Diego to see her oldest son graduate from Marine boot camp. She was thrilled to be doing that; it was the first time she had ever flown in her life. Her son had bought her ticket. "I am so proud of him. He is such a wonderful son, the best kid in the world, and I sure don't deserve such a good kid!"

"Why are you crying?" I asked her, carefully avoiding emphasis on the word *you*.

She sobbed harder and her story came out brokenly at first. Her son would be returning home with her on leave before taking his new military assignment. He had written her and his brothers and sisters almost every day about how much he missed them, all the fun things they would do while he was home, and all the presents he had gotten them. He had always been so good with them and they adored him.

I envied her. She continued, telling me he would finally, this day, have to be told that his brothers and sisters, all four minors, had been taken away from her by the state. Her boyfriend had molested her nine-year-old daughter in her absence. She had trusted him to care for the children while she worked two jobs and went to college at night.

When she graduated, she would be a social worker. It was the second most wonderful thing she had ever done; the first was producing her children. It was very hard, but she had been managing, until this. The state held her responsible and although the boyfriend was in jail, her children were gone.

She was heartbroken. *How*, she wanted to know, was she going to find the words to tell her young Marine that she was such a bad mother to the kids he so loved, that they had been taken away. "How can I *tell* him?"

We both cried. I cried for her pain and for my own. I cried because I now felt admiration and affection for this determined, humble woman; I cried for her children and for Rob. I spoke to her softly, offering ideas for what she might say to her son. I suggested that the state had simply sympathized with the hardship she was under in trying to better herself and care for her kids. The authorities, I said, had reached out to help her in the best possible way under present conditions and laws.

Her children would be provided for in nice, safe homes until she was on her feet and able to get them back. "See," I said, "the state is not telling you that you are a *bad* mother; it is telling you that you are a *good* one, just way, way overburdened. It is recognizing its own responsibility toward you and your family!"

When I finished speaking, she smiled broadly at me through her tears. "Oh, thank you, thank you, thank you! I never looked at it like that!" We sat in silence for a while as the plane entered the approach pattern. I thought she was preparing her talk with her son. I was pondering the fact that I was no longer so worried about mine.

As we were landing, the woman tugged at my arm, "I want to say something that may seem silly to you," she said. "Last night, I lay in bed all night long praying for help to find the right way to tell my son about his brother and sisters. 'Jesus,' I prayed, 'there's nothing between me and my son except a plane trip, please put an angel on that plane who can tell me what to say!' And He did!"

I want to say, reverently, humbly, and in awe that being seen as the answer to someone's prayers diminishes to a very manageable size all other problems! I learned anew that day that God looks at the purity of our hearts, not the stains on our bodies or clothing or lives. That woman was another gift to me.

Rob continued to have repeated near-death incidents in which I would come increasingly to know that God was not yet finished with him. It was on that faith that I began the most difficult plan of all with him, which was a "tough love" approach: he could not live with me without being in a program, remaining sober, and preparing himself for some kind of work. It was very tough to deny my son a place to sleep in a rainstorm when he came to my door soaked and drunk. If he got no sleep on that particular night, neither did I. It was tough to commit to such a plan when it had never worked his entire life.

One of his near-death experiences followed later, after his return to prison in Texas from some forgotten violation. Again, he was released in that state, still on probation.

I wanted Rob's probation transferred to California, so he could be under my care. He was always being released from jail penniless and back on the streets, usually not even to a halfway house. He had more than demonstrated his inability to handle that freedom and responsibility.

Once again, from his letters and our talks on the phone, I observed significant changes in him. I was not sure how these would translate into "normal living." Still, he gained insight and wisdom in leaps and bounds; he expressed concern about my welfare and talked about plans of a future. Hope does burn eternal in a mother's heart!

He obtained permission to come out to visit me where California agreed to accept his probation, as a courtesy. As the probation officer noted, it made far more sense to have him in California where he had family and shelter, than in Texas where he had neither.

Texas demanded, however, that Rob appear in person to sign the release papers and would not be dissuaded from this by either his California probation officer or myself. I put him on a bus this time, with $200 to live on and to return after he had gone before the Texas Probation Board.

The night he arrived in Texas, he was attacked and robbed by several unknown assailants. He was stabbed with a knife in five different places all over his body, dragged into a darkened place and left, apparently for dead. They had taken all his money, watch, and other belongings. Rob crawled to the side of a road and lay there in a pool of blood until a truck driver saw him in his headlights and called an ambulance.

The wounds were deep gashes, not merely punctures. The scars are from three to five inches long. Not one of them struck a vital organ, though each just missed one.

For months afterward, I would wake from horrible dreams, or have difficulty falling asleep, because I would see images of Rob lying there trampled and helpless, watching the knife blade and waiting for the critical stab that would take his life. One scene repeated itself and seemed as vividly clear to me as if I had been there. I could see the light from a distant street lamp reflecting off the knife blade as it was thrust downward into his body again and again, until his blood darkened the metal and the light went out.

Not physically able to show up for the probation transfer hearing, his request was denied and he was eventually sent to a halfway house to finish recovering from his wounds. From there, he obtained work for a moving company some twenty miles away. Without money, he had to charge against his paycheck the money for the uniforms he was required to wear. To get to work at seven-thirty, required that he get up at four o'clock, before anyone else, including the kitchen staff, and take several buses to work.

Without money, he ate no breakfast or lunch. He returned at the end of each day hoping to have arrived before the kitchen was locked for the night. Sometimes he was late. On his first payday, with little left over after uniform deductions, he bought a case of beer for his fellow residents, who had previously shared with him their contraband. He got caught and was kicked out for the violation.

Hoping to still keep his job, he broke into an abandoned shack near the property where the halfway house stood and lived there in isolation, without water or electricity, for many days, walking every morning past the halfway house to the bus stop. He salvaged aluminum siding, dragging the sheets several miles, to be sold for money to live on until his next paycheck.

On a cold, winter night, he built a fire in the fireplace to keep warm and discovered too late that it was only a facade. Having no water to put out the fire, he used his coat to try and smother it. He fled the burning shack and fled the city, certain that he would somehow be arrested for causing the fire. It was the second burning shack he had fled in Texas, the first one having been deliberately set fire to in order to also burn up "satanic demons."

Again, Rob obtained work as a light mechanic for a service station in a Texas coastal town. He slept in his car, bathed in the gulf, and shaved in the service station restroom. He had no friends. He spent his money on alcohol and canned foods. His kind female boss got my name and phone number and called expressing her worries about him.

"He's a sweet kid and a very hard worker, but I worry about him all the time. He's very lonely and, ma'am, he has a drinking problem, I'm sure, because I see his car full of beer cans."

I brought him home. Patrick volunteered to take him in, but Rob was slovenly and depressed. Finally, he left, taking from his brother the few remaining tools he had owned that he had earlier traded to Pat for a radio.

Months passed without word from Rob. He appeared at my door on another rainy day and stayed to sleep and sober up. I told him I'd read *Tough Love* and so he could not stay because he was making no apparent effort to salvage his life. In grim, terrible silence, I drove him two days later to a freeway on-ramp, hating this tough love thing, hating feeling like a failure as a mother, hating that my son lived such a lonely, hopeless life. Months went by without word from him and I came to understand what all is involved in the tough part of tough love.

CHAPTER 19

"I have felt like I had passed the point of no return into the Twilight Zone. *It reminded me of a very bad acid trip. I will be in the south wing soon and it will be better there."*

Patrick was getting married. We didn't know where his brother was; we had tried to get word to him every way possible. Until the very last moment, Patrick believed his brother would show up in time. "It's just Rob's way, Mom, he shows up at the last minute!" He didn't.

He had been arrested in South Carolina and would be sentenced to ten years in prison as a repeat offender. He would ultimately serve four and be paroled to me.

When he finally called to tell me about this news, I began sobbing into the phone. He tried to reassure me; I tried to stop crying so I would not add to his misery. In a second phone call, I asked him why he had gone so long without contacting me. "Because I didn't think you loved me anymore, since you made me leave your house, so I decided I wouldn't love you either."

Ouch. "Okay, then what made you finally call?"

"I thought you needed to know I was in prison so you wouldn't worry for ten years."

"Well, I appreciate that, but if you don't think I love you, what made you call this time?"

"When I heard you crying on the phone last week, I knew you loved me." He still did not know in any enduring way that he was always loved. Love had to be forged anew with him each day. It was defined in terms that I would never quite know.

Rob had spent fifty-seven days in a holding cell in South Carolina, expecting every one of those days to hear his sentence. The suspense every morning and letdown at the end of each day must have caused a tension I can only imagine. There were no distractions, television, music, or visitors. There were only his tangled thoughts and practiced endurance of failure, more familiar than hope. His sentence to prison was initially almost a relief; at least the stress from waiting was ended. He knew his fate.

The length of the sentence was shocking to both of us. It related less to the low value of the used car he had taken, again intoxicated on drugs and alcohol, than from the fact that he was a repeat offender. The car had broken down less than a mile from the lot and a highway patrolman had stopped to render aid. It was almost laughable.

His letters to me were heartbreaking because I knew him beyond his identity as felon. I knew he feared the expectations of just people more than he feared the police. There was always that first letter, written sometime after he had waked one morning to find that the protectiveness of denial was gone. He woke to the full and terrifying reality that stretched interminably before him. He was locked up with the kind of men who most intimidated him with no way to escape from them or from his own demons.

There is an image in my mind of Rob's first prison experiences that matches those of most of his life. It is the picture of the child he was, trudging into the house, friendless, tormented, saying "God made a mistake with me."

But in the first years as a younger adult, the stark terror in prison was even more pronounced, with no relief, no home, no privacy, no brother to laugh with, father to take him camping, or mother to offer comfort.

At any age in which he entered jail or prison, he retained his child-like innocence in many ways. He was also always trapped between loneliness and fear. From his letters, I knew that he was scared all the time. He wondered how he would be different "if being scared goes away."

Judges, as perhaps they must, disregarded the fact that Rob had been under psychiatric care throughout his life since childhood or that he had never done any personal harm to another human being. Rob's life reflected a series of wrong choices, the most condemning ones always those of becoming intoxicated. In that condition, he always forfeited all rational judgment. Yet, sober, his most rational judgments were self-punitive.

His felonies were always the same, stealing cars while intoxicated. He never committed a felony when sober. He liked the self he was when drunk, but that self always betrayed him. Always, the mornings came when he sobered up in jail and faced his mocking demons.

It has always mattered to me that judges ignore that he is slender, handsome, very shy, and very inhibited. The little boy car could pick up hitchhikers because a ride was some *thing* to offer another in exchange for human contact. Conversation was not necessary in such a case; the ride itself was sufficient to a fellow traveler. In prison, he only had a self that few had ever picked for their team. But he best shared that self with me during those times when he could no longer act out his demons but could, instead write them out in long letters.

Alone in his cell, Rob wept, he said, to learn that his cat had died. "Please get another; it must be shown that she was important enough in our lives that we want her honored."

There was a female guard who laughed and joked with the others. He longed so much for her to even smile at him. She did not.

He ached for human warmth, but he was terrified that the threats of rape and possession would become reality. He asked his cellmate to help him kill himself if that should happen. His cellmate reported him as suicidal, so Rob spent three days in solitary confinement "until I figured out that I could just say I'd been kidding." Never once was consideration given for treating his depression. Never once did it occur to him to ask.

"Mom, there must be something wrong with me. Nobody likes me, nobody talks to me, and I have no friends here. I am so very depressed."

He was being set up. Soon, he would be glad for any sort of acceptance, but not yet. He drank strong coffee all day long so that he could remain awake at night, to fend off the predators who stalked him. The guard knew this. She joked with them; she looked through him. He lost weight and became haggard.

I was his lifeline to sanity. He wrote lengthy, sensitive, insightful letters. He had begun to express himself in letters in ways that he could never do orally. His spelling was atrocious, everything written phonetically (fonetikly), but his content was almost poetic. They made me cry, and I discovered that it was worse to be unable to offer him comfort than it was to be always alert to his need for it.

Through his letters, I got to know my son as he was getting to know himself. I liked him. Through my letters to him, he listened as he had never done in person. As I did from his early childhood on, I tried to reinforce his strengths, offer comfort, and give him a hope in himself. But I could little advise him on how to cope with others in prison. That world was totally unknown to me. The rules of conduct there bear only minimal resemblance to those in the free world. He had never mastered the latter; how could he discern those of prison?

He eventually adapted to prison life each time and, in fact, was a model prisoner. Still, it was apparent that all Rob's problems were initially intensified in confinement. The shock, disappointment, pain, shame, and change all combined to cover him in deep grief for a time, as they would for anyone during the first months after entering prison. Most particularly intensified was his fear of people, and how to cope with them. He again found solace in things. Particularly in his relatively minor compulsive need to modify and fix every new radio, television, fan, or headset I sent him over the years. The jails and prisons changed, the problems did not, at least not at first. But he began to examine himself more objectively.

Unable to run, walk, or crawl away from all his fears, he began to confront them. He opened the hood of his own mind and began the process of exploring his own "engine." Typically, he began with his worst instead of his best. But we both learned that he had good tools if few new parts to begin this engine overhaul.

His letters revealed him to be more insightful and more perceptive than I had ever before known him to be. For all the sorrow they often contained, they were marvelous creations to me. However, I learned that he kept most of his worst experiences from me. It was in later face-to-face talks that I learned more about his personal trials behind bars.

He also typically made light mention of major physical assaults on him and then filled a letter with whatever positives he could find to write about. One entire and very amusing letter was devoted to the spectrum of sounds made by the flushing toilet in the next cell.

The following paragraphs are excerpts from Rob's many letters written to me during the years of his twenties from several different jails or prisons. I quote him verbatim, although I have corrected most of his spelling and added some punctuation for clarification. The dominant theme of them is the abject loneliness he felt and the subsequent loss, because of callousness of certain guards, of those things that made prison life tolerable. I've selected only a very few, as much to reveal prison life as to illustrate his thinking.

"I guess people don't like me because of the damage I did to my brain with drugs and all. They are really going against me; tonight they say they are going to give me a blanket party. I'm going to try to talk to a jailer that I think I can trust. I am really skinny now and about as shy as I was when I got out of (residential school)."

In a later letter: "I drew a picture of a car engine and frame, modified to roll on a train track, pulling a line of boxcars up a hill, which represents how I feel."

Some months later, he wrote: "The way I feel now (rejected and isolated) is exactly how I felt during my years in school, except that I have no friends. Also, I've realized that it wasn't the schoolwork I hated so much as it was the other schoolmates I had to deal with while at school. That's probably also what caused my bad grades."

Always, when sober, he confronted the fact that regardless of what his other problems were, it was his loss of self control from intoxication that had the most serious consequences for him: "I had just about learned never to steal cars anymore, and then alcohol comes along and teaches me to steal all over again."

The following made me want to cry because I was so aware of how isolated and lonely he already felt before this impulsive act, and therefore, how painful this had been, "embarrassing" for him, is always an understatement:

"An embarrassing thing happened to me the other day. I was just pacing around the day room, bored, and thinking of how to further improve the performance of my radio. I spotted a wire sticking out of the wall for no apparent reason, so I pulled it down to have a look...there was a pop and a flash and the television went off. I turned around to see thirty angry inmates glaring at me! Blowing the TV in prison is one way to get unpopular real quick! Within three hours, I had received all kinds of threats, so I went to my cell to sleep on it. A friend of mine told the cops I was in extreme danger, so they came and woke me up and had me stand in the hallway for a long time until a new TV could be obtained. The main reason they were so mad is because an important football game was coming on and everyone had bets on it."

In those letters where Rob most needed to communicate intense feelings, he regressed to his identification with cars and prefaced each with a line such as the following, written when he had been in prison six months: "I am going to write this letter about what my mind is going through, imagining my brain as a car engine pulling a lot of weight."

He continued in a very long letter to describe his personal agony: "I was at top speed again but this time with an uphill load, not the wide open high RPM speed my engine enjoyed, but the bogged down struggle to keep moving up the hill (slowing causes depression to increase, stopping would cause a nervous breakdown)....the weight is heavier and heavier now, and the only relief is when the upgrade levels out. Occasionally, it even becomes flat, but never long enough for a good rest, and never does it ever turn into a down grade...this constant abuse is weakening my engine. The temperature gauge is hotter than normal and the oil pressure is always below normal because it's hot too. Normally, I always have an oil cooler when it's needed, that's when I would get stoned."

There had been moments when I'd wondered if my letters mattered to him. I didn't say so, but I discovered otherwise when he wrote this: "I have been up all night re-reading all your old letters." On another occasion, he wrote that he was bummed out because my letters were lost during a transfer to another dorm following a hospital stay (one of several for being attacked). He began saving all his letters again. I still have them. I have a larger stack of every letter he's ever written me, even from residential school at age ten.

"I have only my memories for entertainment." I sadly wondered what of his remembered life was sufficiently entertaining to give him any comfort.

Rob did not lose his sense of humor. It was most apparent when he was in some safe place like the hospital, or solitary confinement, where he was frequently sent for his protection. He noted in one letter that the man in the bed next to him was in there for heart disease, and then added, "I must be in here for spelling disease." One of my favorite of Rob's quotes and humor: "Due to a shortage in paper, this letter will contain no paragraphs."

When Patrick was a child, he called ants "amps." The entire family continued to call them that for years. In the following excerpt, Rob recalls that: "A good radio station out of San Jose is being amped over Soledad. Meanwhile, an amp is walking around my cell. It is limping due to the distance it had to come to get here."

It had been my assumption that prison provided for all Rob's needs. He never asked and it didn't occur to me that he might need supplies, snacks, or even money. I'd seen too much TV, I guess, where prison was often portrayed as little different from the free world except for the surrounding fences. A comment in one of his letters prompted me to inquire about whether or not he could receive packages and if he needed things. I was shocked to learn how desperately inmates need ordinary things from the free world. This next comment prompted my inquiry. Quotes following reflect his appreciation with things his father and I began to send:

"Today I shaved with a razor blade only, no holder. Talk about a blood bath! I turned the sink completely red, but I got it done. With extreme difficulty, I got a close shave." I included safety razors of the kind he was allowed to have in my very first package, sent the same day his letter arrived.

"I just brushed my teeth for the first time in two and a half months. Thank you! It was like Christmas today, two letters from you, toothbrush, shampoo, all the other stuff, and the eighty dollars. I really appreciate them."

I contacted the prison to learn what was allowed and what most inmates most enjoyed:

"Mom, I couldn't have done any better myself choosing an excellent tape collection. I can't say how much I appreciate the trouble you went through to get it. It is the *best* tape collection on the prison yard. In here, owning a tape player makes you instantly popular. That's disgusting, but worth it. On the streets I would never be friends with a person that liked me only for my possessions. But here nobody really has a very big choice of who they hang out with. Anyway, I'm a lot happier now that I can escape into music."

"Dad sent me some paints and brushes, so I'll get to send you some real pictures." It would never have occurred to me to send those, I was so glad his dad had thought of them, Rob was quite artistic and these materials would allow him to be creative. I believe that creating something is essential to peace of mind.

Later, I sent him a radio in his Christmas box; music was also essential to his spirit: "Our electricity to the cells has been off on my row for a ridiculously disgusting entire week. When it finally came back on, it blew out my radio. It somehow managed to destroy every last circuit in it, including the clock and my FM booster. This was a catastrophic blow to my happiness. It triggered the worst and longest depression since getting busted. I didn't come off my bunk for a week, except for an occasional meal. I lost a lot of weight."

On another occasion: "They took away all my pictures and things, while I was in solitary, it bummed me out."

This statement is one of the most common ones made during his incarcerations: "The cops lost all of my belongings again; according to the law here, they have to pay for them, but I know they will get out of it. They also lost the food package request I submitted, so they are sending the package you sent, back to you, and charging the postage for it against my books. The only thing I can do about it is to draw a picture of a "flip off" and send it to the package room officer."

He always searched for something to write about. Food was seldom a favorite topic, but I found this comment amusing: "Today I ate sauerkraut for the first time in my life…sickening."

Rob took classes and obtained his GED. He enjoyed learning in ways he never had before. He retained much of what he read and developed broad interests in many different subjects.

"In my math class, I am teaching myself everything I didn't learn in school. (I need to have a spelling class). My brain is a lot clearer than it used to be. I am reading a very good book about Israel."

He struggled constantly with the challenge of relating to others and still spent most of his time alone. Not knowing how to deepen friendships, he chose the following: "I am trying to avoid my few friends, so that I will be used to it and prepared for when they don't like me anymore. I really can't pinpoint it (why people don't like me), but there is some measure of pleasure from the situation. Maybe it's because I don't have to worry about altering my personality to get people to respect me since they don't anyhow."

"I am in the hospital with a lacerated lower lip, fractured jaw, and a re-fractured nose." There are other injuries he goes on to describe. He had been repeatedly kicked in the face by several inmates; he had tried to crawl under the bunk but they had pulled him out.

The injuries, he notes, can heal, but he will have to go back to face more. Worse, he cannot replace his personal things that he knows will be missing when he gets out of the hospital. While he was in the last time, after being assaulted, all his belongings had been stolen.

He learns to dread that period of agony when he is first returned to his cell even more than he dreads the inevitable next confrontation. He will not know who will need to be avoided, so he avoids them all. He will not know what guards he can trust, so he will trust none. He can never understand just what it is that he says wrong to people, so he says as little as possible.

Saying little further sets him apart. Having lost all his belongings, he will have no solace in music, family pictures, rereading old letters, or anything else that reminds him that out there is someone who really does care.

On another occasion: "You're not going to believe this, but I got beat up again. But this time they took me to a hospital all the way into the city. It was a 'trip' to be in the free world for the first time in ten months. The nurse was even nice to me and she was pretty. I felt like a chained leopard as these people worked on me: A real, live inmate from the notoriously horrible prison just south of them. It must have been a trip for them also. I got written up for being in a 'physical altercation' (I think that means fight)."

There was seldom anything I could write to him of good news that would directly impact Rob, but this reflects one of those few times, written from South Carolina in about 2004: "I received your two latest letters explaining that my Texas hold has been dismissed. That is powerful good news! For the first time in a year, I have allowed myself to think about what it might be like to be free again. I could not have taken another four years; I would have had a major breakdown. Nobody and I mean nobody I've seen in here is smaller than me."

Depression was Rob's constant companion. I am sure that is true for many inmates; it is just that they seldom mention or perhaps even know to identify it. It isn't exactly a tough guy thing to say on the yard that you're depressed. I usually knew when Rob was in very deep depression because I would not hear from him for a few weeks. As I've said, he tried to only write up beat things, but the following excerpts from letters written over many months develops a picture of prison life for him and his subsequent struggles to relate and to cope with predatory type behaviors in others and the resulting depression.

"This place sounds just like a psych ward: black inmates yelling and cursing, whites screaming at the top of their lungs. Gay inmates yelling back and forth to their lovers, talking just like women; and inmates arguing with the guards. Some unknown inmate has been uttering "gaa gaa" continuously (excuse me, I'm having pencil trouble, this one is just one inch long, could you send me some three inch long pencils?) twenty-four hours a day for the last three days. I think his mind has blown a rod through his skull. And to add to it all, are the sounds of inmate TVs and radios blaring everywhere. Iron gates and cell doors slamming, keys jingling, toilets flushing, phones ringing unanswered, alarms going off, etc. Etc. Etc."

"They took away the paints and brushes and stuff that dad sent, because they said I hadn't filed a request to have them sent. I would have, but I didn't know he was going to send them. That was a massive blow."

"I know I have had worse days than yesterday, but I sure can't remember when."

Rob was opening up more and more to me about all his feelings, and suicidal thoughts. He did so in no way seeking pity, but in efforts to both understand himself and to feel understood by someone that cared. He remained in constant fear of being overpowered and raped and had had several other assaults that had required hospitalization. I had been encouraging him to seek counseling or psychiatric care. Doing so, it turns out, is in no way as easy as it sometimes appears to us in the free world. Besides, he feared that it would just set him further apart.

Finally, I got through to the prison psychologist who agreed to see Rob. That is the reference below to "seeing a psychiatrist." However, the psychologist saw Rob one very brief time and then had him moved to a new cell. That was that.

"Well, enough (enoph) sniveling, I just think that because you are my mother and I love you dearly, more than anything in the world, that I should let you know how I feel. You are the only person I can talk to. I have requested to see a psychiatrist and then I will have someone to talk to."

His greatest fears, were of domineering inmates who deliberately intimidated him and I'm sure others like him: "I, myself, am a little more vulnerable to such people than most because of these factors that life has presented me with: I'm shy, have difficulty maintaining in or around a group, I'm uncoordinated physically, therefore a poor fighter, coupled with the fact that I was informed today that due to my light weight, I was only going to get a minimum work day. This shocked me back into the realization that I was still suffering from that age-old, ever-oppressing and very inconvenient (to my pride) 'Skinny B*****d Syndrome.'"

"I am happier as I write you now, because it is nighttime, my depression is worse in the afternoons and after dinner until lock down."

"I'm sitting here admiring my writing with my new pencil. I never knew I could write so well!"

"One thing is for certain, depression makes me write long letters, writing is the one thing that is enjoyable when I'm depressed." From Rob's letters to me and from our later conversations together when he was home again, I learn about the depravity of the prison culture.

One of the most interesting of all Rob's mailings happened during his most recent incarceration. Two days before my birthday in 2011, the postman rang my bell. He handed me a large 12" x 18" inch envelope, of sorts. It had angular pieces of clear tape all over both sides. It was addressed to me at my home which, to Rob's fascination, is half a mile from Route 66, (called "The Mother Road). It was from Rob. Inside were two things: the first, my birthday present from him, an incredible picture drawn with colored pencils on art paper of a mining scene at the turn of the century. The second was a form letter from the post office apologizing for any damage to the contents and advising me what I could do if there was.

I was puzzled; despite a completely mangled envelope, the picture Rob had drawn was miraculously undamaged. After I'd examined and appreciated every detail of it, I next examined the strange, large envelope. It more resembled a crossword puzzle that had been taped together. There were jagged bits of old priority mail envelopes and other pieces of thinner paper in differing shades of white. All the pieces had torn edges and all were loosely overlapped and puckered wherever there was no tape. Inmates are not allowed to have scissors or scotch tape.

A few days later, this explanation arrived in another letter from Rob: "Mom, I tried and tried to get help from the mail room but finally had to do it myself. I know it's a little early, but Happy Birthday! As you can see, I manufactured an envelope out of pieces of old ones that I stuck together with soap. It feels interesting to be making a vehicle to travel back down the Mother Road to my mother. I am confident it will make it." Residue of the soap was barely discernable, and most had flaked off. It was the Postal Service that rescued my priceless piece of art. They, with the help of a loving God who took tender care to deliver a son's labor of love to his mother.

CHAPTER 20

"I have to drink a lot of coffee to deal with these idiots I live with. My mind is passing through territory I've never been through. Sometimes it seems like I died and have gone to hell. My mind may explode if I have to take this much longer. A lot of hardcore people are actually falling in love with me. Last night, someone wrote: 'I love you' on my bed sheet. I guess I shouldn't worry about it, but it's getting to be a constant nightmare." Rob at age 20 in mainstream prison population.

During about a two month period, Rob's letters from prison sounded almost paranoid. I was afraid he was decompensating mentally. I didn't grasp the meanings of his references in each one to being intimidated and pursued "by people who are bigger than me." I naively thought that he would be protected from harm by guards. Nor did I realize that cell doors were open during certain times, so I wrongly thought he'd also be protected by his cell bars. He was writing of his fears increasingly often and then no letters came for several weeks. I worried. As it turned out, Rob finally was raped. It spawned a period of his deepest depression and shame. He did not tell me outright in letters, and he did not call it rape. He said he gave in; therefore, it wasn't rape. He had been terrorized and isolated. He was to be the "possession" of a winning group who were warring over him, at least as he perceived it.

He had already been badly beaten several times; worse, he was being ostracized and intimidated wherever he went in the prison. The pressure had become unbearable. Finally, as I recall the incident, a third party befriended him and offered to defend him against the others if Rob would give in to him. This, too, went on for days. He had not slept or eaten. To gain a friend and ally, to get some peace, to finally sleep, he gave in.

After that event, a letter to me was written in such morbid metaphors that I could not follow his train of thought or references. He wanted me to know about the incident but did not want to tell me outright. His metaphors were ghoulish attacks on himself so filled with venom and self-loathing that I feared he had become psychotic.

The shame from the experience was more painful to him than any beating. In following letters, he wrote indicating his own personal vow to be killed before he would ever submit again. He began working out to build muscles and thereafter he simply stood his ground against others. Doing so over time restored to him some dignity. But it was another deep humiliation he would carry in his heart until the last one some twenty years after would finally be more than he could carry.

Standing up to the kind of men he'd been scared of all his life gave him another bit of a self he found he could respect, even when it resulted in being physically beaten down. As he indicated in one of the excerpts above, he also earned respect from some of the more humane bullies who understood the courage it took for a skinny kid to stand for his own integrity and be willing to take them on.

Not long after that, he was moved to a part of that prison where there were fewer bullies and threats. He did not live so much in terror then. He had wondered how he would be when the terror went away. He discovered the pervasiveness of depression.

From struggling alone with deep depression, he finally became able to contact and identify his feelings. He had no escape from them and nothing but time. He came to realize that he had always been depressed, for as long as he could recall.

Not all of his prison experiences were bad. In time, he had to force himself to be able to socialize with some others and that meant he had to learn how to better read them. Prison would not have been my choice for him to learn how the human mind works. Those to whose rules and attitudes he now had to conform were not representative of society's best. Nor were all of them representative of society's worst. He'd already met the worst in the free world.

Some jail and prison staff seem so antisocial and callous or frustrated and angry that they get away with behaviors for relieving their stress that are denied the inmates whose stress is far greater. Rob lived among men who felt they were the outcasts of society and who then, as human beings will, try to salvage some sense of importance from the very limited resources available. Those "resources" were often weaker or needier human beings. Those men were both inmates and some guards.

However, from the confinement of prison, three talents emerged. He was very gifted at drawing and sketching. Learning that other inmates admired his drawings gave him some self-esteem and some sense of importance. He traded his drawings for cigarettes, and some conversation with people who noticed them. He sent hundreds of his drawings home to me. I had shown many to an artist who thought that Rob would be accepted in art schools on the basis of his raw talent.

Second, he was a surprisingly creative writer. Despite poor spelling and lack of experience in writing, he wrote fiction with astonishing sensitivity, imagery, and metaphor. He started a book in prison and sent his first chapters to me. I was thrilled with this additional talent; I had already been pleased and surprised by his almost poetic letters. They belied his lack of education and detachment at an interpersonal level. In letters and fiction, he expressed intimacy and a broad range of feelings.

His book was misplaced along with other belongings during some intra-prison transfer, and he lost the motivation to start all over or write anything else except letters. These became less and less frequent by the time he entered the South Carolina prison.

Finally, it seemed that he also had a talent in music. The greater talent seemed to be his ability to improvise music. I loved his haunting songs, and I was intrigued by the singular focus he applied to mastering any new maneuver on the guitar. It was the same focus he had applied to repairing his own cars.

Despite my encouraging him for many years to take advantage of his gifts in writing and art, he could not be persuaded to pursue these in any formal training. Rob could not, in his best dreams about himself, see a future where he might "be somebody." He functioned only at a survival level and could not comprehend a life beyond that. Years earlier, in a Texas prison, he had worked as an auto mechanic. Pressure was minimal with respect to time since the work was done without profit. Regardless of his level of skills, he had trouble obtaining work when he was released.

It was a rare job application that did not require that he indicate whether or not he had ever been convicted of a felony. On those few that did not, the fact of his prison experience came out in interviews.

If he lied on the applications, as I finally suggested he do, then he still had no job references to list. His prison experience and his other problems, along with awkward shyness, did not make him competitive in the job market.

He did, however, read a lot in prison. If he did not master a skill or focus his reading on a formal education, he at least became quite knowledgeable in a surprisingly broad range of subjects. It is another very pleasant discovery to have him talk about some topic in a straightforward, knowledgeable manner that seems foreign to the way he otherwise presents himself.

There are few things now that he does not have some knowledge about, yet he rarely engages in a conversation about those topics with anyone. The topics emerge in casual conversation. I might ponder aloud about Lyme disease, because a patient I've just assessed is disabled by it. As I struggled to recall the symptoms, Rob began to recite them, and the fact that it is caused by a tick bite. I commented that I know several people from Oklahoma who have been bitten by ticks without developing Lyme disease; he casually described precisely the kind of tick and where they are found.

On another occasion, he told me in what century rhythm was developed and that prior to that music had been in three-three time, as representative of the Holy Trinity: God, the Son, and the Holy Spirit. He went on to surprise me with a detailed history of music and its mathematical foundations. Sometimes I learned from him about weather or extinct animals or floods and water shortages all over the world.

He was a wealth of information but was unskilled for a job. I love to hear him talk about all these different subjects, although I've had enough car talk to last the rest of my life. I encouraged and praised him; he discounted his knowledge. No one else listened except strangers on the beach or bored drivers who gave him rides.

In the South Carolina prison, where he would be for four years, his gains were reflected in the fact that he made some friends. He also finally succeeded in earlier abandoned efforts and taught himself to play the guitar. He had constructed one out of cardboard. With no real strings, he learned finger positions and the mechanics of guitar playing.

He would then check out the one guitar the prison had, whenever it was available. I sent him an acoustic guitar for Christmas and the intense focus on mastering the instrument made prison life tolerable. He had a productive escape from depression and an entrance into a group of others. Nine months later, he mailed me a homemade tape he had recorded of his music.

Tape recorders are contraband in prison, so he had risked penalty by sneaking to record wherever he could. Usually, that was in a restroom. From time to time, throughout this "concert" Rob put together for my Mother's Day present, was the sound of flushing toilets, a mockery of the applause he would never have.

Nonetheless, I spent a delightful evening listening to my son's voice, now with a southern accent, play, talk to me, and sing some songs. From the far reaches of his memory, he recalled and played some of my favorite ones from his childhood.

I played the tape again and again. I listened intently to how he sounded, what he said, what he did not say. He seemed on the tape just sweet and gentle, cute and funny. I thought it strange that he could still be winsome after all he had gone through. I missed him intensely. He did not sound like the stranger I had come to think of him as being.

In learning that he was going back to prison, for what we had thought would be ten years, I had involuntarily distanced myself and my emotions from him. I could no longer tolerate the pain from these repeat sentences. His life had been one long series of hurts, failures, crises, and trauma for both of us. I could hardly speak his name without feeling intense grief. That I lost all hope for him at least increased my understanding of how hopeless he must seem to himself.

Again, I gave much, much thought to my decision to permit him to come back to live with me after his release from South Carolina. It was Patrick who encouraged me to bring him back to live with me in San Diego instead of remaining in South Carolina. Remaining there would be the same repeated pattern of no support system and no way to live while he scrambled for a job for which he had no skills.

He was released on parole and California again agreed to monitor that for South Carolina. He was otherwise free, but there is no freedom for someone like Rob who is also a parolee. He had chosen to hitchhike home, just for the sheer pleasure of being out in nature again. He made astonishingly good time, getting rides so easily that he arrived just east of Yuma, Arizona, within thirty-six hours.

There, he was arrested. Often wrongly suspected of vagrancy, he was very frequently approached by police and highway patrolmen, having his ID checked and either being released or detained overnight in jail if he had no ID or had no money. There was no way to predict which, it would be at the capricious whim of the officer. It was harassment that he had learned to expect. No charges were made against him at those times because he had not broken any laws.

Returning from South Carolina, he had not been concerned about hitchhiking or about the patrol car that stopped beside him; his debt to society was paid. He was not violating any law and was not a vagrant. He had an identification card that stated he was a paroled felon. Branded. A check was run on him and he was taken to Yuma County Jail.

A five-year-old warrant from Texas, that had been cleared four years earlier, had mistakenly never been deleted from the nationwide computers. I had made the necessary effort to get it cleared in Texas when he went to prison in South Carolina.

Before he could now be released from this jail in Yuma, I would have to get a lawyer in California, in Arizona, and one in Texas. All three working together managed to expedite the release.

The mistake was made by the state of Texas, but they made no apology. Rob sat in jail for the two days it took to have Texas rectify the mistake and notify Yuma that he should be released. That was a very short time considering all that had to be done, but it was an endless time for him.

I had no way of communicating any hope to him that I was getting the matter cleared once and for all. The only information he had been given led him to believe he was to be sent back to Texas to face another four years in prison. He was devastated.

To have come so close to freedom and then have it snatched from him seemed worse than having remained in the South Carolina prison. Once again, some remaining spark of vitality and hope had been snuffed out. He could see the California border out his window, but he thought he would never see his brother or me again.

At ten-thirty in the evening, two days later, Rob called me from an all-night store in Yuma. He had been released, twelve hours earlier than the time I had been given by the jailers. Could I come and get him? He was always being released at the worst possible hours. I had picked him up at varying times throughout the years between midnight and five in the morning. It was a bit comforting to realize that the police never slept, either. Yuma was four hours away.

Patrick offered to drive and we set out to rescue our lost family member. We remarked and almost chuckled that such journeys and circumstances were still so much a part of Rob's, and therefore our own, lives. And suddenly there he was, after four years, shy, grateful, glad, apprehensive.

He had stood outside the store in freezing weather for over four hours. It had not mattered; he had waited four lifetimes. The one certainty he could count on is that his mother and brother would come.

Side by side on the walls of my mind hang two pictures in identical frames: one is of Rob's father taken in the sweltering tropics of Vietnam. He is dressed in fatigues with full combat gear. The other is of my first glance of our son in front of the store in Yuma in the middle of a cold desert night.

Thirty years later, the contrast between the two had narrowed to only the respective lengths of their hair. Both were warriors. Each had tested his mettle in far away places that I could only know from their letters.

Each had been forced to draw upon a courage previously untested and unproven. Under conditions of intense and relentless horror, each rose from his own private sense of hell to forge his own private sense of honor; both preferred death rather than submission to dishonor.

Day by day, both had learned to endure, to overcome terror, to struggle and triumph with their own individual integrity, ultimately only strengthened by the assaults against it. And both, as perhaps have combatants done throughout time, learned to live with the guilt born of reflex efforts to survive.

Their respective worlds were not so much defined by the geography, as by the new relationships. Both were in enemy territory. There the similarities get blurred. The father could identify his enemy but could not always see him. The son could not determine who his enemy might be, although he saw him everywhere. The father was sanctioned to fight; the son was sanctioned if he fought.

There is a morality that governs the military, whether or not all can live up to it. The higher standards of God and country have never been upheld by all, but the standards are there. They are honor, fidelity, and sacrifice to a higher cause. In the military, there is unity of purpose, camaraderie, and the intense focus to bring out the best in each individual. False pride, not dignity, is stripped.

The men and women who defend our nation live by creeds that remind them of that greater cause. Their slogans remind them that they are elite: "The Few and The Proud." They know to whom they belong: "Uncle Sam Wants You." They anticipate gain: "The Marine Corps Builds Men." They are aware of a pride in meeting difficult challenges: "I Never Promised You a Rose Garden."

Prison has its own code of ethics. It more resembles: "Nothing left to lose." Cowardice is defined differently: fairness, honor, and integrity are often seen as weaknesses. Fidelity takes on a perverted twist. Comrades more often exploit and despise. Heroes emerge more often from having successfully "beaten the system" or beaten up someone else.

The father came home a hero with medals of valor decorating his chest. But he came home to a world that had largely betrayed him and scorned the cause for which he had risked his life. He understood the preciousness of the freedoms for which he fought. Still, he forever belonged to a company of honorable men, men whose bonds were tied from having stood together with tenacity of a purpose that transcended that of ordinary human beings.

No heroes come home from prison. No ticker tape parades recognize the valor required to stand against a foe. Freedom is only the safety of a lock-down. No ex-convict walks away from prison wearing medals of honor. There is no honor granted for surviving hell if one's uniform is striped. At best, there is some inner recognition, privately held, but never heralded, that one has stood alone with tenacity of a purpose that transcended that of ordinary human beings.

What defines a hero? When is running from the enemy sometimes cowardice and sometimes courage? Who defines the enemy?

From South Carolina, Rob came home to a world that had seemed to reject him all his life. He had no comrades with whom he could identify, no purpose higher than survival, nothing for which to survive. He had no meaningful relationships with others beside whom he had stood to either triumph or fall. Yet he had a more fierce sense of loyalty to his country than I had ever seen in him. He saw its flaws but declared that America is the greatest country in the world. He worried all the time that it was being weakened by callous, greedy leaders.

He could define his nation but had no way of defining his world, because it only consisted of me and his brother who are not like him. Even we belonged out there where people succeeded in love and accomplishment, out there where others held their heads high, not burdened with guilt and shame from a lifetime of humiliations.

Out there, to even talk about his humiliating experiences was to risk the reminder that he had made his own bed. There is no point at which a person who has never developed a healthy self-image can suddenly become normal. Prison had never held him as captive as his own inability to relate to others in ways that could free his spirit.

His self image had been further injured at every stage of his life. He could not close the gap between what he believed he was and what he believed he should be. His inability did not prevent him from needing what he believed every other person had; it prevented him from achieving those rewards. It clothed him in depression.

Rob arrived home traumatized by experiences, life, and depression. I don't know how much that last false arrest in Yuma cost him in terms of motivation or hope. He had wondered how long he would have to go up before he could come down.

His description from prison of depression was eloquently written in a way only Rob can. He had written that he felt like a car, modified to only run on tracks, pulling a long line of boxcars uphill. He noted his exhaustion from the effort and his greater fear of stalling and therefore of rolling backward into worse depression. For him, it had been four years of another uphill climb to a sudden and totally unexpected fall down. Hope can be more treacherous than despair.

After the initial hours of welcoming and drawing him out with questions, Rob fell into a daily stance I referred to as his "Lincolnesque mode." He sat stiff, expressionless, his hands on chair arms or his knees, staring out at nothing for hours. He looked like the Lincoln Monument in Washington D.C. He would not always immediately hear me when I spoke.

Almost three years after release, he continued to lapse into "Lincolnesque" every time he was struggling with some sense of shame or other inner demons. Crises that followed did not make him withdraw; those he could handle. Shame, defeat, and depression, he could not.

A day or two after his return, we went to visit Patrick and Patrick's wife, Debbie. Rob would meet for the first time his two-year-old niece, Shelby. He had asked about her in every phone call and mentioned her in every letter yet did not now seem eager to meet her.

She climbed all over him, hugging, flirting, and playful. In Shelby's garden, only love grows. Rob barely broke his stiffened posture even when she called him "*Unkal Wob*." He seemed both delighted with and frightened by her.

On our way home, I was perplexed by his actions; I had thought that he would be most comfortable with a small child. I had hoped that through her affectionate acceptance of him, he might find a way to heal at last. "Isn't Shelby precious?" I asked the question, hoping it would lead to an explanation of his reactions to her.

"Yes, she really is. It was a trip to see her, but boy am I glad it's over!" He went on to say that he had been scared to death. "I was afraid I would discover when I met her, that I was a child pervert!" Autistic people have problems with perceiving and processing information from their environments and in judgment.

No, he had no reason to think that. Yes, he thought child perverts were disgusting and incomprehensible. "Well," he said, "everything else is wrong with me. I would not have been surprised to find I was also a pervert!"

Rob began his day with a quart of coffee made from enough coffee beans to produce a gallon with normal robust flavor. Until he had the coffee and one cigarette, he could barely speak. Until I grew accustomed to this behavior, I spent most mornings anxiously wondering if something was very wrong. He slowly came to life about thirty minutes after coffee and a cigarette.

It took weeks and weeks before he began to relax and open up the doors of his heart. It took many months before he felt any kind of comfort in the free world, and at least a year and a half before he could almost believe he was not going to get rearrested at any moment.

When he had been home about a week, he walked out on my front porch, thirty minutes after coffee, smiling and remarking about the beautiful day. I commented that there had been a car theft in the neighborhood the previous night. In mid-stride, he made an immediate one hundred and eighty-degree turn and came back in the house, saying: "They'll think it was me!"

For the first time, he truly seemed like an alien in society, if only because everything was new and strange to him. Not only had technology and society passed him by, but he had entered prison at a much more emotionally immature age than what he was upon his release. He was the former Rob in the sense that he lapsed unexpectedly into periods of being reclusive and largely silent. He still had the habits of coining unusual phrases, asking nonsensical questions, or making the sounds of a car as he traveled from room to room. He remained shy and awkward with most people. He would make a bare-minimum appearance downstairs when I had guests then escape back to his room.

His leave-takings at such times were awkward reflections that he had sat agonizing over how to politely excuse himself. He at first seemed almost helpless in terms of doing anything for himself that required initiative. He would go hungry if I was not home to cook and there were no convenient foods in the freezer. He was an even pickier eater than before.

He told about the poor quality of prison foods and his belief that only the worst ingredients were used. He refused, therefore, to eat most casseroles or dishes such as potato salad. "I don't like foods with foreign objects in them." On one occasion of coming home from dinner at a friend's house, I observed that he was eating as though starved. "I didn't eat much of their food; it was thoroughly vegetable-infested."

In other ways, he was a new Rob. Over time, he became calmer, articulate, open, honest, and had more common sense. He had an air of confidence that derived, I supposed, from having survived so many traumas, as well as having had to interact with the others in his world behind bars. Too, his self-confidence grew from having gained some pride in his guitar playing. With that, he had finally been able, in this last prison term, to break through the barrier of isolation from others. I found myself able to more often discuss normal things with him and rely on his intelligence or perspectives.

CHAPTER 21

"After filling my tank, I only had a dollar and some pennies left, the hitchhiker I'd picked up didn't have any money. We were lucky, the very next McDonald's we came to was having a special of two hamburgers for a dollar. Neither of us had eaten anything all day." Rob, 2003.

We were having a rare, deep and long conversation. He was thirty-two, he had been back home with me for only a short while, we were still reconnecting, but in a more equal way than I'd ever enjoyed with him. I was delighted and amazed at changes I'd seen in him since he'd been home. Again, his intelligence and wealth of knowledge had seemed to gain qualitatively; his history of reading problems seemed long forgotten. The very surprising good is that he was at times much more normal and natural, much more engaging, though not consistently so. However, he was beginning to drink again and in the loneliest of places, by himself, in the desert.

Sitting after dinner and after playing some songs for me on his guitar, Rob began to open his heart. Softly, at first hesitantly, although sober, he volunteered that he had begun drinking again and regretted it. He revealed rare self-insights he had never before shared with me in such depth and emotion. He appealed to me to understand both that he *knew* using drugs and alcohol was wrong, but that it was only when he was under the influence of some substance that he felt like other people.

In the conversation that followed, he did most of the talking. He told me in halting, tear-filled anguish about his lifelong self-hatred and his feelings of never belonging, not to a playgroup, a peer group, or in any other setting outside our home. He stated he did not know what it even felt like to be comfortable or really welcome or wanted anywhere. He *thought* he was, but he did not know for *sure* if he was behaving all right so that I would still want him to live with me.

For two or three hours I sat listening with a breaking heart to Rob tell the story of his life as he had lived it inside the silence of his own wounded heart. He was an adult, but he was still very new at being able to verbalize feelings that he had spent a lifetime mostly acting out. My grief for him was profound, yet I was also astonished by that revelation of insight, his high intelligence, and the emotions that he had held inside all his life.

I heard incredibly painful, tragic perceptions of a reality that had so often been unbearable and so frequently distorted. The distortions were the resulting creations of his own efforts to relate to his childhood world in which he saw himself only as a misfit. I listened to details of his pitiful attempts to make sense of himself, and of his final acceptance that he never would make sense to others. He revealed the humanness of a person who believed he was inhuman.

I looked at him sitting across from me at our dining room table. I saw a handsome, funny, intelligent, talented man. But, when he looked in a mirror, he saw an outsider in a world where he did not belong; someone who still struggled to understand most people and to be at ease with them. He sensed his differences from others rather than any similarities. Finding no one else like him, neither had he found a way to make friends or gain acceptance. He was never obnoxious or unlikable; he just didn't seem to know how to be liked or to think of himself as someone others would find interesting.

Yet he blossomed when he played his guitar. Each time he played for me, it triggered new talks and he began to open up more and more about himself, his life, and what prison had been like. As memories emerged, he often cried in shame and sorrow for all the past miseries that he had held inside. I felt deep sorrow for him, but I also rejoiced in the fact that his ability to talk about rather than act out his emotions was healthy and necessary.

There were more humiliations and more failures with which he had coped for the previous four years. He said the guitar had saved his life. Music expressed his life. He could best communicate his feelings through songs. I began to invite him to play his guitar for my guests, in an effort to ease his presence among strangers.

At first, he would not know when to stop, and I would not want to embarrass him, so the playing continued until others began to start talking to each other again. Typically, he misunderstood that human behavior. He told me that while people might not enjoy his playing, he benefited from forcing himself out of his shyness by playing for them.

Later, I would casually invite him to come and play three songs. He dutifully played the three, picked up his guitar, and retreated back to his room. If he agreed to join us for dinner, he began eating as soon as he was seated, completely bereft of any table manners. He ate without making conversation, finished first, and immediately excused himself from the table. That was a prison habit, as much as present discomfort.

However, around my friend Kathrin, and Kathrin's married daughter, Alisa, Rob grew to be most relaxed, witty, and usually lingering. He thought Alisa was the most beautiful woman he had ever seen. He knew she was absolutely unattainable to him, but he talked for three days about the thrill he had known from just walking with her along the beach one day. "Mom, I felt so proud to have her beside me!"

Once in a very great while, Rob found in some other rare person a quality of acceptance that cast him in his best possible role. When that happened, I retreated to the sidelines, in bittersweet happiness, observing how my son might have been had he not always felt different from others. Kathrin is one of those rare people.

Kathrin insisted on loaning Rob the money to buy a car. I was opposed to this and asked her to not mention it to him, but instead to think about it and to wait and see how he adapted. She ignored me. She had not known Rob all his life, and therefore believed that if he got a truck of his own he could go around doing yards for people and make a living. She offered, he was delighted, and I was voted down.

Again, a solution created more problems. Rob could not get a driver's license without insurance. He could not get insurance without a driver's license. His rates were sky high. He was penalized for not having had a driver's license for years and his fees, because of a six-year-old DUI, were exorbitant. He had no money to pay for these essentials. Each time he met with such an obstacle, I thought with sadness of all others who when newly released from prison might have no family at all who would help or who lacked the time and resources. There are many.

He did not belong to the California parole system; therefore he did not have access to certain benefits doing so might have provided. He belonged to South Carolina, but they had failed to send his transfer papers here after three years of effort to get them to do so. He lived in constant fear that their failure to officially transfer him meant that they would call him back at any time. He could not allow himself to enjoy freedom too much; he knew it could soon be snatched away.

He owed a fifteen-hundred-dollar fine to South Carolina and was informed he must pay it immediately or risk extradition. So, I hurriedly sent in a money order in that amount. It was returned because they had not yet established his account. I sent it a second time on the date I was instructed to but it was returned with no explanation at all. I notified them again and then waited and in time forgot about it until South Carolina suddenly made it our crisis instead of their responsibility, demanding complete payment in terms that suggested Rob had been deliberately refusing to pay. I sent the money order again and proof of all the transactions and his transfer to California finally occurred, months later.

As had been true all his life, changes brought new and bigger crises to be handled. His efforts to become a citizen were met with obstacles or defeat everywhere he turned. He got stopped on routine identification checks so often I wondered if he had some sort of secret mark of felon across his forehead. He would only have his identification checked, but it was always disconcerting and always a reminder that nothing in his world was secure.

He attended AA meetings a mile or two from our house and enjoyed running there and back for the exercise. He got stopped by police and, of all things, was told not to run at night fully dressed because it made him look suspicious. Though he felt he had paid his debt to society, he found that his past continued to hold him in chains.

I became the one most frustrated with the silly red tape that created a halt for him at every turn. I grew ashamed of my own society of petty local officials. It seemed to me that mainly uncaring people staffed every bureaucratic department. They merely shrugged when I would point out that two equally opposing demands were being made of him.

There were further shrugs when I'd point out that he had two coincidental orders to be in two different places at the same time. He was accustomed to such frustrations and accepted them in the despairing passive way he accepted most other defeats.

There were many, many tasks to be undertaken to get him in parole, settled with identification, and otherwise made legitimate. None was a simple procedure, and none provided any semblance of respect from others. I did not know which was the sadder condition: that my fellow human beings treated another as though he was only a thing or that my son accepted such treatment without protest.

Despite resolution to the problems surrounding getting him a car, and getting licensed and insured, Rob was not getting yard work. Doing that required him to initiate contact with strangers to ask for work. This he found as impossible as ever.

Debbie and Patrick tried to help him by making fliers and getting him a job or two. He was a hard worker as long as someone else took the initiative to make the contacts. He would be prompt about returning the calls, following up, and doing the work, but he sat paralyzed when required to sell himself.

Yet he would surprise me by explaining himself confidently to some stranger on some technical matter related to his efforts to comply with whatever regulation he was currently facing. If he was having a problem with his car, he would naively phone repair shops all over town, assuming that each would share his concern, and he'd talk freely, intelligently, and politely about the matter. As long as he had some *thing* to talk about, something he knew about, he was at relative ease.

He lost himself in his guitar, but he was otherwise just as lost as ever in terms of having no goals, skills, or relationships. He went dutifully twice a week to his AA meetings, month after month. After fourteen months, he still did not have one single friend.

He had a sponsor who never called and whose name or face he no longer remembered. In tears, he spoke about the fact that "at least in prison, I had people I was forced to talk with." He noted camaraderie in prison that he now missed. In another of the paradoxes that defined his life, within the walls of prison, Rob had found the most freedom from his greatest fears.

He became, however, more normal and enjoyable to me on a personal basis. As he relaxed more and more in our home, he resumed his former habits of showing affection by using a single word as a sort of code between us and pulling nonsensical pranks. These were welcome signs of his healing I remembered so well.

Pulling some simple prank is Rob's first gesture toward opening the door to his heart. If you do not know that about him, you may be irritated or simply discount him for the act. If you laugh with him, you just might be a safe person. He will test a little more. If you return a prank, the door will open wider and he will let you see the more serious and complex person that he is. More than once, I came home to find all of my lampshades removed, turned upside down, and replaced on the lamps. It delighted me as much as doing it must have delighted him. I'd laugh heartily knowing that Rob, too, loved having his jokes appreciated.

Other times, he would silently wait for the hour or day it might take me to notice that pictures on the walls had been hung upside down. I might find belongings hanging from the ceiling or stuck in the refrigerator. My laughter might often simply be from the joy of having Robbie back. But it was laughter he took as acceptance and so he opened his emotional door a little more.

For at least a year, we passed a small, empty box back and forth in prankish ways. He might stick it under my pillow; I would tape it on the inside of his toilet cover. He put it under the Christmas tree for me; I put it in his Easter basket. It would seem to disappear for weeks and then reappear in my sink or his bureau.

There were many mornings in which I would open my bedroom door to find articles collected there from all over the house—silent messages that signaled our shared bonds. There were mornings then, when he opened his door to find it barricaded with chairs and pillows. He delighted in these acts of love spoken in his language more than the words "I love you."

Every three or four days, "boat" would be the only word he spoke to me as he passed through the room I was in or came downstairs in the morning. "Boat" was a coded reminder of affection and a secret word we shared. As he had in childhood, one word from some movie, song, or event would be adopted to communicate all the positive feelings the event had stirred and then to transfer them to me in some show of love.

"Boat" was adopted from the movie, *Forrest Gump*. It was always pronounced with the two-syllable southern drawl of the movie character. I had taken him to see it a week after he returned home from South Carolina. I had thought when I first saw it that Rob would identify with Forrest, and he did. I had wished then that he might have found the same self-acceptance as had fictional Forrest. Rob loved the movie and said that Forrest had had a wonderful, wonderful life.

"But Jenny died!" I had wailed. It matters more and more to me that movies, at least, have happy endings.

"Mom, no life can be perfect."

"Boating" together was a reminder that there was hope in an imperfect world. Rob would leave cutout or sketched pictures of boats someplace where he knew I would eventually see them. He asked repeatedly when I was going to outsmart him with a "boat incident," as he called such pranks. Months later, he came home to find a large container of water sitting on his bed, with a battery-operated boat floating in the middle. "You out-boated me all right!"

───────◆◆◆───────

There were other ways in which Rob was more normal, more of a man, and responsible. He was eager to please and to help me, but I could not be his entire social life and he did not want or expect me to be. Patrick and his wife, Debbie, were both in graduate school, had two children now, and both worked. They had little time for anyone.

Rob had very much wanted to attend the birth of his nephew, Maclean. He was not allowed inside the delivery room, but he waited all night outside. Outside the room where life began and other loved ones gathered to participate in it.

Patrick was as available to Rob as he could be, but their differences were more striking than ever. Rob's improved ability to relate to others was still episodic and stiff. It was also off-set by an inertia regarding everything else about life. Sadly, it was most normal with a couple of beers, but when had he ever stopped with two?

He obtained a few odd jobs from my friends, but faced daily rejection from job applications. He had passed the "high" he had achieved after about a year, and was sliding down again into the depression of defeat. I was scared. We both seemed to have come up against another impossible barrier.

Drugs and alcohol again became his self-treatment for what came to be an agitated solitariness. He had initially been quite proud of himself that he remained sober and had often said in that first year that he had no desire to drink or use drugs. When he admitted that he had been using again, he told me that he had also been experiencing worsening obsessive thoughts that were unbearable and deeply, deeply shameful.

Also, he believed he was possessed by many different personalities, some of which were "evil." No, he did not think he had multiple personalities; he just thought he was possessed by demons that at any given time, he feared might "cause" him to do things he would later regret. "One of these is someone like Alexander the Great, I'm not saying it *is* Alexander the Great, just someone like him."

I listened to him while trying to draw from all I knew about psychology. I found I knew nothing at all! I could not help him make some sense of himself if I could not detach and place him in some framed category of behavior. I could not detach and he could not be framed. No single picture captured Robbie.

My frustration was heightened by Rob's many inhibitions about such self-disclosure. He never asked for my professional perspective. What he might tell me was that of son to a mother whom he intensely hoped would understand. Was it hope that I would understand without his having to risk the vulnerability of stating his fears in concrete language? Or was it hope that I would help him make sense of chaotic emotions about which he had no understanding? Did he lack the words to define his feelings or did he lack the will to risk rejection by me? He still spoke with his own subjective symbolism and he still expected me to decode. Every time he did, my logic told me one thing, but my mother's heart told me I was letting him down again.

Following each such mutually painful conversation, Rob seemed to be temporarily relieved. Following each, I initially concluded that he was getting worse instead of better. Then, he would suddenly behave normally, happily, and rationally for a while; and I would conclude that the many fragments of his identity were forming a whole and healthier self with whom he could finally live in peace.

Sometimes those good periods were brought on by some small hope: belief that he might get some job for which he had applied or that some "friend" he had met would remain so. More times, it turned out those periods of more apparent normalcy and articulation were because he was using some stimulating drug, typically, methamphetamines.

He kept his relapses secret from me for as long as possible. It was easy to do because I was accustomed all his life to the one predictability about him—unpredictable moods. Initially, his use of drugs was only occasional. I also grew accustomed to his occasional late returns from the beach or out driving. There was no reason for me to suspect that he was staying out late in order to sober up before returning home. Even if there were clues, I could not exercise control over him and I didn't want to. Parole had set his boundaries now.

The one control I personally had over Rob's behavior was to make him leave my home, and I had learned to hate the consequences of that. As had always been true, my almost daily struggle was to decide if I was helping him or only enabling.

CHAPTER 22

*"Mom, I go to places most Christians never go. I go where peo-
ple are depraved and lost. I tell them about Jesus, that He loves
them. Christians need to go to those places, but I don't think
they will."* Rob, 2002.

On the day that the rest of the world mourned the Oklahoma
City bombing tragedy, I mourned Rob's own personal one, as
well. On a morning run in Balboa Park in San Diego, he was
attacked by another assailant, with another knife. There were six
new stab wounds all over his head and the side of his face, and
one that missed his heart by one-half inch.

Another stranger called another ambulance. Another doctor
phoned asking if I was the mother of Robert Bowers; another
hospital emergency room saved his life. And another quiet grief
he would stuff inside with only physical scars to suggest the
greater pain from inner battles.

I later visited the large, darkened spot where he had sat watching his own blood forming a puddle all around him. "I believed I
was dying," he said matter-of-factly. He had had to be forced into
the ambulance. "I told them to leave me there because I didn't
have any insurance or money to pay them. I was too weak and
dizzy to get any farther away."

There were no drugs or alcohol in his system; he had just been
in the wrong place at the wrong time. It was called a hate crime
by the media, San Diego's first. His assailant was never found.

The only bright moment of that time was the comfort and gratitude I felt that Patrick had rushed to help me help his brother. We retrieved his car and guitar from the park and visited him in the hospital. He tried to make light of it and never gave in to self-pity. The two people who loved him unconditionally and who had stood by him all his life flanked him. Whether or not he realized it, it was that love that had kept him human.

Making music on the beach with some ever-changing group of strangers became his only social life. Occasionally, a girl would talk to him and he would come home and tell me about it, delighted and hopeful, but he would never see her again.

He was failing again. The rules and laws and mores of society had always been difficult for him, but now they seemed even more complex and confusing to him. He would grasp one rule of life in the free world only to discover that he had unknowingly broken another. In the beginning, he had gotten parking tickets from expired meters so often that he now parked blocks away from where he needed to be, in some free zone.

He got stopped for not fastening his seat belt just weeks after returning home and within one week of the law going into effect. The officer had told him that he would receive the ticket in the mail, so he set aside the citation and forgot about it. The ticket never came and eventually, the citation cost $450. He had not read the fine print that stated, "If you do not receive a ticket in the mail, you must pay this within thirty days."

Rob had never grasped such nuances. The world was black and white. If the officer said the ticket would come in the mail, then that was that. Taking initiative on his own behalf had never resulted in accomplishment for Rob. And one does not need to take initiative in prison.

Finally, he received a ticket for driving under the influence of alcohol. In previous times, I had let him serve his jail sentence. By now, I knew that he was in at least as much danger in jail as on the streets. Besides, he had not benefited at all from those consequences any more than he ever had in childhood. My choices were to either bail him out or have him go back to prison. He would lose the gains made.

The same conflict that had typified Rob's life presented itself this time. Tough love told me to let him go back to prison. My mother's heart told me he would not benefit from it any more than he ever had. The issues were not which was better or which option would work with him. Instead, they were choices of which would do the least overall harm to him. If I'd had a crystal ball and had been able to foresee that even greater tragedies lay ahead for him, I would have chosen this lesser prison sentence.

I bailed him out and retrieved his truck, never a simple process. I took him to all of his court appearances. Going back to four more years of prison seemed too great a penalty for either of us to pay. Prison meant four more years of his dying inside, to be released again and start all over trying to negotiate his way in society.

As his expenses mounted, he grew increasingly ashamed and overwhelmed. He felt he was going backward rather than forward and could see no way out. I could only do what I had always done, stand by him for the good I knew him to be and try to arrange appropriate consequences for the wrong, no easy task at his age. I listened now to him tell me about personal accountability, responsibility, and integrity, and his own sense that he was not fulfilling these. He agonized, admitting he failed himself in continuing to drink. His conscience was more condemning than anything that society or I could do.

He had to have a breathalyzer on his car, which cost another $900 before it was completed. Additionally, he had to go to DUI School for eighteen months and work community service.

The community service he chose was to pick up trash off highways. This gave him a purpose and meaning. He was up and eager to work early every morning, humming as he prepared his coffee, saying good-bye in good spirits.

Additionally, he went out alone on his days off and picked up trash on those places the work crew missed. He asked me to buy larger, more durable trash bags for his weekend voluntary efforts. He was kind and helpful to the many homeless people he found hiding along the way. He would come home complaining about the callousness toward them of others in the crew. \

His community service time ended and he was again without a purpose. He kept the orange safety vest he had been required to wear hanging in his closet, as though keeping a souvenir breast-plate of a moment of glory.

When it became apparent that he was again drinking, I sent him to another drug and alcohol rehabilitation program. My choices for him could no longer be the "best possible;" my finances were too strained. The choices had to be the best available under the circumstances. I had heard favorable mention of this program, sponsored by a religious group. It was similar to the one he had fled eleven years before.

Seven days later, I answered my door to a drenched Rob. "I've just come home to get my things and some dry clothes. I won't stay. I'll go somewhere else." He stayed, because I wanted him to. Where else would he have gone?

He had left his group at their church and walked seven miles to my home in a downpour. "I can't take it anymore. I guess I'm just a failure even there!" He had been required to pray until he could speak in tongues. Doing so would then demonstrate to him and everyone around that then and only in that way had the Holy Spirit, and therefore sobriety, descended upon him. He had prayed and prayed for hours and been prayed over for more hours until exhausted, but he never spoke in tongues. God didn't want him, he concluded.

Finally, I showed him from passages in the Bible that God's love was not exclusive to only those who spoke in tongues. It took several hours of talking to try and undo that sense of abject rejection by a god he saw as only condemning. I don't think I ever sounded sufficiently convincing.

Rob's parole officer came regularly. She liked him and told me each time that he was the easiest parolee she had. She, too, thought he was a good person, "sweet," and really trying to go straight. He was disarmingly honest except for the risks he took in using drugs and alcohol.

In every other way, he was completely trustworthy and trying to be a law-abiding citizen. He was actually relieved to get the breathalyzer. He wanted the device, because it imposed discipline and controls he admitted he lacked.

The device was "foolproof" for about one year. Then the idea of circumventing it became the greater challenge. His first occasion of bypassing the breathalyzer occurred out of necessity when his car broke down miles from help.

The barren, desolate desert was his favorite terrain. It had been all his life. His idea of success was to own a gas station and repair shop in an area I regarded as the most forlorn spot on earth. He seemed compelled to go there every two or three months, despite the risk of getting caught by leaving the county—a parole violation. He would go to get drunk, sober up, then drive back home. I had cautioned him repeatedly not to go without permission from his parole officer.

His flattened voice on the telephone stated, "Mom, I've been arrested in El Centro." I was so shocked, devastated, and furious, I impulsively hung up on him without learning any further details. He was supposed to be at work in San Diego.

"It's over and all for nothing!" My hope for victory had never been as forceful as Rob's belief in defeat. He would be going back to South Carolina for certain. I sat huddled in grief, trying to convince myself that this was for the best, knowing that it was his responsibility to keep himself out of prison. I suspected that it was I who was most unwilling to have that happen.

My self-arguments included: he had not been able to cope in the free world and he had not been able to maintain sobriety or become productive. He had not achieved any sense of belonging or of peace. Maybe prison was where he belonged. Maybe prison was where a part of him wanted to be. Social isolation was now more painful than isolation from mainstream society. Breaking the law was more personally acceptable than failure to be self-supportive.

After I rationalized my way to accepting this inevitability, I cried in protest. Prison was not where he belonged! We weren't finished trying; he was not going to benefit in any way by going back. Now I needed to talk with him. El Centro is a desert town about 140 miles from where I lived in San Diego.

I could not call my son in jail, and he did not call back. A few hours later, a highway patrolman called, "Are you the mother of Robert Bowers?" Flashbacks.

It turned out that Rob had not broken any law. He had been working for a few weeks as a laborer for a slate and marble contractor. He had left the job early on a Thursday after overhearing a conversation that he had wrongly thought was in reference to him. It was derogatory and he thought it meant that he was going to be fired.

It was the only fulltime job Rob had gotten since release. He had done maintenance work for a condominium complex, but the jobs had all been completed. Some of my friends and acquaintances hired him to repair their cars. He had also been hired by a series of small auto repair shops but had been let go at the end of each day because he was slow or became distracted. It was crushing to him to return home and tell me he had lost another job.

He was desperate to prove himself on this one. He had worked long, back-breaking hours, loading heavy slabs of marble. He had repaired and improved every piece of equipment. He had to be told what to do, but he did what he was told. He had even refused to join his coworkers in drinking beer there on the property after work.

Having given his all, and believing that he had failed even at this, he sought out the desert where all his demons were allowed to run rampant and where he was free from the strain of reining them in. He worked through this latest failure, arrived at some ability to live with himself, and stuffed his demons back inside and trekked back across the sand dunes to his truck.

Rob had parked his truck at a rest stop and walked out into the desert. When he returned hours later, highway patrol cars surrounded him, hand-cuffed him, and took him to jail in El Centro, California. They had run a routine check on his license plate and discovered a nine-year-old outstanding warrant for his arrest in Barstow, California. He had stolen a sandwich and a carton of milk.

It was a relief to know that Rob had not broken the law this time. But I was angry with myself for having hung up on him. It certainly meant he would not call back. I told the officer I'd hung up on Rob and asked him to have Rob call me when he could, not believing the man would go to the trouble to do so, but he did.

Rob had been taken thirty-five miles west from where his truck was parked to the El Centro jail. It didn't matter to the officer who had a choice of towing companies that he was heaping further inconvenience and cost to his arrestee. By this time, I was as accustomed to such lack of concern as was Rob. His truck had been towed twenty miles further east from the point of arrest to an impound yard in Yuma, although there were towing companies and impound yards in El Centro where the jail was located.

Each time he was arrested, there was never only the fine or the sentence to be paid and then have the matter done with. Always, there were secondary difficulties heaped upon him (and others like him!) that are usually more punitive than the direct consequence to the misdeed.

In this arrest, based on the old theft of returned food, Rob was surrounded by more highway patrol cars and officers than necessary. He had been forced down on his knees, handcuffed, and then carried off to jail barefoot and shirtless. He had chuckled in telling me, with an acute sense of the ridiculousness, rather than becoming angry over it.

He was arrested on the misdemeanor charge from nine years before and his truck was impounded. In his truck were his guitar and tools, the only property of value that he owned. He also believed that he would now be going back to prison.

He had only two dollars, and was fifty-five miles away from where his truck was locked up with an initial fee of $200 before he could retrieve it, if he could at all. The impound costs mounted each day he was in custody. A three day Memorial weekend lay just ahead during which the impound yard would be closed but the impound fees would accrue.

It would not be their problem how he would retrieve a truck and the rest of his belongings. It was not worth their consideration to simply ask that the truck be taken to El Centro, since that is where he would be. He has left more cars in impound yards than he has wrecked, under just those circumstances—away from home, no money to retrieve them or his belongings inside.

Telephone calls to El Centro indicated that they intended to extradite Rob to Barstow's jail. If I ever understood the logic next explained to me, I cannot recall it, but he could be bailed out of El Centro because he had not broken a law there; however he could not be bailed out if he got to Barstow.

I contacted an attorney who advised me to get Rob out of jail immediately. If he ended up in custody in Barstow, then South Carolina would be notified. We still wrongfully assumed that the Barstow crime must have been more serious and therefore that he would be sent back to prison for at least the duration of his parole. He had to be rescued before he was shipped out the following afternoon.

I arranged to connect with a bail bondsman in El Centro and take the day off from work. My friend Kathrin volunteered to accompany me on this long day's journey. We became lost in El Centro and so arrived later than planned at the jail. It took several more hours to arrange for the bond, pay it, and arrange for Rob to get out. I was not given a specific time he would be released, only that it would be sometime between then and midnight.

It was four o'clock. I telephone the impound yard to say I was leaving the jail right then and asked them to please remain open until I got there. "We close at five o'clock."

I pleaded.

"We will close at five after five!"

Kathrin drove ninety-five miles an hour; she was a woman possessed. I advised her frantically that more tickets were written along that one stretch of highway than almost any other in California. "Well, that's just a risk I'll have to take. We are not going to let those suckers defeat us!"

Flying down the highway, the engine suddenly quit and the car slowed until it stopped completely. Together, we pushed it, now without power steering, to the shoulder. It was not out of gas.

The time was twenty minutes to five. The sign we had just passed announced that we were nineteen miles from the tiny town wherein somewhere there is an impound yard with Rob's truck.

Kathrin piled out and immediately began to try and flag down a passerby. In between passing cars, I fumbled with my cell phone and found I had no signal.

A school teacher picked us up. He was driving a van full of handicapped children from a hospital in San Diego back to Yuma. Less than five minutes had passed since we'd pulled over. He knew the location of the impound yard.

I picked the most likely looking shack of all as the possible office. Inside were three men in rough shirts and overalls sitting around a swamp cooler.

A breathalyzer device apparently requires some practice. I'd had none. I sat out in the hot desert sun, ruining my silk suit, blowing again and again through the mouth piece. I followed the directions exactly and pressed the buttons in the correct order. Red lights, green lights, and tones happened but the truck did not start. At six o'clock, the men pushed the truck outside the gates. They were more than happy to accommodate us, since they would now be towing Kathrin's car.

We were equal distance between El Centro, California, and Yuma, Arizona, therefore they would tow us to Yuma. We didn't want to go farther on to Yuma. "Ok," the driver told us, "but it will cost you three times as much to have the car towed to El Centro as it will to Yuma." Huh?

The driver did not then tell us that he lived in Yuma. We three, with Rob's guitar and case, wedged ourselves into the one seat of the tow truck. The floor gearshift was there as well, I sat in the middle straddling it. He drove us west twenty miles to the car, then back east fifty-five more miles to Yuma, through Yuma, and on to the far eastern side. We passed many repair shops along the way, but he knew of one he has "heard" stayed open late into the night. We would definitely get the car fixed that night.

He boasted that it was cool for this time of year, only 105 degrees, so he hadn't needed to fix his air conditioner. I didn't even respond.

When we arrived, someone called out to him by his first name before we'd even come to a stop. "Pete, there's no way in the world we can get to that car tonight!" The jerk did us the favor of driving us to the airport, the only place we could rent a car.

Kathrin and I were disheveled, hot, thirsty, starved, broke, and worried, but still in good spirits. It was 7:30 p.m., Rob had not been released. We stopped for dinner at an inexpensive looking restaurant that boasted specials: prime rib or scampi.

I ordered the scampi and iced tea. The waiter returned, "We're out of scampi." I chose the second special. I sipped at the too bitter tea. He returned and told me they were out of prime rib. I'd have a hamburger and a glass of red wine. He returned again empty handed, they did not have any more red wine. "A Coke, then. *Are you out of ice?*" We laughed at the humor of it all; the situation at the restaurant reflected the entire day.

After dinner, we drove the eighty miles back west to El Centro and retrieved Rob, clad only in pants, and sporting a crude haircut. He had paid a fellow inmate his last two dollars to get it cut because, "Well, that's how he made a living, Mom."

CHAPTER 23

"I guess the book about me is never going to be published, but it should be, even though it will be embarrassing, people still need to know what alcohol and drug abuse can cause a person to do."
Rob from prison, 2010

A month later, Rob and I drove the 180 miles to Barstow courts. It was another sad, sweet time with him. He brought along a tape recording he'd made for me of songs he wanted me to hear and thought I would like. I was always surprised by how well he knew me.

Several songs prompted tears from us both; I stopped the tape and asked him to explain what about the lyrics most appealed to him. Love; love lost, unrequited, never experienced. Lovelessness and loneliness and isolation from intimacy were the themes of the lyrics that expressed his soul.

In court, I listened to the thirteen cases that went before the judge ahead of Rob. Not one of them received any leniency. I thought that either he had been on the bench too long, or I was too much of a pushover. Rob's name was called and I walked up with him. The judge seemed taken aback and asked if I was his lawyer.

"Oh. Well, can, uh, can Robert, uh, can Robert speak for himself?" I was *so* tempted to say no, and would have, I *think*, except that it would have embarrassed Rob. I thought also that there seemed to be a touch of the criminal mind in me!

Rob was set free. "Mom power is awesome!" marveled Rob.

He began spending free time on the beach, playing his guitar, and acquiring friends about whom he spoke but did not bring home. He did still bring an occasional homeless person for a meal, shower, and a blanket before returning them to the beach. They would talk to me about their mothers back home. I encouraged each one to contact his mom and let her know he was all right.

On one occasion, Rob allowed one of these to sleep in the bed of his pickup in our garage; he was too exhausted himself from having worked all day to drive again. I nervously supported his every act of kindness, knowing other mothers had done so for him in previous times. I also understood that he was repaying that generosity. We were repaying it.

He was continuing in his DUI program. It was a weekly meeting with a group of others who had been arrested for driving under the influence. Rob felt intimidated by them all and believed himself to be the only real loser there. He also had a difficult time understanding why these other men, all of whom had jobs, nice cars, and girlfriends or wives, would have risked drinking and driving. The only thing he believed he had in common with any of them was the fact of their mutual violations.

Rob discovered an over-the-counter cold medication that he could "legitimately" abuse. As it turned out, he was taking in any one day amounts equivalent to a month's supply, not that anyone would have needed to take it for a whole month.

He overdosed on it in attempts again to self-medicate and to quiet his self-talk and inner conflicts. He abused it to such a degree that instead of finding peace, he became psychotic, paranoid, and mean. I did not know what was causing this behavior that steadily worsened over a two-week period. I was truly frightened and exhausted by his uncharacteristic behaviors.

He left bizarre notes for me all over the house warning me of impending doom and evil. He lost his temper with me and accused me of irrational things. He argued against the America he loved, stating belligerently that all forms of American government were evil and were about to be overturned by him and his friends. He did not sleep at all, and I slept very little.

He exploded one day and I discovered his medication abuse. He had been emphatically denying it. I called poison control and learned overdosing on the cold medication could trigger extreme paranoia and psychosis, especially in someone with Rob's problems. I sent him to a psychiatrist and then placed him in another drug treatment program in San Diego. He was there about five weeks.

The program encouraged him to reveal his innermost thoughts and fears. He finally did, and they immediately placed him back on an anti-psychotic medication and gave him an early discharge. He did not fit. He had more problems than just drugs and alcohol. He finally did stabilize on the medication. I had tried to get him into the County Mental Health Hospital, but he was "not severe enough."

For a time, he remained stable, although he had used up all the medication, as prescribed. He returned to being the same Rob: sweet, kind, funny, and spontaneous with me, or at other times, for inexplicable reasons, isolated and withdrawn.

He was given his job back at the marble company where, according to his boss, he was actually regarded with respect, but as eccentric. He grew to feel comfortable there with some of his coworkers after he had begun taking his guitar to play on his lunch hour. He seemed proud, if tired, all the time. Two and a half months later, the business closed in San Diego and relocated to Las Vegas.

Again, he began acting disturbed, although not overtly psychotic. His behavior was the same that I had always associated with his feeling shame and guilt about some matter he was not yet ready to reveal, although I believed this time it was the loss of the job. He would make friends about whom he'd seem delighted, and then lose them, grieving each time, and struggling again and again to come to terms with rejection.

Losing his job was a great disappointment. It meant he would have to start all over with the months of denials and employment rejections and the most dreaded initial applications. He admitted that he was having his fantasies and obsessive thoughts again. But there was more.

"Mom, do you remember that I told you I was possessed by someone like Alexander the Great? I mentioned him as one of them (his demons), because he was a homosexual." Then silence. I waited. Again, it seemed that Rob had expected me to discern from his brief reference to Alexander the Great months before that the one salient aspect of that man was his homosexuality. I didn't know if the man was homosexual, but if I had known, that would probably have been the last thing I would have thought about in defining him.

For the next several months, Rob talked and struggled painfully with whether or not he was a homosexual. It was, he said, driving him crazy. I listened and probed anytime he needed to talk about it. Little by little, the pieces of this latest challenge fit together to form a whole.

First, he believed he was a homosexual because "no girls like me." Second, he must be a homosexual, because he had not been able to have sex with the oil field prostitute years before.

No girl ever approached him or initiated friendship. Of course he did not approach them; he was too shy. He said he would not know what to say to one. But girls liked other guys and flirted with them. No girl flirted with him, but lots of guys did; therefore, he must be homosexual.

"Rob," I asked, "when you have sexual fantasies, what are they about?"

"Death, dying, burning up, wrecked cars, burning cars, dead bodies." He forced these out and reminded me he had already told me many times.

"I remember, but don't you ever have pleasing sexual thoughts?"

"Yes, sometimes."

"Are they with men or women?"

"Women, of course!"

"Why, 'of course?'"

"Because that's who I would love."

As the pieces of his struggle formed a picture, it was one again of feelings of being a misfit, being lonely, and fearing others. Whenever he discussed his attitudes about homosexuals, it was in the context of hating the thought but longing for companionship and affection. He saw that longing for love and companionship as a weakness and an affliction. "It has gotten me in trouble all my life."

Only homosexuals now befriended him on the beach, he said. They flattered him. They did him favors, provided him with drugs and alcohol, bought him meals, played music, talked to him, respected his opinions, and accepted him. His choice had been to either accept all that because he was starved for it or to have no companionship at all and no one at all who made him feel that he mattered.

However, it was not the homosexuality of this group of new-found friends that was the concern for me. It was the fact that they were themselves outcasts by all respectable people, heterosexuals and homosexuals, alike.

He had grown up in a heterosexual home that had at least tolerance for homosexuality, if no understanding about the cause of it. His loathing of it was mostly from prison experiences. No doubt it had also been born from his earliest experiences including molestation at residential school, sodomized rape by a man at age fifteen, as well as his other prison experiences.

However tolerant I might be of others' homosexuality, it is not a choice I would have made for Rob. Who, given a choice, would want their child to be placed in the high-risk position of contracting AIDS and of further rejection by most of society? Either one is a guarantee of a slow death. Nonetheless, I was not about to condemn him if indeed he was a homosexual. But he was not convincing himself or me that he actually was.

I told him he must get an AIDS test. "I don't need an AIDS test. I haven't had sex with anyone; that's why they quit being my friend." As in any previous self-conclusions Rob drew, I could no more follow his logic on this than any other. He seemed always to draw from many fragments of his own life and reduce himself to the least flattering one.

He had thought first that he was a car. Not just any car, but a broken one. Then he was an alien. At age nine, the painted words on our street stated he was "retarded," so that must be the worst thing in the world to be. In early adolescence he was a "weirdo." Later, he was a "drug abuser," then "vagrant." If he felt any normal affection for his own niece, that might mean he was a "pervert." Permanently a "criminal;" forever a "failure."

Whatever he was, it was in his mind the lowest form of humanity. The group he perceived as equally as rejected by society as he was that of homeless, jobless homosexuals. That fact, along with his own experiences and later grateful appreciation of their attention, suggested to him another identity.

With the information about his conflicts he shared with me, I remained outwardly neutral, trying only to be a sounding board as he struggled with this latest identity crisis. I struggled against imagining him ultimately dying of AIDS. Better, I thought, was death in a fiery crash.

As with every other "self" he had settled on in the past, he disliked this one at least as much. It did not fit his inner values; it just fit his inner needs for attention and belongingness. "Homosexual" gave new form to never-ending inner chaos.

Rob had shared his worries with Patrick, who then shared them with his father. Both rallied with compassion. His dad wrote a letter expressing that he would love him, regardless, but cautioning him about the dangers and risk of AIDS.

Rob found no comfort in that compassion, because it only seemed to support one side of the conflict he was in. The other side being that he did not feel like a homosexual. He did not desire a male, sexually. He did not, he said, even desire sex.

He desperately desired to belong and to make music and be accepted. He only wanted companionship on his terms but his had never been a match with any others. He also needed escape and isolation time and could not comfortably balance the demands of friendship with those inner pressures.

I'm sure he was selective with the information he shared with me, but this new and troubled arena of "relating" to this latest identity group offered some possibilities. Childlike, he would grumble about how unfair someone behaved or how disloyal was another. He would relate some confrontation he had made to some person whose behavior he disapproved.

I used our discussions about his relationship problems as opportunities to again try and teach him about the necessary give and take and about the primary importance of choosing friends who helped you be your best. It was awkward and sometimes contrived because actually choosing friends was totally alien to him. Yet, when he gave out of friendship, he received nothing of value back in return. Other than refusing to engage in sexual activity, he otherwise knew no boundaries; if you cared about a person you were loyal. So he was loyal in giving money, rides, and food to his friends.

If I pointed out that he was being exploited, he was hurt. That, of course, meant that some things had not changed for him since childhood. He still wrestled with the thought that "they don't like me for me." He could not permit himself to believe that the only friendships he had were based on the material things he could give.

I didn't know how he was handling all other things in his mind, but I could see that he was walking a tightrope again, the tense tightrope between his conflicts and his enjoyment of having friends around him for the first time in his life.

The single attractive feature for him of anyone is his or her interest in making music. For the first time in two years, he answered the phone when it rang because more calls came for him than for me.

He had plans almost every day. It was the first time in his life that he had plans for fun with friends. He was working hard at improving his guitar playing and now had people with whom to practice. He decided he would soon be good enough to make a living at music. That illusive goal justified his lack of employment. And it held at bay his fear that he would never be anything worthwhile.

At thirty-three, it looked as if he had entered adolescence, in every sense and struggle of the stage. I lived with this in quiet tension, with some hope but more fear. I told myself perhaps it truly was a long-delayed but necessary stage of finally learning how to relate to peers.

There were girls in the group and he brought one home. Though he had a crush on her, she was the girlfriend of another man. That man mistreated her so Rob rescued her, rather than having her sleep on the streets.

I learned of her presence when Rob joined me downstairs early the next morning before I left for work. "Mom, I brought a girl home last night; she's too shy to come down and meet you."

This is a first. Would I prefer that he sleep with a homeless girl, in my home, about whom I know nothing, or that he have no girlfriend? Would I prefer that he bring home a girl instead of a guy? I would prefer that he sleep in peace.

"Where did she sleep?"

"With me, but don't worry, we didn't have sex. She's in love with Jeff." Would I prefer him to have had sex with a homeless girl in my home, or that he be undesirable to any girl?

"I thought you said Jeff was a homosexual."

"He is. I guess he's both. He treats her very badly, I've tried to get her to like me instead, but sadly, she doesn't, except as a friend."

More than concern about his lack of work and adolescent-like focus on pleasure were my deepening worries about the kinds of friends with whom he was associating. They seemed like marginal people who functioned in life even less effectively than he. They survived by exploiting other people.

Rob came home amazed to tell me that Jeff told him he was in love with him. No one had ever told him that before. Rob literally agonized over the next several weeks about whether or not the man who told him he loved him was sincere or exploitive. In time Rob concluded, with pain, that Jeff was insincere and toying with him as he'd toyed with the pretty girl and other men. In accepting the truth of Jeff, Rob again concluded he was unlovable.

His friends tended to party even more than he wanted. They were not employed, had no permanent residence, and seemed to have no desire to change that lifestyle. He volunteered all this to me and admitted he did not respect or excuse them anymore than he did himself.

However, his friends also engaged in conversations beyond the superficial, about matters of new interest to Rob—politics and current events. He had not found anyone since prison who would treat him as an equal in that respect. For reasons he did not disclose, he would avoid them all for days, determined that he would never see any of them again and then loneliness would cause him to return.

I could only wait to see if he would grow beyond this stage and emerge with the goals of a young adult. Instead, he began using drugs more and more often. Finally, his lifestyle seemed to be too extreme for his own conscience. He was embarrassed about not working and frightened about getting more and more into drugs.

He had been exploited by several of his "best friends" who had he said "only pretended to really care about me." He became angry that he had allowed himself to be talked into being used by "acting as a bodyguard" or driving them all over in his car. He had drawn the line when they had tried to get him to panhandle on the streets for money. Disgusted, he could finally become more objective about their characters.

Typically, he would stereotype the world on the basis of his own unique perceptions: "We've just become a society of prostitutes." "Even police use sex to trick you." "If you don't have sex, you don't fit in, so I can't be their friend." "Since I'm not verifiably straight or gay, I don't fit in." "I have to lie to fit in and I don't want to do that, so I don't fit in."

I marveled as much at his manner of speaking as I did his conclusions. And I was reminded again that Robbie was almost obsessed with being honest and authentic, even at the cost of friendships.

He talked to me about needing to get out of San Diego for a few months in order to get away from the drug-abusing crowd. That left only wandering the country alone.

It seemed to me that Rob was most in need of strong male companionship and guidance from males who would be good role models and whom he would respect. I thought he was hungrier for and more receptive to that now than at any previous time in his life.

In all of our many talks, and in having observed him day in and day out for the past twenty-six months, I did not doubt that he had basically good moral values, despite behaviors to the contrary. In fact, I was surprised by the strength of the foundations of moral integrity in which he believed. In many ways, watching the behaviors of these new "friends" made him more aware of what he did not want to become.

Given his history and experiences, I would have been less surprised to find him bitter, callous, and hostile toward moral and ethical standards. Instead, he just didn't think he could uphold them. He violated his own moral and ethical values and beliefs, as he said, "Because that's who I am." But he needed to have the good reinforced for him by other good men whom he respected and that was not to be.

CHAPTER 24

---◆---

"All my life, I remember dad telling me I should stand up and fight for myself. Never do I remember him teaching me how to fight." Rob in a note left on his bed New Year's Eve, 2002

On New Year's Eve, I was dressed to go out to a black-tie dinner party. For the first time ever, Rob looked at me with tears in his eyes and asked if he could go with me! He didn't even have a suit, much less a tux. He would be miserable at such a party. This was so unlike him I was confused; ordinarily he strongly avoided these kinds of functions and certainly didn't fit in. I don't remember what all I said, but I recall feeling torn between staying home with him and the commitment I had to others. It wasn't his habit to ask me to stay home with him or ask to go to such things with me. He agreed he would not enjoy himself and I left, vaguely uncomfortable about it. I returned after midnight to an empty house.

The ringing of the phone woke me. I assumed it to be the psychiatric hospital where I worked calling about a patient being assessed. "Is this the mother of Robert Bowers?"

The voice belonged to an emergency room physician. Rob had been brought in by ambulance earlier in the evening from a freeway intersection near our house. He was struck by a hit- and-run driver while out jogging and was found alongside a freeway. His legs had several compound fractures, he had a head injury, and he was not yet stabilized enough for surgery.

I sat beside his bed, holding his hand, watching him sleep. He had IVs and bandages, smeared blood all over his body, and mangled-looking legs in partial casts that looked like gauze wrappings. I didn't cry. The pain in my heart was way too deep for tears.

I tried not to wonder if these traumas would ever end or, if they finally were to end, then how? How would that kind of normalcy look?

He partially wakened, smiled weakly at me, and begged me for water. His lips were dry, cracked, and bleeding. I wanted to give him a big glass of fresh cold water , but I was not allowed to give him anything. I gently dabbed his lips with moistened swabs, frustrated that once again, what I could do for him was so very little in contrast to what he needed. Out of his blurred haze, he whispered, "Thank you for being here, Mom." He was still so sedated that he did not recall that he'd already been denied a drink several times. He asked adding, "I'm *so* thirsty!"

I was *so* relieved! I'd been more scared about the extent of his head injury than the injuries to his legs. I didn't yet know that his legs were seriously broken or that he was about to be operated on by an orthopedic surgeon who had been special ordered by God just for Rob.

Finally, he was stabilized enough so that he could undergo surgery. His surgery took many, many hours. One leg was broken in over thirty places; the other in fourteen. It was this leg, with fewer breaks, however, that would cause the most trouble.

A day or two later I met with his surgeon and thanked him for staying with it for so long and doing such an incredible job on his surgery. He told me that, like Rob, he, too, had Attention Deficit Disorder and that seven of his nine children also have it. He stated that also like Rob, he can either be scattered or can gather all his attention and focus for prolonged periods on something of interest, like patiently, painstakingly piecing back together a man's almost crushed legs.

At no time did this man or any of the hospital staff on the trauma and treatment team ever treat Rob with anything but respect and dignity. He received their best. In turn, as so often happened when he was treated with respect, he related to them as an equal.

Rob would need more surgeries, but he would eventually walk again. A steel rod was permanently inserted into one leg. The other required an external stabilizer—what I thought of as a combination brace-like, humorously, Martian-like device. It included a metal wrap around frame that encircled his leg. From that were both vertical and horizontal pins and rods piercing through his flesh into the various pieces of bone to hold them in place for knitting and new bone growth. A later surgery was needed to remove that and install an upgraded version of the external stabilizer.

Rob was in the hospital for one month. He coded twice because of sudden severe drops in his blood pressure and breathing difficulties, but his head injury seemed to have no permanent effect. His pain was intense and he had a morphine pump.

I was apprehensive about his having control over his own morphine. I checked from time to time with his nurses and learned that he was a model patient who never complained, despite obvious inconveniences, and never abused his morphine. In fact, they said he used less than was prescribed. As with any other institution that he cannot leave, he cooperated completely and meticulously with every requirement.

Rob was discharged to a nursing home where he would receive some additional needed care. Mine was a two-story home with the bedrooms and baths upstairs; he could not manage stairs for many months after.

I worked an afternoon shift and every morning I visited Rob in the nursing home for about two hours. I brought him treats and nutrients to compensate for the inexpensive food and the weak, powdered milk served there. He was fortunate that there was a charming patio outside his sliding glass door. Flowers bloomed, cats played, and birds sang. He made the most of the situation and usually kept his sense of humor although he had many complaints about the loud snoring and unclean habits of his roommate. To my delight, he began assuming somewhat of a leadership role in the facility. He felt there was not enough respect for the rights of others and so he talked with staff and those he regarded as the worst offenders, but he did so without offending. He was liked by all!

I saw again in public now the very significant developments in Rob that I'd seen with staff at the hospital and so often at home. He had a great, quirky, off-the-wall sense of humor that was delightful. Although he avoided formal group gatherings, when he absolutely had to be in them, he exhibited more and more confidence and interaction. He was much more outgoing but never intrusive. He had strong notions of how things ought to be (a lack of cleanliness in others was one major issue) and could assert leadership in ways to improve things in the home.

He made friends there among the young and old. He was more spontaneous and he enjoyed clowning and entertaining them without self-consciousness. He knew he was accepted and enjoyed there. He got away with popping wheelies in his wheelchair down the long hall and of course racing it with all the sounds of gears changing and wheels cornering amid appreciative laughter of older folks who seemed not to have had any laughs in years.

We had long conversations about the fact that he acted so much better when he was completely detoxed and that he liked himself so much more. He acknowledged that he must remain sober. He knew he had once again just missed death and that there must be something purposeful about his life. A friend of mine committed to taking Rob to AA meetings, hauling his wheelchair there and back, and befriended him in a way I hoped would further contribute to Rob's newfound sense of belonging.

Robbie fell in love! He was unabashedly, head-over-heels in love. Her name was "Mary" and she was pretty, spontaneous, lively, and quirky like him. Like him, she broke rules she found ridiculous and took personal risks for adventure. They laughed together and they enjoyed their constrained life together, she sneaking into his room from her own late at night.

Rob could still put no weight on his legs, so he was confined to bed or his wheelchair, but he transferred readily and would not be held back. His legs now truly were his wheels. With Mary standing on the cross bar behind his chair, they sailed down streets and back allies to the bottom of hills as fast as they could get the chair to roll, shrieking with joy and laughter. They sometimes tumbled over, disregarding the potential and seemingly probable damage to his healing legs. Sometimes she pushed him on flat areas; other times he wheeled them both in order to build muscle in his upper body. They were almost inseparable.

Rob and Mary were adopted a bit by employees in the little café they visited and those in other surrounding businesses who now watched out for them from their windows. More than once, these folks rushed to the rescue after Rob and Mary rolled off a curb too fast and fell over, laughing fearlessly. The local people saw only two carefree people who added a bit of spice to their workdays.

Some weekends, Mary left the facility to go home to be with her family. At those times, Rob entertained himself by taking a city bus, with a wheelchair lift, east out of town several miles into the mountains and coasted his wheelchair downhill all the way back. He traveled as far as twenty miles up into the mountains on the wheelchair and rolled back down to town. He had learned the hard way that if he rode on the side of the lane he would tip over, so he rode down the middle of the road whenever he could. When I learned of all this, I just thanked God for all those hearty, adventurous, and loyal angels he'd commissioned for the duration of Rob's life.

Mary was healing from a liver disease; she was an alcoholic. Like Rob, she must never drink again. But she did and then he did. And then the heartache began for two sweethearts who cannot, must not, but who drink anyway. She bought the alcohol while on a weekend with her mother and brought it to his room. They intended to have only a little but to Rob's astonishment it only took a little for Mary to become very intoxicated.

The first time it happened, they had left the facility in order to better sneak their contraband alcohol. They drank and chatted and then rode the wheelchair down the hill at breakneck speed and they fell. Mary fell off and Rob and the chair fall over. She was too drunk and ill to right herself and he, unable to withstand her weight on his legs, refused to leave her and so stayed with her in the alley all night long.

The pattern was repeated, and each time Mary became more intoxicated, Rob stayed more sober to care for her. Mary, sweet when sober, was a mean, loud, hostile drunk, no longer happy, carefree or fun. It was now Rob's turn to admonish her, plead with her, and argue with her that she could not drink, because her personality could not handle it any better than her diseased liver. He vowed to never drink again if she would never drink again. She agreed, but she could not stop for very long.

Mary was asked to leave the facility; she was no longer able to conceal her drinking and she had become a mixture of grief and love for Rob. He talked to me about her every day, but he realized that there was nothing anyone else could do. He was sad and defeated by the quarreling and missed the fun. He received the news that she must leave with mixed emotions.

I arranged to take him on an outing the next day so that he would not be left to watch while she was moved out by her mother. At the end of the day, I helped him back into the wheelchair from my car and pushed him to the facility door just as it opened and Mary stepped out with her mother. We all four stop as though on some cue, startled, expectant. Rob and Mary looked in each other's eyes for a very long moment, their mothers forgotten. Neither of them said a word and again as if on cue, she and her mother walked past him and out of his life.

A month or two later, Mary invited Rob by phone to her new apartment in San Diego. To travel from his facility in El Cajon to her apartment near the beach required several hours; he had to wait for a specific bus with a wheelchair lift and make multiple transfers, waiting in between for a bus that would accommodate his chair. He made the trip with no small amount of effort only to find no one at home. He would never see her again or try to contact her. He told me about it, his eyes reddening; then he never mentioned Mary again. It was another one of those hurts that goes too deep for tears. But I was grateful for that special time and special love in his life; grateful that though only for a season, he had found a whimsical, playful, laughing, loving girl who appreciated him. I do not have his stoicism; I grieved. I wanted something good in his life to turn out well and to last forever.

In time, Rob returned home to stay, he was allowed to spend some time on crutches; he was still sporting the leg device. However, I worked full-time so he was holed up in his room again too much of the time, with no visitors or companionship except occasional outings and movies with my friends and me. He was dependent on me for his meals but continued to amuse and worry neighbors by riding his wheelchair too fast down our steep hills. Still, that was insufficient stimulation to occupy his life. A neighbor man thought to entertain him while I was at work and brought him some alcohol; they began drinking in the afternoons and so relapse occurred, at first concealed.

In applying for aid to help pay Rob's medical bills, I was told that I should have had him on disability all this time. It had never occurred to me! I doubted that he would meet criteria for it. However, we applied, he was denied, and I lost hope. Friends propped me up when I lost hope and I tried to prop Rob up when he did. He rather liked what alcohol did in that respect more than what I did, but nevertheless, "we" apply again for disability, and then again. Social Security referred him for a psychological evaluation. The psychologist obtained a release of information from Rob and phoned me.

The man was astonished, he told me, that we had gone that many years without applying for Social Security. He also told me that Rob better met criteria for disability than most people he had assessed. He talked with empathy and understanding about all the struggles he knew Rob had experienced all his life. That man confirmed my belief that Rob was really not able to hold down a job. He assured me this was not from any lack of intelligence, but because of his autism and the secondary problems that have emerged from it. He recommended Rob for benefits. My income suddenly went further and Rob became suddenly "rich" at age forty!

His riches didn't just come from the retroactive Social Security amount he received dating back to the initial time of application. Around this same time, he received money from an earlier insurance claim filed on his behalf from injuries sustained while doing painting and maintenance work. I talked to him about how to open a checking account but I made the mistake of sending him to the bank to do it on his own. It was the first checking account he had ever held.

Social Security would make direct deposits. However, for whatever reason, the bank had the checks deposited into a savings account instead of a straight checking account. That meant that there was an unexpected thirty-three dollar transfer fee deducted from his savings every time he withdrew even five dollars cash from his ATM, and that meant he ran out of money every month long before his own deductions indicated he should.

Being "rich" and having a steady income brought mixed blessings. He was lighthearted about the fact that he had an income and would not be depending on me; he was thrilled to be able to pore through used music stores and pawnshops at will. Shopping almost whenever he wanted was a totally new and wonderful thing. He was surprisingly frugal, avoided paying full price, shunned new when used was just as good, and he became more independent in healthy ways.

But a small but steady income paid out at any ATM in the country eventually meant he could drink more, buy alcohol to win friends, and not starve if he had to leave home in order to drink. He began to again travel and roam. He was finished with his crutches, had the stabilizer removed, and was now working to strengthen his legs, determined to regain his former running capacity. Having also sold his truck because vehicles only caused him trouble, he was back to hitchhiking, which only caused him a little less trouble.

On one of his journeys up the coast of California, he bought a racing bike in San Luis Obispo and rode it the three hundred miles back home. It was exhausting and fraught with some perils along the way, but he was very pleased with himself for succeeding at that. He stayed home a few months and headed out again.

This time he was picked up by a woman. A fun, laughing, risk-taking, music-loving, redhead with the same kind of quirky perception on life Rob enjoyed. She was the mother of three children and she invited Rob into their lives. Rob repaired her house, landscaped her backyard, and together the whole family built a natural habitat in it. They made music together on the back porch on warm evenings and in the candle-lit living room when it was cold. He defended her against neighbors who both say intimidated her. They allegedly harassed her for no reason other than the fact that her long red hair did not match the tight black curls of the obvious African-American heritage her children shared. Rob's sense of righteousness was outraged by such prejudice. He thought she was a good mother. "Carolyn" phoned me to introduce herself and to let me know that Rob was there and was safe and to ask me if he was safe around her children. This was new!

She was wise enough to at least want to know if his mother was as involved in his life as he had been indicating. She was impressed with his hard work and his guitar playing, "and his hair; I just love his long blond hair." This, too, was new. Cautiously optimistic, with emphasis on the "cautious," I awaited further news about this almost-too-good-to-be-true happening.

She would, it turned out, provide and smoke weed with Rob, but she didn't want him to drink alcohol. When after two months of sobriety, he drank again, she asked him to leave. He came home, disappointed, but admitted that he had blown the relationship by drinking. He told me how this relationship with Carolyn would have been the perfect thing for both: "She needs a man to help her with the house and the children, and I need a ready-made family, because it's pretty obvious I shouldn't have children of my own!"

He talked fondly of happy times they shared. He protected her and the children, provided for them in many ways and did all the repairs and chores that fulfill the masculine role. It was apparent to me that she was also eccentric and enough of a non-conformist to accept him in every way except the drinking. I was pleased about that.

Carolyn wrote me, hoping I would send the message on to Rob, "wherever he is." She missed him. Back he went to her home in northern California, a thousand miles away. They phoned me. Carolyn, it turned out, was a bit quirky because she suffered a severe head injury some years back. Her quirkiness and her black children, Rob assured me, have together caused the small town people to look for ways to take her children from her. I was suspicious and thought there must be surely more to it than what they were saying.

As he had done most of his adult life, Rob asked me to fix the problem for Carolyn. I told them I could do nothing; both pled with me to do whatever I could to intervene with the authorities there on her behalf. Rob had assured her that I had good Mom power. I heard no more from them, but a few weeks later I opened Rob's bank statement and saw from his ATM withdrawals that he was no longer at Carolyn's house.

Despite my emphasizing there was nothing I could do, Carolyn drove the 1,000 miles to San Diego without my inviting her and phoned asking to see me that evening. She wanted me to evaluate her for the courts. That behavior gave me clues about her problems that the others had already seen in her. I agreed to see her the next day at the psychiatric hospital.

She brought stacks of her legal and psychiatric paperwork. She also brought photographs of her children in a wide variety of happy family home settings and celebrations. In the photographs, there were obvious indications of affection, comfort, and a lack of fear. Her house appeared warm and homey, with appropriate seasonal decorations at varying times. These were not staged photographs; they were collections over the years.

Carolyn also brought letters of support for her situation, a newspaper article featuring positive things about her and her family, and the phone number of her attorney, whom I called. He and I agreed that there were many strange things about her, but one of them did not seem to be that she was an inadequate mother.

Rob returned to her home and all went well for a few weeks until Carolyn gave a party where all her friends, including Rob, got drunk. Her friends stole Rob's ATM card after he allowed them to watch him use it to withdraw cash. All his Social Security money for the month was withdrawn and he was beaten up when he confronted them.

I don't know if the whole problem that night was all Rob's responsibility, but his decision to drink again certainly was. Once that kind of out-of-control drunkenness enters into any scene, only mayhem and loss result. He had not become angry until hit with the humiliating combination of being robbed and beaten up by men he'd befriended and for whom he'd bought more alcohol. Rejection by Carolyn was apparently the last straw. His reaction at the end of the ordeal was to kick out her windshield and hers was to rightfully then kick him out of her house.

Hitchhiking his way south back home to heal, Rob stopped off in one of his favorite places. He drank Southern Comfort, sitting on a bench in a pleasant park setting in the pretty, little city of San Luis Obispo, California.

EPILOGUE

Tears rolled down his cheeks as Rob initially read random pages from this manuscript. It took a minute before he could speak, "Mom, you've turned my ugly life into something beautiful! If just one person can be helped by reading my story, then everything I've gone through in my whole life will be worth it!" That is the Rob I know. The prison mail system does not allow him to have the entire manuscript received at once. So, I sent him twenty pages of it at a time for him to read and allow me to include the material. From time to time since then he has written me his hopes that his story will be told because "people need to know about these things before it's too late!"

I know I speak for other parents and other individuals who have disabilities or are imprisoned. I think too often the two are related. There's a very high incidence of learning disabilities and such in prison inmates. But, I can only tell Rob's story, not at all to defend him or to seek pity for him or to make excuses. Rather, as he has said, I write for him and for others like him who have no voice of their own. I write for parents that they may gain insight into the behaviors, motives, and pain of their "different" child. Earlier in the book I commented that while decisions have consequences, they also have reasons. The reasons, I again suggest, can only be understood when the pieces of a man's broken life can be fitted together. I've tried to do that in this book because broken people feel pain, too.

With every new research finding on autism and on all developmental and learning disabilities, I gain new awareness of the density of the fog that my son struggled through all his life. I also gain a profound respect for the unpredicted qualitative gains he's made in his cognitive development.

He had just turned three the first time I took him to a child psychologist. That man declared, with a smile on his face: "Robbie may only grow up to be a vegetable, but he'll be a happy one!" He is neither.

In Rob's lifetime, probably nothing significant will become known about the causes and specifics of autism. Therefore, we may not learn whether his early problems were all symptomatic of the one condition, or if, as seems most likely, he has several different conditions. His delayed ability to bond to me, his stereotyped behaviors, his narrowed focus on only cars, odd communication patterns, and his awkwardness with other children were most certainly the results of autism, as was his inability to figure other people out. The severity of the impact on his personality formation of this one deficiency cannot be over-emphasized, showing up in part in his perceptions first that he was a car and then that he was "an alien" who didn't belong on this planet, and that he was "unwanted" by almost everyone but his family.

He was classically dyslexic and clearly deficient in his capacity to focus, attend, and concentrate. His visual perception was impaired and probably his auditory perception as well. Certainly, his physician believed he was deaf. I've since come to suspect the seeming deafness was due to his impairment in processing all information.

He didn't learn to read or write until well after the age when such a lack profoundly impacted his already fragile self-concept and added to an enduring personal shame. He still has difficulty with cause and effect, and telling his right from left.

His childhood problems also included being bullied most of his schoolboy years and having cruel teachers at vulnerable stages of childhood and no close friends to buffer that pain. When he looks back, it is the bullying that hurts the most. Next is his then inability to control bowel and bladder, or in some ways worst of all, to form meaningful, lasting friendships. Our frequent moves may have rescued him from neighborhood bullies, but it also prevented him from having the opportunity to form attachments.

In childhood, he was molested. By mid-adolescence he had also experienced severe and humiliating sexual assaults and very violent knife-stabbings. By early adulthood, he continued to suffer physical beatings and finally imprisonment with its times of prolonged, intense fear for his life and its constant threats of harm to his person. Added to that is his having for a third or fourth time been left for dead on the side of a road, this time when he was struck by a hit-and-run driver.

The police estimate the driver was going at least sixty-five miles an hour when Rob was struck and knocked over 250 feet through the air from the point of impact. Rob has never worked through the pain of any of these experiences. The accumulation of those traumas is overpowering for even a healthy sense of self.

But deep compassion for others has always been a striking contrast to his awkwardness with them. For instance, he did not disclose any information the police sought in an effort to identify the hit-and-run driver. When I asked him why he would not want the person arrested and made to pay for what he'd done, Rob's answer brought tears to my eyes, "They were driving an old Buick. They probably were poor and scared; maybe they were even illegals. There's no good reason to just ruin their lives." That was only months before he stabbed a man.

It is believed that autism has genetic origins, as does alcoholism. From scientific research we have now learned a lot more than was available to Rob even as a young adult. We know that both conditions (addiction and autism) have direct brain and neurotransmitter relationships and brain anomalies, and that alcohol as well as all other addictions can cause further permanent brain damage. We believe that the part of the brain, the amygdala, in which both emotions and faces are "decoded" in normal infants seem to be "detoured" in autistics to the part of the brain that decodes objects and things...like cars. There is a correspondence to Rob's expressing himself best in automobile terms and seeming to project all his emotions onto cars and other motor mechanical devices. "Cars do too have feelings!"

Further, the deficiency in Rob's capacities to assess risks, to prioritize, to discern people's motives and moods, and to make good decisions also seem related to difficulties in information processing common to many autistic individuals.

Science and experience also give us reason to believe that most of these individuals need strict adherence to routines and have great difficulty breaking the mindset reflected in repeated behavior patterns. Again, this has significant implications for addiction and any habitual behavior dysfunctional or otherwise. It is quite conceivable that all of Rob's more compulsive behaviors have their origins in autism. This would include his continuing to build his models in his room and destroy his favorite toy cars and later stealing and wrecking cars, suggesting that these behaviors were not merely bad conduct but more likely the idiosyncratic means he used to express a behavioral mindset reflective of autism.

This is not at all to suggest that autistic individuals steal cars or routinely break parental rules. But rather repeating the same acts over and over despite serious consequences and even in opposition to one's own wishes looks very much like the indications found in many autistic individuals of obsessive-compulsive type behaviors. Rob was repeating self-defeating kinds of behaviors as early as age two and three when neither rewards for good behavior nor punishments for unwanted behaviors were the least bit effective. That is why his evaluation team at age five concluded that we needed to resort to extreme measures, including beating him, in order to socialize him. I have wondered many times if he would have been very different had I resorted to beating him for his misbehavior at age five.

My role as his mother has always demanded that I remain in a dynamic tension between unconditional love and being the bearer of society's standards. In love, I have listened to, delighted in, and marveled at his creative, whimsical perspectives. In love, I have acknowledged my dislike for many of his acts and focused on the better person I know him to be. It has always been easier to forgive him than to condemn.

As his gatekeeper to society, I have struggled hard quite literally against his private inner world that contradicted everything I knew to be true; and I've struggled to reign in his more whimsical perspectives so that they might fit into a more productive and fruitful mold.

Fruitful would include having friendships with psychologically healthier people. Productivity would mean some development and application of his talents in a way that even if only in prison might still give him a sense of contribution and accomplishment. Turn him loose on a road gang to clean up the area, he'd work harder than anyone. Give him an engine to repair and it would be done meticulously. Let him play his guitar in a band and he could momentarily forget that a locked cell awaited him at the end of the day. Then do something like that for as many inmates as possible. At the end of their sentences, we'd have more parolees staying out for good.

The absolutely worst thing a parent can imagine is that a son or daughter will kill someone and go away to prison. I doubt that many parents even have the capacity to imagine that; I didn't. It contradicts everything we hope and dream for our children, and so when it happens, it feels like our own worst failure. Deep inside, there is that sense that we have done something terribly wrong in our parenting, yet we still don't know what we should have done differently.

Nowadays, when I hear news of a tragedy, my heart goes out equally to the parents of the victims and those of the perpetrators. I hear on occasion the Columbine and other school shootings brought up in the context that the parents should have known or should have suspected something. I don't think so. There is no place in the mind or heart of a parent or spouse, for that matter, where there can be anchored such a notion that someone for whom they would readily give their own life could actually take one.

It is tragic that a man, a stranger, lost his life at the hands of my son; and tragic that the man he killed merely symbolized the lifetime of assaults done against Rob. That man's fate was settled nearly forty years earlier, in a tragedy that had been in the making since Rob entered kindergarten, maybe since he entered that cardboard wardrobe box.

I hate that he has taken a life, but I love and respect the man he is. I respect Rob for the inner strength that kept him struggling to cope against such fierce odds and that helped him retain a basic gentle, kind nature. He has strong ethical values and this, too, seems paradoxical considering that he is in prison for murder. His strength is quiet and deep, yet I know he also has symptoms of Post Traumatic Stress Disorder.

I know, as with most things about his psychological processes, his symptoms show up in ways unique to him, ways with which he's struggled to live without complaint as one traumatic experience after another has accumulated over his lifetime. I think one of those symptoms is that he ultimately catastrophized and overreacted to again being beaten up and humiliated.

Sometimes when I visit him in prison, we have to cut our visit short if he happens to have a guard in attendance whose practice it is to observe the inmates using the bathroom. In that Rob is still unable to use the bathroom while being observed, he waits as long as he can and then must end the visit so as to return to his cell where he has more privacy. He's learned not to drink too much coffee during the visits. Fortunately, most guards are not that dedicated. Sometimes, too, he just sits and stares into space, as though he has checked out, or as though he is hearing drums his mother still cannot.

Most autistic children need sameness, routine, and stability. Yet, Rob's childhood was filled with almost constant change through our relocations. As a career military man, his father was absent during critical years and then we divorced. I even continued moving around after the children and I were no longer a part of the military. I foolishly believed that I was the needed stability in their lives.

Also, treatment was hampered by his preference for alcohol over psychiatric medications, although he was on medications during significant portions of his life. Medications never provided the emotional numbness he needed. All of his pathological or traumatic experiences combined were so profound I am still astonished that he is actually so normal and so enjoyable.

Rob's *lifestyle* is probably not representative of autistic adults; his has so many other intervening problems that it is not possible to distinguish them. They are interrelated. A person who is not autistic might have made a wiser choice at any stage of life and certainly on the day in question. But a person who is not autistic might not have gotten himself into that situation in the first place where he was unable to discern the mood of the man he finally stabbed. Still, a person who is not autistic might never have been confused about how the world operates or failed to make the sort of friendships that are supportive during times when life grinds us down.

Studies show that the largest majority of autistic individuals are not able to live completely alone without at least some regular guidance, structure, and support from family or community agencies. There are some in college and on jobs, (in mathematics and engineering, to name two areas) but all struggle in widely varying degrees with many of the same life challenges as has Rob. That most are not able to live completely independently expresses their problems. The degrees of struggle to adapt and conform to society vary because autism is a spectrum. The symptoms run along a continuum from mild to severe. Probably no two autistic individuals are alike in the manifestations of their symptoms.

It is another tragedy that prison is the only place where a man like Rob can be sent. He has a debt to society and he has demonstrated an inability to live in it without harm to himself or others, but that is not where my son belongs. Society simply doesn't have a better place.

With little stimulation or variation to his routine now, Rob tries to write often from prison, acknowledging he has nothing to write about but telling me it is the least he can do to "try and make up for all the pain I've caused you." I think about that pain…it *never* goes away, but he misunderstands. It isn't for myself. Love always trumps whatever problems it brings. The pain is for him; it always has been.

In a recent visit, I offered to delete anything about his story he didn't want disclosed. He struggled a moment and said, "No, I'm not proud of it, but it might help someone if they see even what just alcohol can do to a person." That, too, is the Rob I know.

God's hand has so often been on Rob's shoulder that I've finally learned He can do what I cannot; and I've finally grasped that any human's value is simply that he or she is, not in what he or she does. No one gets to heaven on their good behavior. Because of Rob, I tend to see others as heroes in ways I would not previously have done. Because of Rob, there was never a day at the psychiatric hospital where I worked that I did not feel humbled by some patient whose courage in facing life far exceeded mine. Usually, it was the disheveled, odd one whose life story always included loneliness, rejection, and persecution. Yet, like Rob, he or she found something to smile about and something in life to appreciate and something to give to someone in greater need. If I have any heroes, it would be those chronically mentally ill individuals.

I have also journeyed with my son to places I would otherwise never have gone. If he has not found peace at the end of any road, I finally have. I have learned that criminals have hearts; that not everyone in prison is a criminal, and not every criminal is in prison. On the other hand, I've learned that some criminals don't have hearts, some are depraved, and that people shouldn't get away with hurting other people, not even stealing their cars.

I've learned that God has offered free therapy to everyone who asks. He calls it grace, mercy, and forgiveness, toward ourselves, toward others who have hurt us, toward those we have hurt. One of the most profound discoveries I've made is that God's capacity to heal is much, much larger than any harm or pain one human being can inflict on another. That knowledge gives me enormous peace.

Through Rob's eyes, I have made other important discoveries: I've discovered that courage is often greatest among those in whom it is never seen. And I've learned that love is always complex but never failing. It is wholly contained in the trust of one's own child and in crying for him when his own grief is beyond tears. Love is standing beside your very guilty son and lending him your own dignity when he has none. It is knowing the nightmares of prison that he faces and accepting that he has to go there, and love is leaving judgment to the courts but finding it is not lessened by seeing truths you desperately wish were otherwise.

Love is also befriending when no one else will, liking when no one else does, feeling unashamed to call him brother, picking him to be on your team even when you know you'll lose, and showing that forgiveness is always bigger than any hurt or offense.